Badiou and Philosophy

Critical Connections

A series of edited collections forging new connections between contemporary critical theorists and a wide range of research areas, such as critical and cultural theory, gender studies, film, literature, music, philosophy and politics.

Series Editors
Ian Buchanan, University of Wollongong
James Williams, University of Dundee

Editorial Advisory Board

Nick Hewlett
Gregg Lambert
Todd May
John Mullarkey
Paul Patton
Marc Rölli
Alison Ross
Kathrin Thiele
Frédéric Worms

Titles available in the series

Agamben and Colonialism edited by Marcelo Svirsky and Simone Bignall
Laruelle and Non-Philosophy edited by John Mullarkey and Anthony Paul Smith
Badiou and Philosophy edited by Sean Bowden and Simon Duffy

Forthcoming titles

Rancière and Film edited by Paul Bowman
Virilio and Visual Culture edited by John Armitage and Ryan Bishop

Visit the Critical Connections website at
www.euppublishing.com/series/crcs

Badiou and Philosophy

Edited by Sean Bowden and Simon Duffy

EDINBURGH
University Press

Edinburgh University Press Ltd
22 George Square, Edinburgh EH8 9LF

www.euppublishing.com

Typeset in 11/13 Adobe Sabon
by Servis Filmsetting Ltd, Stockport, Cheshire, and
printed and bound in Great Britain by
CPI Group (UK) Ltd, Croydon, CR0 4YY

A CIP record for this book is available from the British Library

ISBN 978 0 7486 4352 3 (hardback)
ISBN 978 0 7486 4351 6 (paperback)
ISBN 978 0 7486 4353 0 (webready PDF)
ISBN 978 0 7486 6833 5 (epub)
ISBN 978 0 7486 6834 2 (Amazon ebook)

Contents

III. Philosophical Figures

Acknowledgements

The editors would like to express their gratitude to the following people: Miriam Bankovsky, Ian Buchanan, Sandra Field, Paul Patton and James Williams. A special mention is also due to Carol Macdonald and all the team at Edinburgh University Press.

An early version of Chapter 3 was published as 'Alain Badiou: Problematics and the Different Senses of Being in *Being and Event*', *Parrhesia*, 5 (2008), pp. 32–47. The editors gratefully acknowledge the permission of *Parrhesia* and its editors to republish some of this material.

Abbreviations

BE   *Being and Event*, trans. Oliver Feltham (London: Continuum, 2005)

C   *Conditions*, trans. Steven Corcoran (London: Continuum, 2009)

CH   *The Communist Hypothesis*, trans. David Macey and Steven Corcoran (London: Verso, 2010)

CM   *The Concept of Model: An Introduction to the Materialist Epistemology of Mathematics*, trans. Zachary Luke Fraser and Tzuchien Tho (Melbourne: re.press, 2007)

D   *Deleuze: The Clamour of Being*, trans. Louise Burchill (Minneapolis, MN: University of Minnesota Press, 2000)

E   *Ethics: An Essay on the Understanding of Evil*, trans. Peter Hallward (London: Continuum, 2001)

LW   *Logics of Worlds*, trans. Alberto Toscano (London: Continuum, 2009)

M   *Metapolitics*, trans. Jason Barker (London: Verso, 2005)

MP   *Manifesto for Philosophy*, trans. Norman Madarasz (Albany, NY: SUNY Press, 1999)

MS   *Meaning of Sarkozy*, trans. David Fernback (London: Verso, 2008)

NN   *Number and Numbers*, trans. Robin Mackay (Cambridge: Polity, 2008)

PP   *Pocket Pantheon*, trans. David Macey (London: Verso, 2009)

SM   *Second Manifesto for Philosophy*, trans. Louise Burchill (Cambridge: Polity, 2011)

TC   *The Century*, trans. Alberto Toscano (Cambridge: Polity, 2007)

TO   *Briefings on Existence: A Short Treatise on Transitory*

Ontology, trans. Norman Madarasz (New York: SUNY Press, 2006)

TS   *Theory of the Subject*, trans. Bruno Bosteels (London: Continuum, 2009)

TW   *Theoretical Writings*, trans. Alberto Toscano and Ray Brassier (London: Continuum, 2004)

Contributors

Adam J. Bartlett lectures in the School of Culture and Communication at the University of Melbourne, Australia. He is the author of *Badiou and Plato: An Education by Truths* (Edinburgh University Press, 2011), and has contributed to and edited, with Justin Clemens, *Alain Badiou: Key Concepts* (Acumen, 2010) and, with Justin Clemens and Paul Ashton, *The Praxis of Alain Badiou* (re.press, 2006).

Anindya Bhattacharyya recently completed his MA at Kingston University, London, under the supervision of Professor Peter Hallward. He is currently completing a study of Badiou's ontology and has published a number of reviews of Badiou's work in *Radical Philosophy* and the *Socialist Review*. He is a full time journalist and activist with *The Socialist Worker*.

Sean Bowden is an Alfred Deakin Postdoctoral Research Fellow at Deakin University, Australia. He is the author of *The Priority of Events: Deleuze's Logic of Sense* (Edinburgh University Press, 2011) and has published a number of articles and book chapters on Badiou, Deleuze and Simondon.

Justin Clemens is a Lecturer in English at the University of Melbourne, Australia. In addition to the edited collections with Adam J. Bartlett, he is the editor, with Oliver Feltham, of Alain Badiou, *Infinite Thought: Truth and the Return of Philosophy* (Continuum, 2003). He is also the author of *The Romanticism of Contemporary Theory* (Ashgate, 2003) and, with D. Pettman, of *Avoiding the Subject* (Amsterdam University Press, 2004).

Simon Duffy is a Research Associate in the Department of Philosophy at the University of Sydney, Australia. He is the author of *The Logic of Expression: Quality, Quantity and Intensity in Spinoza, Hegel and Deleuze* (Ashgate, 2006) and is the editor of *Virtual Mathematics: The Logic of Difference* (Clinamen, 2006). He recently translated the French collection of the work of Albert Lautman, *Mathematics, Ideas and the Physical Real* (Continuum, 2011).

Graham Harman is an Associate Professor of Philosophy at the American University in Cairo, Egypt. He is the author of, among other works, *Quentin Meillassoux: Philosophy in the Making* (Edinburgh University Press, 2011), *Towards Speculative Realism: Essays and Lectures* (Zero Books, 2010), *Prince of Networks: Bruno Latour and Metaphysics* (re.press, 2009) and *Heidegger Explained: From Phenomenon to Thing* (Open Court, 2007).

Talia Morag is a PhD Candidate in the Department of Philosophy at the University of Sydney, Australia. Her research project is entitled *The Looping Effect – Mind-Dependence of the Realities Studied by Science and Psychoanalysis*. She is the author of 'La Pathologie mathématique – du sublime mathématique chez Kant à la pathologie de l'obsessionnel chez Freud', *Cahiers Critiques de Philosophie*, 3 (2007), pp. 77–98, and 'Alain Badiou within Neo-Pragmatism: Objectivity and Change', *Cardozo Law Review*, 29: 5 (2008), pp. 2239–67.

Ed Pluth is an Associate Professor in the Department of Philosophy at California State University, USA. He is the author of *Alain Badiou: An Introduction* (Polity Press, 2009) and *Signifiers and Acts: Freedom in Lacan's Theory of the Subject* (SUNY Press, 2007).

Nina Power is a Senior Lecturer in Philosophy at Roehampton University, UK. She is editor and translator, with Alberto Toscano, of Alain Badiou, *Political Writings* (Columbia University Press, forthcoming), the author of *One-Dimensional Woman* (Zero Books, 2009) and editor, with Alberto Toscano, of Alain Badiou, *On Beckett* (Clinamen Press, 2003).

Jon Roffe is the founding convenor of and lecturer at the Melbourne School of Continental Philosophy, Australia. He is the author of *Badiou's Deleuze* (Acumen, 2011) and has co-edited with Graham Jones *Deleuze's Philosophical Lineage* (Edinburgh University Press, 2009) and with Jack Reynolds *Understanding Derrida* (Continuum, 2004). He is also a member of the editorial board of *Parrhesia*.

Brian A. Smith recently completed his PhD in Philosophy at the University of Dundee, UK, with a thesis entitled *Philosophies of the Event: The Continuing Problem of Subjectivity and Freedom*. He is the author of 'The Limits of the Subject in Badiou's Being and Event', in Paul Ashton, A. J. Bartlett and Justin Clemens (eds), *The Praxis of Alain Badiou* (re.press, 2006).

Tzuchien Tho recently completed his PhD in Philosophy at the University of Georgia, USA, and is now a researcher associated with the Centre International d'Etude de la Philosophie Française Contemporaine, Paris. He is the author of 'Remarks on aphaeresis: Alain Badiou's method of subtraction between Plato and Aristotle', *Filosofski Vestnik*, 31: 3 (2010), and 'The consistency of inconsistency: Alain Badiou and the limits of mathematical ontology', *Symposium: Canadian Journal for Continental Philosophy*, 2 (2008). He is also the translator of Badiou's *The Concept of Model* (re.press, 2007).

James Williams is Professor of Philosophy, University of Dundee, UK. He is the author of *Gilles Deleuze's Philosophy of Time: A Critical Introduction and Guide* (Edinburgh University Press, 2011), *Gilles Deleuze's Logic of Sense: A Critical Introduction and Guide* (Edinburgh University Press, 2008), *The Transversal Thought of Gilles Deleuze* (Clinamen, 2005), *Understanding Poststructuralism* (Acumen, 2005) and *Gilles Deleuze's Difference and Repetition: A Critical Introduction and Guide* (Edinburgh University Press, 2003).

Badiou's Philosophical Heritage

Sean Bowden and Simon Duffy

In the wake of the numerous translations of Badiou's works that have appeared in recent years, including the translation of the second volume of his major work, *Logics of Worlds: Being and Event II*, there has been a marked increase in interest in the philosophical underpinnings of his *oeuvre*. The papers brought together in this volume provide a range of incisive and critical engagements with Badiou's philosophical heritage and the philosophical problems his work engages, both directly and indirectly. Our aim is to offer a balanced assessment of the ways in which Badiou responds to various philosophical thinkers, arguments and traditions, and of the arguments that he employs to do so.

The volume is divided into three sections: I. Philosophy's Mathematical Condition; II. Philosophical Notions and Orientations; and III. Philosophical Figures. The first explores the philosophico-mathematical underpinnings of Badiou's *oeuvre*. The next engages with a number of key philosophical concepts and orientations that provide a critical context for an engagement with Badiou's work. And the third offers in-depth analyses of some of the key thinkers that constitute a large part of Badiou's philosophical heritage.

This present, introductory chapter explores a number of Badiou's remarks which explicitly treat the relation of his work to the discipline of philosophy more generally, and gives an overview of the ground that will be covered throughout the collection. We will also here make a few general comments about the importance, for Badiou, of philosophy's 'mathematical condition'.

Badiou and Philosophy

As is well known, in his first *Manifesto for Philosophy*, Badiou argues that philosophy has certain extra-philosophical 'conditions' which are required for it to take place. These conditions, which are of four types, are the 'generic' or 'truth procedures' resulting from major upheavals or events in the fields of science, politics, art and love. The specific role of philosophy is to propose a unified conceptual space for – or, as Badiou also puts it, to think the 'compossibility' of – its contemporary conditions (MP 33–7). In so doing, philosophy is able to seize upon and elaborate, in novel ways, those new possibilities of existence which are nascent in its external, evental conditions.

At the same time, however, still following Badiou's *Manifesto for Philosophy*, philosophy since Descartes has *internally* maintained certain 'nodal concepts' which organise the thinking of these external and diverse conditions within the same conceptual space. These nodal concepts are, for Badiou, being, truth and the subject (MP 32; see also SM 117–18). Of course, these concepts have their specific correlates in each case, depending on the particular philosophical system under consideration. In Badiou's own philosophy, as is well known, these correlates include notions such as the State, the event and fidelity. And as Ed Pluth and James Williams show in Chapters 6 and 7 of this volume, certain conceptions of materialism and time also have a decisive role to play in Badiou's philosophical system. What is crucial in any case, as Badiou argues, is that the deployment of the philosophical concepts of being, truth and the subject is grounded in certain events having occurred in the domains of science, politics, art and love (MP 38, 79–80). In other words, philosophy's external conditions somehow clarify and orient the task of philosophy, even in the concepts which philosophy internally deploys.

What, then, are the contemporary, conditioning events whose compossibility Badiou feels himself obliged to think, and how exactly do they bear on the philosophical concepts of the subject, truth and being? Firstly, with political events such as May '68 and the Chinese Cultural Revolution, as well as with the advent of a new discourse on love in Lacanian psychoanalysis, Badiou declares that we have seen the emergence of a new kind of dialectics whose terms – that is, the political or amorous *subject* – need not refer to a given or objective essence, such as a class or a sexual essence.

This is a crucial point for Badiou, many of the details of which are examined here in the chapters by Nina Power, and Justin Clemens and Adam Bartlett. Secondly, with the artistic event associated with the poetry of Hölderlin, Mallarmé and Celan (among others), Badiou arrives at the idea that *truth* – here, poetic truth – need not entail a reference to an object. Finally, in the order of science and the matheme, the event which is the development of set theory from Cantor to Paul Cohen has given us the concept of an 'indiscernible' or 'generic multiplicity' (that is, a multiple falling under no particular determinant), allowing us to rigorously think the truth of the *being qua being* of any given multiple as pure multiplicity 'without one' (MP 79–96). The importance of this last event for Badiou's philosophy is examined throughout the collection, but most particularly in the papers comprising the first section.

So how do the nodal concepts of philosophy organise the thinking together of these events, even as these events clarify the meaning of the concepts of being, truth and the subject? Firstly, it is by declaring that a truth has no need of the category of the object because truth is itself an indiscernible or generic multiple which, as the result of an infinite procedure, will have been 'subtracted' from all exact designations and their corresponding discerned multiples. Secondly, it is by arguing that such a 'truth procedure' is founded upon the affirmation of an 'undecidable' event which comes to supplement a given multiple-situation. The infinity of multiples comprising this given situation are then 'verified' as being connected in some way to the supplementary event, which in turn leads to the ongoing production, within multiple-being itself, of the truth of this event-supplemented situation as a purely generic multiple. Finally, it is by affirming that while truth has no necessary relation to a given object, it is inseparable from a subject: the subject being that which verifies the connection of the infinity of multiples comprising a situation to the supplementary event and, in so doing, must be thought of as a finite fragment of this infinite generic procedure (MP 95–6, 108). It is in this schematic way that Badiou's philosophy thinks the compossibility of the truth procedures which have their origin in the aforementioned contemporary events in the domains of science, politics, art and love.

All this is not to say, however, that by affirming the dependence of philosophy on extra-philosophical conditions the specificity of philosophy collapses. Indeed, Badiou makes it clear in *Manifesto* that insofar as philosophy must systematically think the compossibility of all four of its very disparate conditions, it cannot be 'sutured' to or identified with any particular one of them (MP 65–6). Moreover, as Badiou explicitly states in the introduction to *Being and Event*, philosophy circulates not only between its conditions, but also between these conditions and its own history (BE 3).[1] The independence of the discipline of philosophy is thus also due to the relationship it maintains with its own history. In fact, it is clear from a brief glance at the table of contents of any of Badiou's major works that significant portions of his *oeuvre* are dedicated to analyses of numerous venerable philosophers and the concepts and themes they addressed. Plato, Descartes and Hegel are singled out by Badiou, in typical exaggerated fashion, as 'the only three crucial philosophers' (LW 527). But as Brian Smith and Graham Harman convincingly demonstrate in their contributions to this volume, philosophers such as Sartre and Heidegger were also indispensable for Badiou.

But two further things also follow from Badiou's assertion that philosophy is inseparable from its own history and concepts. Firstly, as he makes clear in texts such as *Metapolitics* and *Logics of Worlds*, citing Althusser and Sylvain Lazarus, it follows that the 'effects' of philosophy's external conditions on philosophy in some sense remain internal to philosophy (M 54–5; LW 518–19). And secondly, it follows that philosophy should, at least in principle, be able to discuss these internal, conditioned effects in specifically philosophical terms. Indeed, with regard to this last point, Talia Morag argues in Chapter 8 that Badiou could enter into a productive dialogue with contemporary neo-pragmatists about the philosophical importance of sets. And in Chapter 13, Jon Roffe, among other things, laments the philosophical discussion that could have taken place between Deleuze and Badiou on the questions of 'multiple being' and the relationship between mathematics and ontology.

Some twenty years after the publication of the first *Manifesto for Philosophy*, Badiou published his *Second Manifesto for Philosophy*. He argues that the first *Manifesto* was concerned above all to assert the existence of philosophy against the attempts to declare its 'death' by exclusively 'suturing' it either to science (analytic philosophy, positivism), politics (dogmatic Marxism), art (Nietzscheans and Heideggerians) or love (Levinasians, Lacanian 'anti-philosophy'). By the time of the publication of the *Second*

Manifesto, however, Badiou thinks that philosophy's 'inexistence' is no longer the whole problem. The problem now is that philosophy is 'everywhere'. Philosophy has become ubiquitous, but it has also become servile, assimilated with 'conservative morality' and the uncritical defence of 'democratic dogma' (SM 67–9). Asserting the existence of philosophy will thus no longer simply amount to thinking the systematic compossibility of all four of its conditions in the manner outlined above (MP 65). It must also involve a certain 'de-moralising' of philosophy, which is to say that philosophy must become a little 'reckless', 'corrupt the youth' and destabilise dominant opinion (SM 69–71). In other words, the primary mode of philosophy must become the polemic if philosophy is to avoid being merely another means of legitimising the legal and ethical status quo.[2]

Of course, Badiou thinks that philosophy's commitment to universal truths is its own distinct means of de-moralising itself (SM 71–2). Indeed, it is clear that that fidelity to a truth which is always in excess of the status quo is inevitably conflictual. But surely philosophy's polemical attitude must also be carried into the domain of philosophy itself, in order to avoid the consolidation of new, philosophical status quos. Moreover, a point which is relevant to this present volume, perhaps philosophy's combative attitude must also be brought to philosophical commentary, if only to prevent uncritical scholarship mistaking itself for the elaboration of new possibilities for thought.

So it appears that we can now draw upon a number of the points examined above in order to contextualise this project, in terms Badiou would approve of, as a critical and, at times, combative examination of Badiou's relation to, impact on and relevance for the discipline of philosophy. The collection as a whole is thus characterised by the way in which it brings together a number of critical studies of Badiou's relation to various philosophers (Althusser, Deleuze, Heidegger, Lautman, Marx, Plato, Quine, Sartre), philosophical concepts (being, events, freedom, the infinite, the subject, time, truth) and philosophical movements or orientations (communism, Marxism, materialism, neo-pragmatism). The volume also examines Badiou's relationship to a number of thinkers who, while not themselves philosophers (at least in the standard sense of that term), have nevertheless had major impacts on philosophical thought: the psychoanalyst and 'anti-philosopher' Lacan, but also mathematicians such as Cantor, Cohen,

Grothendieck, Eilenberg and Mac Lane. Indeed, the significance of mathematical thought for Badiou's philosophy cannot be under-estimated, and so we have devoted an entire section to examining philosophy's 'mathematical condition'. Some general remarks on this topic are thus also warranted here, by way of introduction.

Philosophy's Mathematical Condition

Mathematics has a dual function in Badiou's philosophy. On the one hand, mathematics plays the central role in the determination of Badiou's ontology. And on the other hand, mathematics has the privileged status of being the paradigm of science and of scientific enquiry in general, and is therefore instrumental in the determination of science as a truth procedure.

Science, including mathematics, proceeds by following experimental lines of enquiry that are established by new discoveries. What differentiates mathematics from science is that it is only in mathematics that a problem can be solved unequivocally. Badiou maintains that, insofar as thought formulates a problem, it is only in mathematics that it can or will definitively be solved, however long it takes. He notes that the history of mathematics is littered with examples of breakthroughs that resulted from proving or disproving conjectures first proposed by the Greeks more than two thousand years ago. What this means for Badiou is that mathematics does not acknowledge categories such as the unthinkable or the unthought, which he characterises as spiritualist because they exceed the resources of human reason, or those according to which we cannot resolve problems nor respond to questions, such as sceptical categories. Science in general, on the other hand, struggles in this respect, and is deemed by Badiou not to be reliable on this point. What is distinct about mathematics as a science is its abstract axiomatic foundation. And he argues that it is this foundation that provides the infrastructure for the characterisation of being qua being. According to Badiou, 'mathematics teaches us about what must be said concerning what is; and not about what it is permissible to say concerning what we think there is.'[3]

Badiou considers Cantor's invention of set theory to be the archetypal event that allows mathematics to henceforth and retrospectively be understood as the science of being qua being. The much debated proposition from *Being and Event*, that 'mathematics is ontology' (BE 4), is a philosophical idea that is conditioned by this event. The general ontology that Badiou develops in *Being and Event* draws upon a number of subsequent developments in mathematics that show felicity to this event, namely the Zermelo-Fraenkel axiomatisation of set theory and the open series of extensions of these axioms, including in particular those by Kurt Gödel, who introduced the notion of constructible sets, and Paul Cohen, who developed the method of forcing and generic sets. Tzuchien Tho examines the implications of this Cantorian event and the problems it poses for Badiou in Chapter 2.

The characterisation of mathematics as ontology has a direct bearing on how Badiou understands the nature of the relation between science and mathematics. For example, he considers physics to be 'the investigation of matter, the very concept of matter', and he argues that 'the more you decompose the concept of matter into its most elementary constituents, the more you move into a field of reality which can only be named or identified with increasingly complex mathematical operations' (E 130). Badiou endorses the fact that in nearly all scientific theories, the structures of physical systems are modelled or described in terms of mathematical structures. Mathematics is generally considered to be applied in this way when the scientist postulates that a given area of the physical world exemplifies a certain mathematical structure. However, Badiou goes further than this. Rather than there being an analogical relation between the structure of the physical world and the mathematical theory that allows it to be modelled or reconstructed, Badiou considers mathematics to actually articulate being itself. Mathematics doesn't just provide a description, representation or interpretation of being. Mathematics itself is what can be thought of being *simpliciter*.[4] It is for this reason that Badiou maintains that axiomatic set theory is the science of being as pure multiplicity, or of 'the presentation of presentation' (BE 27), that is, of the presentation of what is presented in a situation. What this means is that Badiou figures mathematics itself as that which guarantees the access of the natural sciences to presented reality.

With the proposition 'mathematics is ontology', Badiou consigns the task of ontology to mathematics, and in so doing liberates philosophy from the burden of the Heideggerian question of being. However, this doesn't liberate philosophy completely from dealing with the problems associated with the *Seinsfrage*, but rather recasts the role of philosophy in this respect from its historical preoccupation with ontology to the task of metaontology. Sean

Bowden looks at some of the dialectical implications of this shift from ontology to metaontology in Chapter 3, and Simon Duffy examines the importance of Plato to Badiou for making this move in Chapter 4. One of the tasks of philosophy as metaontology is to articulate the relation to being that is displayed by the truth procedures operating in the different generic procedures. Because mathematics, as the basis of science, itself belongs to one of these four generic procedures, philosophy must remain attentive to those truth procedures in mathematics that follow experimental lines of enquiry and that continue to develop new articulations of the presentation of being qua being. This line of research is evident in a number of Badiou's subsequent texts, including *Numbers and Number*, where Badiou draws upon the development of surreal numbers to extend the universe of ordinals up to the reals, and in *Logics of Worlds*, where Badiou attempts to address his dependence on set theory in *Being and Event* by deploying a category-theoretic presentation of set theory, namely topos theory. Yet just how successful Badiou is in respecting the implications of the experimental lines of enquiry that mathematics opens up for the presentation of being qua being remains an open question.

Category theory is the programme in mathematics that has established itself as an alternative power of unification in mathematics that challenges the dominant role set theory has traditionally played in this respect. Although category theory does appear to be the historical continuation of set theory, the concept of 'categorisation' is not a technical refinement of the concept of set but rather represents a profound conceptual change in mathematics. Category theory allows you to work on mathematical structures without the need to first reduce them to sets. Despite this, Badiou's deployment of category theory in *Logics of Worlds* restricts itself to topos theory, which is the category-theoretic presentation of set theory. This narrow deployment of category theory betrays Badiou's work as being both overly bound to its early set-theoretical underpinnings, and as being quite limited in its exploration of the full richness of what category theory has to offer for the presentation of being qua being. The extent to which this can be understood to pose problems for Badiou's work is explored by Anindya Bhattacharyya in Chapter 5.

The Cantorian event, the dialectic, Plato and Category theory – these are the issues that orient the papers on Badiou and mathematics in the first section of this volume.

Badiou: Critical Connections

As noted at the outset, this volume is divided into three sections: 'Philosophy's Mathematical Condition', 'Philosophical Notions and Orientations' and 'Philosophical Figures'. Each section, in turn, is comprised of four chapters.

In the first group of chapters, in his piece 'What Is Post-Cantorian Thought? Transfinitude and the Conditions of Philosophy', Tzuchien Tho begins by examining the role of Cantor in Badiou's thought. Tho provides an account of what would constitute a post-Cantorian context of thought, and of how Badiou's work can be understood to be post-Cantorian. On the one hand, Cantor's development of the transfinite for mathematically fixing the coordinates of the concept of the infinite represents a significant development in the history of mathematics. On the other hand, however, this work has far-reaching ontological implications. Through Cantor's provision of a transfinite multiplicity, the metaphysical reliance on unity to render the multiplicity of being intelligible and consistent could be overcome with a discourse on multiplicity that is uncoupled from a horizon of unity and totality. The formal sense of the infinite derived from the mathematical legacy of Cantor's work represents a definitive shift from the dialectic between the one and the multiple. What is at stake in this problematic is the very basis of Badiou's mathematical ontology, and Tho's work provides a clear account of the contours of this problematic and of how Badiou negotiates them.

Sean Bowden's chapter, entitled 'The Set-Theoretical Nature of Badiou's Ontology and Lautman's Dialectic of Problematic Ideas', reconstructs the nature of Badiou's 'debt' to the French philosopher of mathematics, Albert Lautman – a debt to which Badiou alludes in *Being and Event* but never explains in any detail. Bowden shows that Badiou's assertion that set theory is ontology depends upon what Lautman would call a 'dialectic of problematic Ideas' – a line of thought which runs counter to more standard accounts of Badiou's metaontology which rather focus on the importance of the 'doctrine of conditions'. Following the work of Lautman, Bowden argues that Badiou's set-theory ontology is grounded insofar as it resolves a series of 'ontological problems' which can be expressed in the form of 'dialectical couples' such as the one and the multiple, Nature as poem and Nature as Idea, the finite and the infinite, and the continuous and the discrete. Bowden demonstrates how the Zermelo-Fraenkel axioms (which are, for Badiou, the 'laws of being') together resolve this series of opposed notions. In concluding, Bowden also indicates some of the potential problems of Badiou's Lautmanian heritage, including the idea that Badiou is left without a unified conception of being, since being is said in one way for the ontological situation in its dependence on a prior dialectic of problematic Ideas, and in another way for what the ontological situation, so determined, can say of situational being in general.

In 'Badiou's Platonism: The Mathematical Ideas of Post-Cantorian Set Theory', Simon Duffy examines the importance of Plato to the mathematical basis of Badiou's ontology, and how Plato is instrumental in determining how Badiou positions his philosophy in relation to those approaches to the philosophy of mathematics that endorse an orthodox Platonic realism. Badiou's Platonism bears little resemblance to this orthodoxy. Like Plato, Badiou insists on the primacy of the eternal and immutable abstraction of the mathematico-ontological Idea. However, Badiou's reconstructed Platonism champions the mathematics of post-Cantorian set theory, which itself affirms the irreducible multiplicity of being. In effect, Badiou reorients mathematical Platonism from an epistemological to an ontological problematic, a move that relies on the plausibility of rejecting the empiricist ontology underlying orthodox mathematical Platonism. To draw a connection between these two approaches to Platonism and to determine what sets them radically apart, Duffy focuses on the use that they each make of model theory to further their respective arguments.

Rounding out this section, Anindya Bhattacharyya investigates what is at stake for Badiou's ontology in the shift from set theory, in *Being and Event*, to the theory of categories and topoi in *Logics of Worlds*. 'Sets, Categories and Topoi: Approaches to Ontology in Badiou's Later Work' shows that while Badiou remains committed to the declaration that 'mathematics is ontology', the contrast between set-theoretical and categorical 'foundations' of mathematics is a stark one. The strategy that Badiou adopts to bridge the gap between sets and categories is to make use of topoi, which are the categorical generalisation of sets. However, this still leaves Badiou's ontology indirectly anchored in the 'foundational' ontological questions presented in set theory. Bhattacharyya suggests that Badiou's ontology can be radicalised further by stripping it of its residual attachment to classical set theory, and that this will allow one to maintain Badiou's subordination of philosophy to its mathematical condition while radically transforming the content of the mathematical ontology that condition prescribes.

The following section, 'Philosophical Notions and Orientations', commences with Ed Pluth's chapter, 'The Black Sheep of Materialism: The Theory of the Subject'. Pluth argues that there are multiple senses of materialism at work in Badiou's philosophy, only some of which are justified. The sense of materialism crucial to Badiou's later work is that materialism equalises or levels down what might otherwise be construed as distinct regions and orders of being. At first glance this would appear to expose Badiou to the criticism of being a monist, and Pluth endorses this criticism by arguing that Badiou's attempt to use matter as a name for being in *Theory of the Subject* represents a monistic stumbling block for his position at the time. However, Pluth also finds within the same text a more promising line of reasoning, according to which the primary category of a materialism need not be matter but rather the 'conceptual black sheep' of materialism, namely the subject itself. Pluth provides an account of the theory of the subject as presented in the *Theory of the Subject*, and of why Badiou feels that a theory of the subject is required for the development of an adequate materialist philosophy. In doing so, Pluth mounts a defence of what some consider to be the overly religious character of some of the language that Badiou uses to thematise the subject and its relation to truth.

James Williams' contribution explores and then critiques Badiou's approach to time in both *Being and Event* and *Logics of Worlds*. In 'A Critique of Alain Badiou's Denial of Time in his Philosophy of Events', Williams objects to the account of time bound up with Badiou's idea of fidelity to eternal truths. For Williams, eternal truths are fictions, and the world's only character is that of becoming. So it follows that, for him, subjective commitment to eternal truths entails a threefold denial of: the passing quality of truths, the passing quality of the world and worldly things, and ordinary and valuable modes of temporal existence bound up with this world of becoming. In the sacrifice of becoming to eternal truths, Williams thus sees a potential for violence – if not direct and necessary violence, then at least a 'violence of consequences'. Badiou's eternal truths are potentially, for Williams, 'lethal fictions'.

In 'Doing Without Ontology: A Quinean Pragmatist Approach to Badiou', Talia Morag identifies two mutually exclusive roles that set theory plays in Badiou's philosophy. One that is straightforwardly metaphysical is concerned with the question of the creation of new kinds of objects. The other Morag identifies as implicitly pragmatic and is related to questions about what kinds of objects there are. By pursuing a discussion of the latter in relation to the texts *Being and Event* and *Logics of Worlds*, Morag aims to demonstrate on the one hand that Badiou can contribute to contemporary neo-pragmatism, insofar as the new Badiouian picture of reality can actually give content to contemporary pragmatist theses about the nature of sets. On the other hand, Morag aims to show that, from a pragmatic point of view, that is if we begin our ontological enquiry not with mathematics but instead with our explanatory practices, then Badiou's philosophy can be released from what she characterises as its inflated ontology.

Finally, Nina Power's contribution to this volume, 'Towards a New Political Subject? Badiou Between Marx and Althusser', brings to light a set of tensions which define Badiou's ongoing work on the political subject. Following Power, Badiou occupies a narrow theoretical ground between Communism and Marxism, between Althusserian anti-humanism and the humanism of the early Marx, between an acknowledgement of the historically unique potential in the current state of global capital and an affirmation of transhistorical communist invariants, and between a commitment to a purely 'generic humanity' and the necessity of naming the political subject for practical purposes. Power traces the difficult line that Badiou feels himself forced to tread with regard to the political subject. On the one hand, she shows how Badiou's Communism dehistoricises Marxism using, in part, Althusser's critique of historical materialism and associated critique of the subject as a mere effect of ideology. But on the other hand, Power argues that Badiou, contra Althusser, never relinquishes a more substantive notion of the subject as 'generic humanity'. The question remains, however, as to how we are to think this political subject in concrete terms when its concept has been emptied of all content.

The third and final section of the collection examines Badiou's relation to a number of philosophical figures who have been central to the elaboration of Badiou's *oeuvre*. Justin Clemens' and Adam J. Bartlett's article tracks Badiou's complex engagement with Lacan from *Theory of the Subject* through to *Logics of Worlds*, showing that having worked through Lacan's particular brand of 'anti-philosophy' was crucial for Badiou. They explicate a number of decisive instances where Badiou's thought was informed as much by its proximity to Lacan's as by the effort to overcome it in specifically philosophical directions. The issues they address include: the question of the subject and its relationship to the articulation of truth; the doctrine of philosophy's extra-philosophical 'conditions'; philosophy's relation to 'anti-philosophy' as well as to sophistry; the question of 'the localisation of the void'; the relationship between the matheme and love; and the formal theory of the body developed in *Logics of Worlds*. In each of these cases, Clemens and Bartlett show how Badiou engages with Lacan in a nuanced and sympathetic way while also revealing certain impasses in his thought – impasses whose resolution take Badiou beyond Lacan without simple repudiation.

Following on from this, in 'Badiou and Sartre: Freedom, from Imagination to Chance', Brian A. Smith examines the importance of Sartre for the formation of Badiou's thought. As Smith shows, Badiou remains faithful to Sartre as a philosopher of decision, sharing his commitment to the relationship between freedom and decision. At the same time, however, it is demonstrated how Badiou, in his attempt to re-found the political subject, pushes beyond the Sartrean conception of the subject or for-itself as the substantial ontological ground of change and free action. For Badiou, change and freedom – and indeed the subject itself – rather depend upon something which is in excess of given, ontologically stable situations, namely the event. Smith traces the contours of Badiou's explicit and implicit engagement with Sartre from *Theory of the Subject* through to *Being and Event*, examining in detail Sartre's varying accounts of freedom, Badiou's critique of Sartre's notion of the group, the use Badiou makes of Lacan to get beyond Sartre in *Theory of the Subject*, and the final rigorous formulation of the relationship, to be found in *Being and Event*, between the situation, the event, decision, freedom, the subject and group action.

In 'Badiou's Relation to Heidegger in *Theory of the Subject*', Graham Harman examines Badiou's admiration of Heidegger as one of the central thinkers of our time in connection with his early work, *Theory of the Subject*. Harman investigates the points of congruence and tension between these two thinkers, specifically the extent to which Badiou can be said draw upon the main Heideggerian thesis of the ontological difference, and the adequacy of this engagement. As to whether Badiou's interpretation of the ontological difference in Heidegger is correct, Harman concludes that despite being unorthodox, Badiou's instincts are basically correct. Heidegger emerges as a key ally in Badiou's deviation from both Hegel and Lacan, and a key figure for the subsequent developments in Badiou's thought.

Finally, in 'One Divides into Two: Badiou's Critique of Deleuze', Jon Roffe sheds new light on Badiou's provocative reading of Deleuze in *The Clamor of Being*. Contrary to many of the responses to this work, both positive and negative, Roffe points out a number of facts which have not previously been discussed. Firstly, *The Clamor of Being*'s major claim – that Deleuze is a philosopher of the One – is not so much intended to be a criticism of Deleuze as to present a point of contrast between the two philosophers. Secondly, the only substantial critical point that Badiou pursues in *The Clamor of Being* bears on Deleuze's formulation of the relation between the virtual and the actual. In short, Badiou reads Deleuze as introducing an indefensible notion of a 'virtual image' in order to cover over a flaw in his account of the virtual-actual relationship in *Difference and Repetition*. As Roffe shows, however, Badiou's reading of Deleuze on this point fails to take into consideration the mathematical, Kantian and Maimonian account of the virtual-actual relationship to be found in *Difference and Repetition*. Furthermore, Badiou reconstructs the concept of the 'virtual image' in *Difference and Repetition* with reference to Deleuze's discussion of the 'virtual image' in the much later text, *The Time Image*. As Roffe demonstrates, however, what is named by the term 'virtual image' in each of these works is very different, meaning that Badiou's main critique of Deleuze in *The Clamor of Being* ultimately fails.

Overall, what emerges from these essays is a critical snapshot of Badiou's relationship to, impact on and importance for the discipline of philosophy. Contrary to the popular image of Badiou as a radical and even iconoclastic figure, he appears here as a thinker engaged, whether directly or indirectly, with some of philosophy's most central and time-honoured figures and concerns. It is hoped that the many critical lines of enquiry opened up by the studies comprising this volume can be pursued more fully elsewhere, and to productive effect, to the benefit not only of Badiou studies, but also philosophy's open future.

Notes

1. See also on this point, Oliver Feltham's 'Translator's Preface' to *Being and Event*, where he writes that, for Badiou, 'philosophy must remain mobile by circulating between a plurality of its conditions and its own history' (BE xix).

2. For an excellent discussion of this point, see Oliver Feltham's entry, 'Philosophy', in A. J. Bartlett and Justin Clemens (eds), *Alain Badiou: Key Concepts* (Durham, NC: Acumen, 2010), pp. 22–3.

3. Alain Badiou, 'Mathematics and philosophy', trans. Simon Duffy, in Simon Duffy (ed.), *Virtual Mathematics: The Logic of Difference* (Manchester: Clinamen Press, 2006), p. 25.

4. See Peter Hallward, *Badiou: A Subject to Truth* (Minneapolis, MN: University of Minnesota Press, 2003), p. 55.

I. Philosophy's Mathematical Condition

2

What Is Post-Cantorian Thought? Transfinitude and the Conditions of Philosophy

Tzuchien Tho

What Can Post-Cantorian Thought Be?

From the perspective of the history of mathematics, the work of Georg Cantor represents a major turning point. The development of the transfinite, the development of orders of infinity measuring larger than the countable or denumerable infinite pushed mathematics beyond the centuries old debate about the negative, potential and virtual infinite toward a true 'banalization' of the infinite (E 25–6). On the other hand, Cantor's early development of set theory, deeply correlated with the transfinite, became the start of what was to become the hallmark of the greater part of modern mathematics. With subsequent foundational projects of axiomatisation and rigorisation, Cantor's work ushered in a new period of crisis, paradoxes and synthesis. It was in the context of these paradoxes and inconsistencies that D. Hilbert, the 'faithful Cantorian subject' of his day, emphasised that, 'No one shall be able to drive us from the paradise that Cantor created for us.'[1]

Despite the undeniable influence of Cantor, it is rather difficult to pinpoint what something like post-Cantorian thought, whether in mathematics or otherwise, would be. The shape of modern mathematics, especially with respect to foundational questions, was formed equally through the work of R. Dedekind, G. Frege, B. Russell and others. Cantor's critics openly mocked his contributions as 'philosophical' or even 'theological'. If we add to this account the immense contributions of the subsequent rise of intuitionism and abstract algebra, it seems deeply injudicious to understand modern mathematics as 'Cantorian' in the strict sense. While Cantor's influence is spread widely across modern mathematics, proposing a post-Cantorian historical epoch of thought seems to risk diluting any sense that can be gathered from the term 'Cantorian'.

Despite Badiou's reference to 'post-Cantorian' thought, the axiomatisation of set theory by E. Zermelo and A. Fraenkel remains at the core of his project of mathematical ontology (BE 3). Here we must underline the distance this has with Cantor's own settheoretical contributions. From this distance between Zermelo-Fraenkel set theory (ZF set theory) and Cantor's own work, I point to two places where Badiou's use of mathematics could lead one to question how important Cantor really is for him.

The first example is evidently the central (meta)ontological argument in *Being and Event*. Even a cursory scan of the book will reveal that it is axiomatic set theory that takes centre stage, a development that even Badiou acknowledges as owing more to Frege, Russell, Zermelo, Fraenkel, Von Neumann and indeed Bourbaki. The truly explosive parts of the book concern the controversies surrounding the axiom of choice, forcing and generic sets. This is at a certain distance from Cantor's own concerns. Cantor's theorem and his version of the continuum hypothesis do make short appearances in the text but are interpreted systematically through set theory's eventual canonical form.

A second example concerns the ontology of numbers themselves. Published two years after *Being and Event*, Badiou's *Number and Numbers*, which could be read as a separate and prolonged 'meditation' accompanying *Being and Event*, sought to address the region of ontology that concerns the central mathematical entity, numbers. In this project, Badiou does indeed approach the subject with an unambiguous set-theoretical approach through the work of J. H. Conway and D. Knuth. Here, however, outside of necessary nods toward Cantor's work concerning the concept of wellordering and the measure of sets, it is Dedekind's contribution to analysis and number theory that is the cornerstone of this work.

These two aspects of Badiou's work to date, central to his overall relationship to mathematics, seem to call into question the degree to which Cantor really figures in his work. No doubt, Badiou's *Logics of Worlds* presents yet another dimension of his relationship with mathematics which take the Grothendieck topoi and categories as his central concerns.

The relation between Badiou and Cantor would not be so difficult if not for Badiou's own understanding of the evental nature of Cantor's work. Badiou understands genuine historical transformations, events, as being rooted in sharp discontinuity. The event in this understanding is not an activation of some latent possibility but rather an interruption of impossibility whose radicality is immeasurably 'more than' the sum of its differential causes. To recall some of his favourite examples of this, the eruption of the French Revolution was more than the sum of its economic, cultural and political causes (BE 180). The event of love between two people is also something that exceeds the combined elements of their encounter and relationship (BE 232). In the tradition of Koyre, Bachelard, Canguilhem and Althusser, Badiou understands historical transformations in terms of a discontinuous novelty that is irreducible to the situation within which it arises. In this same tradition, the consequences of a historical transformation mark out its own historicity following the path of its own immanent conditions which are uncertain and undecidable from the point of view of its origin. Conditioned by the event, the activity of thought becomes unmoored from the certainty of what Badiou calls 'natural' or naturalised situations, where the historical eruption of the event throws things into suspension. Thinking under the condition of the event is to think in the context where relations are unbound and pre-established orderings collapse (D 124).

If we accept Badiou's understanding of history along the lines of the theory of the event, Cantor's work and the epoch of mathematical *thought* that he ushered in did provide something that can be understood as a discontinuous eruption in the history of mathematics. Despite reservations about how best to trace Cantor's concrete influence in the development of set theory, number theory, analysis and the afterlives of the transfinite, there seems to be no way of uncoupling the advent of modern mathematics and Cantor's enormous but not always obvious influence. The difficulty here arises not with Badiou's understanding of Cantor's wide and profound influence in the rise of modern mathematics any more than the historical shift ushered in by the politics of the French Revolution. The difficulty with understanding the post-Cantorian concerns the ambiguous nature of this 'post'.

Sharing in but departing from the tradition of Koyre, Bachelard and others which privileges historical discontinuity, Badiou takes the history of breaks, ruptures and irreducible transformations into a stronger context of difference. History is itself a break with ontology and not simply the interruption of a sedimented regime of objective knowledge or the regulative framing of experience. Indeed, much of Badiou's mature work has been dedicated to the elaboration of this deep separation between being and event.

From the perspective of *Being and Event*, this radical difference is aimed both at the construction of an ontological theory that overcomes the metaphysics of the one and, in turn, the subjective and historical consequences of such an overcoming. In a more formulaic expression, if the difference that grounds Badiou's project of mathematical ontology is the difference between being and event such that 'the event is forbidden, ontology rejects it', then how do we situate the Cantorian event that is itself the situating of ontology itself (BE 184)?

The attempt to understand Cantor's role in Badiou's thought as ushering in a 'post-Cantorian' context of thought risks this uncomfortable circularity. The root of the problem is that Badiou understands Cantor as introducing a transformation of the nature of difference itself. Cantor's evental re-situation of ontological discourse reaches down to the core of ontological difference and, by consequence, situates the difference between being and event. If this theorising of Cantor's historical difference remained at the level of a scientific transformation in a more stratified manner, the problem may not be quite as profound. That is, if the means by which we grasp the very discontinuity that Cantor represents was not due to Cantor's reorganisation of that discontinuity itself, we could then file it under the context of the history of science. It is this very reflexivity that I believe is the real legacy of Cantor in Badiou's thought. My task in what follows is thus to unfold this reflexivity through Badiou's treatment of Cantor in its ontological and historical senses.

Ontology and Metaphysics

In order to enter into our problematics concerning Cantor, some themes in Badiou's mathematical ontology must first be laid out. This should commence with the separation of ontology from philosophy underlined by the founding expression of his mathematical ontology, 'mathematics = ontology' (BE 6). As he explains, the identification of ontology with mathematics not only frees ontology to do its work, but allows us to return to philosophy with a new basis. In the introductory remarks of *Being and Event*, Badiou puts forth the thesis quite delicately, remarking that, 'The thesis that I support does not in any way declare that being is mathematical ... It affirms that mathematics, throughout the entirety of its historical becoming, pronounces what is expressible of being qua being' (BE 8). Here Badiou proposes an account whereby the fundamental paradoxes of ontology, starting from its Parmenidean-Platonic aporiae of the inexistence of the pure multiple circulating between the one, the many, the same, the other and change become redeemed in modern mathematics. While mathematics have always already been the becoming of ontology, it is with G. Cantor and R. Dedekind's historical opening toward the transfinite and set theory that the metaphysical shadow over ontology can be definitively undone and the separation 'mathematics = ontology' can be effected. As he argues elsewhere:

> At this point, enlightened by the Cantorian grounding of mathematics, we can assert ontology to be nothing other than mathematics itself. This has been the case ever since its Greek origin. However, mathematics has managed only with considerable difficulty and at the cost of toil and tiresome recasting to ensure the free play of its own conditions. (TO 40)

As such, the identity between mathematics and ontology has always been the case but it is a historically dynamic identity. The impedance that renders this identity historically dynamic is precisely the 'metaphysical temptation' present in both philosophy and mathematics/ontology. This temptation has in turn always rendered the relation between mathematics and ontology, this self-recognition, inactual. For Badiou then, the difference made by Cantor is the actualisation of mathematics as ontology. This difference, however enormous, still seems far from 'evental'.

What is this metaphysical temptation and what is the nature of Cantor's 'enlightenment'? To answer this question, we begin by sketching out the larger vision of Badiou's mathematical ontology. As readers of Badiou are familiar, his ontological project is a non-representational and anti-metaphysical one. This means first of all that ontology's consistent unfolding can only be effected by untangling itself from metaphysics. This separation from metaphysics is the untangling of the question of being from the criteria of the one or unity. In its various expressions, metaphysics attempts to address reality through the speculative construction of its principles of organisation. This metaphysical mode of thinking, however, has always been mired in treating reality, the world or being under the mode of the one. In such a manner, metaphysical thought has traditionally reproduced versions of unification,

whether from 'above' by means of a transcendent hypostasisation
or from 'below' by means of an immanent plenitude. Following
the powerful interventions of both Hegel and Heidegger, Badiou
takes seriously the problem that metaphysics cannot escape the
reflexivity inherent in thinking being. From the position of unity,
metaphysics can only address beings but neither the address itself
nor the distinction between being and beings. As such, the metaphysical treatment of being immediately slips, in its various expressions, into the address of beings, entities, objects. Indeed, ontology
or the treatment of being qua being has continually failed to meet
its own questioning insofar as metaphysics has always treated the
question of being qua *beings*. This 'qua' has been the reflexive
mark of the problem, the 'qua' as the externalisation of being
as such to beings. Badiou's rejection of metaphysics is the rejection of the treatment of being as beings at the point of its 'empty
generality', that of 'beings' (TO 34). The immanent reflexivity of
ontological thought and being qua being can only be grasped by
its subtraction from the one and the total. Yet, as Badiou is well
aware, without the one or the effect of a unifying totality, being
is no-thing. Here Badiou reminds us of Leibniz's metaphysical-
ontological maxim, 'What is not *a* being is not a *being*' (BE 23). As
the emblem, for Badiou, of metaphysical thought, it is in affirming
the conditional as such that he ironically delivers the very task
of ontological thought separated from metaphysics. Ontology is
as such the treatment of this 'not *a* being', being as such taken
up in thought as the void-multiple. As such, this nothing is not
to be understood in a metaphysical sense as naught. Rather, the
'nothing' of being, an expression of the reflexivity of ontology,
is precisely the pure multiplicity, a multiplicity not composed of
unities and which presents what is in principle not-presentable.

For Badiou, this actual task of the presentation of the no-thing
is precisely identified with set theory. Through Russell's 'paradox'
of the set of all sets, Badiou affirms the untotalisability of sets.
This means that in the set-theoretical presentation of the universe
of sets as a delineated discourse of ontology, there is no set of all
sets and hence no overarching unity to multiplicity. Through the
axiomatisation projects in set theory, Badiou affirms ontology as
a theory of the nothing insofar as the void set $\{\emptyset\}$, a set which is
literally 'of nothing', provides the fundamental concept of difference. The independence proofs for the continuum hypothesis and
the axiom of choice provide even wider horizons for the unfolding

of multiplicity where rational consistency is separated from the guardianship of unity.

My aim here is not to address the deeper issues present in Badiou's more robust development of ontology through axiomatic set theory. No doubt, it is in evaluating the details of axiomatic set theory and its contemporary developments that different complications will both demonstrate and challenge the power and limits of this ontological vision. What this sketch aims to provide is a vision of the stakes of Badiou's mathematical ontology. Whether or not one finds Badiou's positive arguments concerning ontology convincing, one can without much trouble understand that a transformation in how we reckon with the fundamental constraints of the distinction between the one, the multiple and the nothing constitutes a fundamental transformation in the very means by which we treat the gap between being and beings as well as the structure of beings or entities themselves.

The very recognition of the stakes of Badiou's mathematical ontology implies, as Badiou underlines, the historical and dialectical subtraction of philosophy from metaphysics itself. As he remarks:

> It is true that philosophy exposes the category of truth to the unifying, metaphysical power of the One. And it is no less true that philosophy exposes this power to the subtractive defection of mathematics. This is why every singular philosophy is less of an actualization of its metaphysical destiny than it is an endeavour, under the mathematical condition, to be subtracted from it. (TO 42)

The part of ontology that philosophy constantly submitted to the metaphysically problematic guardianship of the one, posed as the criterion of truth, is also the part that remained dialectically subtracted as mathematics. It was mathematics that consistently supplied the framework for closing the gaps between metaphysics and its historical reinvention of the dialectic between one and multiplicity. From Plato's indefinite dyad to Leibniz's infinitely aggregating monads, the tension between the one and the multiple was continuously reworked within mathematics and in turn circulated problematically within philosophy.

Although affirming the mathematical subtraction of the philosophical problem of the one and the multiple in our sketch above, I do wish to underline the actual lack of Cantor's presence in all of this. In Badiou's own presentation, Frege's set-theoretical arithmetic, Russell's paradox concerning totality, Zermelo and Fraenkel's axiomatisation, Von Neumann's theory of ordinals, Gödel's undecidability, Bourbaki's naming of the void and Cohen's forcing of the generic sets all make significant contributions. There is no doubt that there is a certain gap between Cantor and the later developments of axiomatic set theory. As Badiou explains, 'The Cantorian presentation of sets was subsequently shown to be not so much a particular theory, than the very space of the mathematically thinkable' (TO 42). The elaboration of this very space would then serve as the guiding question in continuing our investigation. What then is Cantor's contribution to Badiou's ontology?

Mathematical Subtraction from Metaphysics

Along with Leibniz's maxim, Badiou also employs Plato to formulate the historical thread of the subtraction of philosophy from metaphysics. In various places, Badiou develops the central formulation of the historically dynamic dialectic of being, starting with the Eleatic maxim 'If the one is not, nothing is' found at the end of Plato's *Parmenides* dialogue.[2] What Badiou argues is that, under the statement of this conditional, what Plato investigates is not simply the implications of unity's essential relation to intelligibility but also the possibility that 'the one is not'.

The *Parmenides* dialogue as a whole treats the obvious reliance of the theory of forms on unity. That is, if the Platonic theory of forms purports to account for the intelligibility of things through a formal unity (the like and unlike, the greater and smaller, rest and motion), the forms themselves seem to require some 'one' on the basis of which this intelligibility is engendered. The dialogue begins with a young Socrates proposing a version of the theory of forms only to be quickly refuted by a wiser and more experienced Parmenides who then agrees to take his young interlocutors through a series of investigations in the dialectical style (as opposed to Socrates' speech). In a series of multiple approaches to this 'one', the dialogue leads us to an aporetic state where there can be no conclusion to be had on the existence of the one but only an agreement on the idea that 'if one is not then nothing is'. In this conceptual mode, Badiou privileges the aporetic power of Platonist philosophy over its doctrinal aspects. Hence for Badiou, it is neither the doctrine of recollection nor the participatory theory of the forms that constitute the active kernel of Plato's insights.

To get at the conceptual kernel, Badiou goes a bit further in his interpretation of the *Parmenides* dialogue. The aporetic unfolding in the dialogue occurs in the context of a dialectic where the various hypotheses on the one's being or non-being are entertained. Towards the end of the dialogue, the possibility of the one's non-being is drawn out into the possibility of an inconsistent multiplicity, a multiplicity without one. Such a possibility is posited by Plato in a 'dream within sleep',[3] a world of inconsistent multiplicity where the great becomes small and the small great: in the place of one, there would be many, a disoriented 'nocturne' with no fulcrum of evaluation and no metric of measurement. The significance of this, for Badiou, is that this is not simply a hypothesis made just to be discarded but is in fact the positive attempt to think something that opens the path to a real concept of inconsistent multiplicity that, according to Badiou, only comes to be fulfilled in Cantor's development of transfinitude and set theory in the late nineteenth century. In this, the terminological distinction between *plithos* (πλῆθος) and *polla* (πολλά) forms the two sides of multiplicity, the inconsistent multiple-without-one and the consistent multiple of composed ones (BE 35). In this way, the impasses encountered in Plato's work on the one and the multiple come to find resolution in Cantor's invention of a new form of multiplicity. Plato's impossible dream is thus Cantor's transfinite paradise (BE 32).

There are two conceptual sides of Badiou's account of ontology's historicity here. The first side concerns infinite multiplicity and the second concerns its consistency. For the first point, the paradoxes of the infinite can be read as intimately tied to the entire development of mathematics from antiquity to the present. The struggle for an alternative articulation of the infinite beyond the ancient Greek negative sense has been at the centre of the crucial turning points in mathematical history: the development of mathematical physics in the sixteenth century, the infinitesimal calculus in the seventeenth, the concept of limit in the eighteenth, the development of the transfinite in the nineteenth and proofs concerning the numbering of the continuum in the twentieth. Even though the mathematical use of the infinite and the infinitesimal, whether considered as 'mathematical fictions' or otherwise, were commonplace in Cantor's time, he introduced a proof with a deeply ontological implication. The definitive mark of the positivity of the infinite was Cantor's development of the evaluation of different orders of infinity. Beyond the denumerable infinity, the infinity of the 'count', there are orders of infinity that elude the count, in excess of and measuring beyond what the denumerable infinite can cover. With the structure of transfinitude orders in place, the conditions were set for the 'banalisation' or relativisation of the infinite. The centuries old grappling with the first order of infinity and its accompanying metaphysical implications were literally neutralised, shifting our very means for examining the structure and nature of multiplicity.

The other side of this historical reading of the transfinite concerns consistency. The fundamental opposition to an infinite that would be more than a potential or a virtual one lay in the contradictory senses of the infinite. The idea of an infinite number, magnitude or quantity is a self-defeating one. In order to establish something like an infinite number or sum, one would either have to produce an infinite totality which is contradictory, or place its consistency under suspension by the means of a 'fictionalisation' such as was practised by the founders of the calculus. Outside of this tremendous development of this latter method and the achievements in making this fictional or virtual infinite rigorous through the notion of the limit, the conjunction of infinity and unity, the path of the actual infinite, had a more difficult task since an infinite number, entity and the like appear so apparently inconsistent. Cantor's work adds a new page to this long history of the relation between infinity and unity by displacing the criterion of unity toward a notion of 'set' or 'collection'. The sum of the countable numbers hence can have an infinite measure that is strictly a 'unity' or indeed a 'totality' of countable numbers, a consistent set. Here, the unbinding of the first infinite with the notion of the 'greatest number' allows us to understand that since it is the smallest in the series of transfinite numbers, it does not suffer from traditional inconsistencies of the infinite. This uncoupling of infinity from totality allows for a consistent notion of infinity to venture into regions of infinities of greater measure, the transfinite.

In Badiou's historical reading of the subtraction from metaphysics and the one, these two sides of Cantor's intervention constitute a definitive shift in the dialectic between the one and the multiple. If the eventual transformation in mathematics-ontology brought about by Cantor represents anything in Badiou, it is constituted by these two sides of the transfinite: this transformation of both the nature of infinite multiplicity and the unhinging of consistency and unity. Through Cantor's transfinite, the metaphysical reliance on unity to render the multiplicity of being intelligible and consistent could be overcome with a discourse on multiplicity that is not couched on the horizon of counting or the one. The multiple as *plithos* (πλῆθος) opens up a path for thinking multiplicity that shifts the grounds for how difference is articulated. Here, a number of different themes in Badiou's philosophy line up to deliver the same essential point: the death of God, the passion of the real, the identification of the ontology of mathematics. Affirming that 'if the one is not, then nothing is', the inexistence of the one, totality, underlined precisely by the transfinite separation between unity and consistency, brings us to a new appreciation of the consequence that 'nothing is'. Indeed, axiomatic set theory understood in its ontological capacity is the very activity of unfolding the structure of this 'nothing' and Badiou proceeds toward axiomatic set theory to give a more robust development of this.

The situating or localisation of mathematical ontology in this historical subtraction of mathematics from the metaphysical guardianship of the one indeed highlights the sense of the identity of set theory and ontology but there remains a certain gap in answering the stated problematic that we began with. The historical account of the subtraction from the one indeed places Cantor in the continuity of the history of thinking multiplicity. No doubt this historical account is retroactive in nature and it is Cantor himself that allows us to reinterpret Plato's *Parmenides* along the lines of a history of subtraction. As such, this narrative of subtraction is itself an effect of a discontinuity. How does this localisation of ontology within the historical subtraction of mathematics cast light on Cantor's reflexive status in Badiou's thought?

The Point of Impossibility

In light of this narrative of subtraction, which seemingly puts Cantor somewhere in the middle of a historically and dialectically constituted continuity between Plato, ancient Greek mathematics and the latest developments in mathematics, this continuity has allowed Badiou to underline the significance of Cantor's work but does raise questions concerning Cantor as an 'event'.

In order to address this question, we should dig a little deeper into the controversies surrounding Cantor's own work. Here, we return to the distance between Cantor and axiomatic set theory. Cantor can undoubtedly be credited as an early contributor to the development of set theory. His position concerning sets was, however, something that was rejected from its later canonical version, the ZF axiomatic set theory. The issue concerns the problem of the definition of set, *Menge*. In basic terms, this concerns the very passage from what is understood as the naive set theory of Cantor and the axiomatic set theory introduced later by Zermelo and reworked by Fraenkel. In Cantor's *Contributions to the Founding of the Theory of Transfinite Numbers*, Cantor defines an 'aggregate' [*Menge*] as a 'collection into a whole [*Zusammenfassung su einem Ganzen*] M of definite and separate objects m of our intuition or our thought'.[4] We can compare this to the contemporaneous work of Dedekind who also provides a version of this naive set theory through the concept of 'system' which is 'an aggregate, a manifold, a totality' of things, which are in turn 'every object of our thought'.[5] In the development of set theory after Cantor and Dedekind, these appeals to intuition, 'thought' or 'objects of thought' encountered immediate limits.

One of these limits, a central outcome of this appeal to intuition, was immediately obvious to Cantor and would eventually become a defining issue of the axiomatisation projects. In his famous letter to Dedekind in 1899, the question that Cantor asked himself concerned what sort of multiplicity would constitute a set in its rigorous sense. Could there, for instance, be a set of all (ordinal) numbers? Predating Russell's paradox by two years and echoing Burali-Forti's paradox a few years before, Cantor recognised that such a set would be contradictory to the very notion of the ordering of the size of sets (cardinality), the cornerstone to the concept of the transfinite. Simply put, if there was a set of all numbers, and if this were indeed a set, there would be a number δ greater than the number that measures the set. In turn, the number δ would have to belong to this original set since it is a set of *all* numbers. As such, 'δ would thus be greater than δ which is a contradiction.'[6] In a mathematical sense, we could say that this set of all numbers is too 'large' to be measured, even with the transfinite numbers (which are themselves numbers). This problem recalls traditional paradoxes of the infinite concerning the number of all numbers but is indeed separated from the notion of the 'count' in a strict sense. As Russell will later show, the problem is to be pinpointed at the notion of the naive intensional notion of sets. The intensional reference to sets by means of a property or an object of thought falters precisely because there can be an intensional object 'set of all sets' which is contradictory. The appeal to intuition in the definition of sets has thus to be replaced with a minimalist one, in ZF set theory, constituted by the relation of belonging ($\in$). In contemporary terms, a set is simply defined by what belongs ($\in$) to it, which are themselves sets.

In this same letter, Cantor aimed to circumvent the contradiction by underlining the exclusive conditions of his original definition of sets. Here Cantor insisted that a set must be consistent, underlined by his idea of 'definite and separate' in his original definition; but such a condition requires some overarching concept of unity and thus restricts those very multiplicities which are not appropriately ordered. This illustrates the fact that the problem is not a paradox and the problems of the inconsistent 'set of all sets' in Russell or the 'number of all numbers' in Cantor constitute an inconsistency and should lead us back to problems in the premises of set definition. On Badiou's own treatment of this issue, I cite his quotation of Cantor in full:

> On the one hand, a multiplicity may be such that the affirmation according to which all its elements 'are together' leads to a contradiction, such that it is impossible to conceive the multiplicity as a unity, as a 'finite thing'. These multiplicities, I name them absolutely infinite multiplicities, or inconsistent . . . When, on the other hand, the totality of the elements of a multiplicity can be thought without contradiction as 'being together', such that their collection in 'a thing' is possible, I name it a consistent multiplicity or a set. (BE 42)

This tricky passage contains a number of different problems. There is a problem with translation that appears to indicate that sets could only be finite. Oliver Feltham's translation here mirrors Badiou's own reference to Cantor. This is inaccurate since the very context of these statements concerns Cantor's questions about the transfinite sets themselves. In the now standard translation by Stefan Bauer-Mengelberg and Jean Van Heijenoort, the same problematic sentence is translated as: 'For a multiplicity can be such that the assumption that all of its elements "are together" leads to a contradiction, so that it is impossible to conceive of the multiplicity as a unity, as "one finished thing". Such multiplicities I call absolutely infinite or inconsistent multiplicities.'[7] This translation correctly renders the fact that Cantor was not speaking of the finitude of transfinite sets but rather the consistency of certain transfinite sets. This distinction between consistent and inconsistent multiplicities, the first being sets and the latter being 'absolute infinite' multiplicities, played a central role in the formalisation of set theory in the decades to come. Indeed, the definition of 'set' through the conceptual dependence on the loosely intuitional notion of unity, 'one finished thing', places unity before multiplicity and renders the set dependent on the 'objects' defined by their properties and constituted by intuition. Badiou affirms that the axiomatic projects in set theory have the virtue of *not* relying on this Cantorian appeal to property or intuition. As such:

> Yet the one and the multiple do not form a 'unity of contraries', since the first is not whilst the second is the very form of any presentation of being. Axiomatization is required such that the multiple, left to the implicitness of its counting rule, be delivered without concept, that is, without implying the being-of-the-one. (BE 43)

This fundamental rejection of the definition of the set concept is crucial to Badiou's set-theoretical ontology. As he argues:

> In Zermelo and Fraenkel's stabilized elaboration, there is no other nondefined primitive term or value possible for the variables apart from sets. Hence, every element of a set is itself a set. This accomplishes the idea that every multiple is a multiple of multiples, with no reference to units of any kind. (OT 41)

That is, as Badiou is well aware, ZF set theory is not a Cantorian one. It is rather one that eschews Cantor's original definition of the concept of the set, a theory of sets that rejects the definition of set provided by Cantor as well as one that rejects any definition other than an immanent one constituted by the minimal relation of belonging ($\in$).

Badiou's mathematical ontology depends on the maturation of set theory from its naive and intuitional background to its axiomatic formulation. As we remarked earlier, it is the axiomatic development of set theory that is precisely what provides Badiou with the fundamental connection between ontology and mathematics. With the relation of belonging, Badiou asserts that, 'The sign $\in$, *unbeing* of any one, determines in a uniform manner, the presentation of "something" as indexed to the multiple' (BE 44). In addition, the sign of the void ∅, itself a multiple, is 'the sole term from which ontology's compositions without concept weave themselves' (BE 57). These two aspects of axiomatic set theory explicitly distance themselves from Cantor's naive conception of sets, built on an appeal to intuition to furnish the 'objects' that would aggregate to form a set. It is this distance that constitutes the ground of Badiou's ontology. As Badiou explains:

> There is no question about it: the 'first' present multiplicity without concept has to be a multiple of nothing, because if it was a multiple of something, that something would then be in the position of the one. And it is necessary, thereafter, that the axiomatic rule solely authorize compositions on the basis of this multiple-of-nothing, which is to say on the basis of the void. (BE 58)

I emphasise here that this observation is made precisely on the basis of the distance from naive set theory and in turn philosophically qualifies the 'multiple-of-nothing' as the basis of Badiou's mathematical ontology.

To constitute the grounds of an immanent multiplicity constituted by the void, the no-thing of the rejection of metaphysics, thought through the conceptual power of set theory, we must first recognise the historical transformation that Cantor himself constitutes. Here, we must return our focus on the inconsistent multiplicity, the multiplicity precisely rejected by Cantor as capable of forming a set. As Badiou argues:

> However, one could also argue that Cantor, in a brilliant anticipation, saw that the absolute point of being of the multiple is not its consistency – thus its dependence upon a procedure of the count-as-one – but its inconsistency, a multiple-deployment that no unity gather together. (BE 42)

Badiou highlights precisely what axiomatic set theory sought to overcome. It is not the rigorisation or the making-consistent of the notion of set that Badiou underlines as the greatest insight of Cantor but rather its apparent weakness. Leaving to one side, for the moment, what axiomatic set theory will eventually bring about, we can reinterpret Cantor's exclusion of the inconsistent multiplicity as forming a site encircled by two terms. There is, on the one hand, consistent multiplicities understood as sets, and on the other hand, inconsistent, absolute multiplicity understood as inconsistent multiplicity. The latter is the opposing side of a distinction that preserves the elaboration of the transfinite cardinals that is excluded from a presentation as an ordered set. This expansive unending transfinite measure was one that constituted, for Cantor, the absolute, God. This absolute is inconsistent precisely in that it transcends any one. As Badiou argues:

> Cantor's thought thus wavers between onto-theology – for which the absolute is thought as a supreme infinite being, thus as trans-mathematical, in-numerable, as a form of the one so radical that no multiple can consist therein – and mathematical ontology, in which consistency provides a theory of inconsistency, in that which proves an obstacle to it (paradoxical multiplicity) is its point of impossibility, and thus, quite simply, is not. Consequently, it fixes the point of non-being from whence it can be established that there is a presentation of being. (BE 42)

Cantor thus undoes the one by means of the absolute itself. It is this paradoxical emergence of the absolute that reveals, in a global sense, that the 'one' is an effect of the very operation that reveals the absolutely inconsistent multiple grounds of the count. In this undoing, however, Cantor, as Badiou explains, provides the 'point of non-being' or the 'point of impossibility' that is itself the context wherein ontology achieves its grounds for articulating the difference between being and beings. That is, from a strictly mathematical perspective, Cantor's treatment of the definition of set was something to be overcome insofar as it led to inconsistency and unrigorous distinctions. For Badiou, it is not simply the correct mathematical 'solution', the exclusion of the paradoxical set, eventually cleaned up in axiomatic set theory, that illuminates the establishment of mathematical ontology. As a concrete instance mirroring the overcoming of the metaphysical priority of the one and the total, it is precisely this entanglement between consistent and inconsistent multiplicities, in Cantor's last-ditch metaphysical-theological supplement, that situates the limits of mathematical ontology within the horizon of Cantor's inconsistent and absolute multiple.

On the one hand, Badiou affirms that it is from this 'point of impossibility', an evental site opened up by Cantor's struggle with the consequences of his transfinitude, that provides the grounds and hence the limits of mathematical ontology identified with axiomatic set theory. This point is not so straightforward, however. As Badiou explains:

> At the core of its presentation, Set Theory is nothing else than the theory's body of axioms . . . The upshot of this is that the essence of thought of the pure multiple does not require a dialectical principle. Furthermore, the freedom of thinking in harmony with Being is in the axiomatic decision – and not in the intuition of a norm. (OT 42)

No doubt, if we consider the ontological separation from philosophy as the constitution of ontology as a mathematical discourse enclosed by the limits of set theory, this 'cutting of the Gordian knot' would present itself without its external dialectical constraints. On the other hand, however, the arrival at this very subtraction of ontology as mathematics places the transformation of the thought of multiplicity within the historical passage – formulated retroactively and reflexively through Cantor himself – that reaches as far back as Plato's treatment in the *Parmenides*. In Badiou's own treatment of Cantor, this dialectical conflict can be localised at the point of the difficulty that Cantor faced in his own definition of set. In this, the separation between ontology and philosophy may well render ontology as axiomatic set theory undialectical. However, it is this very separation that places ontology within a concrete and historical 'situation' that not only renders the grounds for mathematical ontology coherent but also underlines ontology's consistent treatment of the inconsistent multiple. In short, it is the dialectical situation of ontology within the thought of the inconsistent multiple that renders ontological discourse itself undialectical.

In this series of localisations, the localisation of the consistent multiples within the inconsistent absolute multiples, the localisation of axiomatic set theory within the historicity of its grounds, we gather a more precise picture of Badiou's relationship with Cantor. The structure provided by the axioms of set theory produces an immanence wherein the identification between mathematics and ontology can be established. This immanence, however, provides the very means of outlining the historical understanding of how the consistent multiples within set theory relate with being's inconsistent multiplicity. Insofar as the void $\varnothing$ sutures this inconsistent multiplicity as 'nothing' in the syntax of ZF set theory, the neutralisation of this paradoxical ground grants set theory's immanent enclosure while at the same time allows this 'theory of the void' to be exactly and precisely a theory of inconsistent multiplicity (BE 67–9). As such, mathematical ontology localises inconsistent multiplicity, the point of impossibility encountered in Cantor's work, through the subsequent developments in axiomatic set theory including the struggles with the independence proofs which unfold the undecidable nature of inconsistent multiplicity. It is, however, equally true that the historical twists concerning inconsistent multiplicity localises axiomatic set theory. It is in this light that, as Badiou aims to establish in *Being and Event*, 'mathematics is the historicity of the discourse on being qua being' (BE 13). Indeed, while it is clear that mathematics does not require this historicity to create a consistent discourse concerning multiplicity, it is this very historicity that allows us to grasp it, philosophically, from its point of subtraction. This mutual implication, ontology's reflexive localisation, encircles the very site opened up by Cantor's work.

Concluding Remarks

We make a return to the question posed at the start of our investigation. How can the event be taken as separated from ontology if the very constitution of mathematical ontology is itself an event? Through our investigation, we can answer this question in the following way. What was opened up by Cantor was not so much a 'paradise' as a problematic site that allows for the historical and dialectical reading of the constitution of mathematical ontology which in turn renders coherent the inconsistent grounds of this subtraction of ontology from metaphysics. At the same time, this subtraction is inactual unless it is exercised and elaborated immanently within the limits of what is subtracted. The effect of this problematic site is the positive articulation of mathematical ontology but at the cost of distancing itself from this very site. As such, the localisation of ontology within its history is the localisation of this history in mathematical ontology.

As paradoxical as it seems, this circularity is precisely what was opened up by Cantor's 'point of impossibility', a site whose consequences are drawn temporally forward into the development of set theory and also backward to deliver a history of subtraction. The conceptual development of the transfinite brought the historical dialectic concerning the one and the multiple, concentrated traditionally within problems of infinity, to a new stage of articulation, a historical stage with its own paradoxes, problematics and unresolved problems. On the other hand, it is in the context of these problematics that ontology, as mathematics, achieved, with axiomatic set theory, 'the free play of its own conditions' (OT 40). Through this site, ontology's reflexive grasping of its own conditions is of course 'nothing' for mathematics in the strict sense but it is also this 'nothing' that will be the very condition for the unfolding of its immanent discourse.

I terminate this investigation with one of Badiou's more poetic treatments of Cantor. In Badiou's recent *Second Manifesto for Philosophy*, in the chapter on '*Ideation*', he uses Cantor's life as an example of a life that took on the exacting burdens of a truth. Following the model of a 'life worth living' given in Plato's allegory of the cave, Badiou reads Cantor's life as being split asunder by his development of the transfinite cardinals. Divided between the implications of his mathematical work and the fear of the absolute-divine, Cantor was, in Badiou's parable, undone by his unwitting encroachment on God's domain by rendering the orders of infinity accessible. As Cantor admitted to Dedekind, 'I see it, but I don't believe it' (SM 114). This split between seeing and believing testified to a deep subjective split that is inherent in the irreconcilable dynamics of a truth. In succumbing to madness in his final years, Cantor never strayed from the path of fidelity which in turn allowed its violence to wreak havoc on his psyche: a true life.

Whether Cantor's madness can be attributed to his work is of course contestable. It is this madness, however, that is underlined by Badiou. What can be gathered from this parable extends beyond the model of a courageous subjective encounter with truth. As one of Plato's allegorical captives who climbs to the light just to be blinded by it, Cantor certainly represented, for Badiou, a model for the ethical encounter with truth. However, here again, what Badiou underlines is neither the courageous struggle with truth nor the positive results that can be gained from this struggle. What the parable illustrates is the opening up of a site, the point of impossibility where an event interrupts in such a way that, regardless of its positive results, it remains undecidable and interminable. Irreducible to any positive naming, the position of Cantor's proper name can finally only be minimally identified with this madness.

Notes

1. David Hilbert, 'On the infinite', in Jean Van Heijenoort (ed.), *From Frege to Gödel* (Cambridge, MA: Harvard University Press, 1967), pp. 367–92, at p. 376.
2. Plato, 'Parmenides', in John M. Cooper (ed.), *Plato: Complete Works* (Indianapolis, IN and Cambridge: Hackett, 1997), pp. 359–97, at p. 397.
3. Ibid., p. 395.
4. Georg Cantor, *Contributions to the Founding of the Theory of Transfinite Numbers* (New York: Dover, 1915), p. 85.
5. Richard Dedekind, *Essays on the Theory of Numbers* (New York: Dover, 1963), pp. 44–5.
6. Georg Cantor, 'Letter to Dedekind', in Jean Van Heijenoort (ed.), *From Frege to Gödel* (Cambridge, MA: Harvard University Press, 1967), pp. 113–17, at p. 115.
7. Cantor, 'Letter to Dedekind', p. 114.

3

The Set-Theoretical Nature of Badiou's Ontology and Lautman's Dialectic of Problematic Ideas

Sean Bowden

In the notes to *Being and Event*, Badiou declares: '[Albert] Lautman's writings are nothing less than admirable and what I owe to them, even in the very foundational intuitions for this book, is immeasurable' (BE 482). Nowhere in his published work, however, does Badiou explain in detail what he believes he owes to the philosophy of Lautman. In an interview with Tzuchien Tho, Badiou remarks that even though Lautman's primary and secondary theses for his *doctorat d'état* were published in 1938, it was only well after the 1977 publication of Lautman's collected works that he became familiar with them (CM 82).[1] This would certainly explain the lack of explicit engagement with Lautman's writings prior to the publication of *Being and Event*. But even after 1988, Badiou primarily invokes the figure of Lautman for illustrative purposes, or to suggest a very general affinity. Thus, in *Logics of Worlds*, Badiou inscribes himself, but without indicating what such an inscription amounts to, in the French tradition of 'mathematising idealism' which includes Brunschvicg, Cavaillès, Lautman, Desanti, Althusser and Lacan (LW 7). In *Metapolitics*, Badiou eulogises Lautman, both a philosopher of mathematics and active member of the French Resistance who was captured and shot by the Nazis in 1944, as one of the 'exemplary resistant figures of French philosophy' (M 4–5). Finally, in the first *Manifesto for Philosophy*, Badiou cites Lautman as an ally insofar as he, like Badiou, is an openly Platonic philosopher standing in opposition to the more general twentieth-century trend of Nietzschean anti-Platonism (MP 100–1). In each of these instances, it is clear that Badiou invokes the name of Lautman for purposes other than concrete conceptual or argumentative support.

Three exceptions to this tendency, however, can be found in *Briefings on Existence*: a note to the essay 'Philosophy and

Mathematics', originally published in *Conditions*, and the short interview with Tzuchien Tho mentioned above published alongside the English translation of *The Concept of Model*. In these three texts, Badiou indicates a more substantial philosophical affiliation with, and perhaps a philosophical debt to, Lautman.

In *Briefings on Existence*, Lautman's work is cited in support of Badiou's thesis, defended from the time of *Being and Event* onwards, that 'mathematics thinks being qua being' or that 'set theory is ontology'. He writes: 'As Albert Lautman's works in particular demonstrated, as far back as the 1930s, every significant and innovative fragment of real mathematics can and ought to evoke, as a condition of existence, its ontological identification' (TO 60 – translation modified).[2] But how exactly does Badiou understand this apparently Lautmanian idea, which he believes himself to share, that mathematics evokes – and as a 'condition of existence' no less – its ontological identification?

We ought firstly to recall that, for Badiou, the proposition 'set theory is ontology' is a philosophical and not a mathematical proposition (TO 59). In *Manifesto for Philosophy*, Badiou argues that this particular proposition is grounded in his own philosophy insofar as this latter has successfully been able to 'compossibilise' a number of contemporary, extra-philosophical 'conditions' or 'generic truth procedures'. Because the development of set theory from Cantor to Paul Cohen is one such truth procedure, within the conditioned philosophical space that Badiou constructs, the philosophical thinking of being qua being can be effectively handed over to set theory (MP 33–9, 79–81). Indeed, this metaontological justification of the 'set theory is ontology' thesis is the one normally discussed in the secondary literature.[3]

In *Briefings on Existence*, however, Badiou adds a specifically Lautmanian element to his account of the justification of the philosophical proposition that set theory is ontology. He writes that while it is indeed a matter of philosophy 'identifying what its own conditions are', it is also necessary for 'real mathematics to be crossed reflexively' (TO, 59). In other words, the grounding of the proposition that mathematics thinks being qua being is not simply a matter of philosophy welcoming within its 'space of compossibility' a novel, set-theoretical translation of well-established philosophical and ontological concepts. It is also a matter of philosophy fully entering into and traversing mathematical discourse (but without itself becoming mathematical discourse) in order to discover how mathematics thinks being qua being in its *own* unique terms.

Badiou makes a similar point in a note to 'Philosophy and Mathematics' – the second text mentioned above. Here, Badiou makes it clear that his and Lautman's (as well as Cavaillès' and Desanti's) philosophical relation to mathematics is a matter of treating mathematics 'as a singular site of thinking, whose events and procedures must be retraced from *within* the philosophical act' (TW 244). And indeed, this sounds very close to the way Lautman expresses his own position on the issue of mathematical philosophy:

> Mathematical philosophy . . . consists not so much in retrieving a logical problem of classical metaphysics within a mathematical theory, than in grasping the structure of this theory globally in order to identify the logical problem that happens to be both defined and resolved by the very existence of this theory.[4]

Finally, in the interview with Tho, Badiou explicitly aligns himself with Lautman's unique brand of 'dialectical Platonism' (CM 92–3).[5] Badiou's comments here, coupled with the remarks just examined, throw a little more light on his belief that he shares with Lautman the idea that mathematics elicits, as a condition of existence, its ontological identification, and hence also that he owes to Lautman's writings some of the fundamental intuitions for his philosophical undertaking in *Being and Event*. In the interview with Tho, Badiou alludes to two aspects of Lautman's work which will be examined further below. The first aspect is that Lautman understands there to be a 'dialectic of Ideas' which drives the historical development of mathematics (as its 'condition of existence'), giving to mathematics its philosophical value and, as Badiou would say, its 'ontological identification'. The second aspect of Lautman's work to which Badiou alludes is that there is a dialectal interpenetration of, on the one hand, the abstract Ideas governing the development of mathematics and, on the other hand, the concrete theories in which such development is successively embodied. Indeed, as Badiou appears to read Lautman, it is because certain abstract 'ontological' Ideas are both transcendent and immanent with respect to concrete mathematical theory that philosophy must fully enter into and traverse mathematical discourse in order to discover how mathematics evokes, in its own terms, its ontological character.

In line with textual evidence such as this, this chapter proposes to explore in greater depth the precise nature of the debt that Badiou owes to Lautman in *Being and Event*. The chapter's thesis is that Badiou's assertion that set theory is ontology is grounded upon what Lautman calls a 'dialectic of problematic Ideas'. More specifically, it will be argued here that the proposition that set theory is ontology is grounded insofar as set theory simultaneously defines and resolves, in its own terms, a connected series of philosophical – or, more precisely, ontological – problems. As will be seen, following Lautman's work, these problems can be expressed in the form of yet-to-be-determined relationships between a number of opposed notions belonging to the history of philosophy and ontology: the one and the multiple, Nature as poem and Nature as Idea, the finite and the infinite, and the continuous and the discrete. In what follows, I shall demonstrate exactly how the Zermelo-Fraenkel (ZF) axioms which found Badiou's set-theory ontology together resolve this series of dialectical couples. In concluding, I will also raise a problem which ensues from Badiou's Lautmanian heritage. But let us first of all examine the major lines of Albert Lautman's only recently translated work.

Albert Lautman and the Dialectic of Problematic Ideas

Lautman distinguished several layers of mathematical reality. Apart from mathematical facts, objects and theories, Lautman also argued for the existence of a 'dialectic of Ideas' which governs the development of mathematical theories and provides them with their unity, meaning and philosophical value.[6] This dialectic is constituted by pairs of opposites (same and other, whole and part, continuous and discrete, essence and existence, etc.), and the Ideas of this dialectic present themselves as the problem of establishing relationships between these opposed notions.[7] As prior 'questions' or 'logical concerns' relative to mathematical discourse, these problematic Ideas are transcendent with respect to mathematics and can be posed outside of mathematics. Indeed, many of the pairs of opposites analysed by Lautman can be found in the history of philosophy. However, since the Ideas, in order to be thought concretely, require an appropriate 'matter' in which they can be thought, any effort to respond to the problems that they pose is to effectively constitute mathematical theory. In this sense, therefore, the dialectic must equally be said to be immanent to mathematics.[8] As Lautman puts it, an 'intimate link thus exists between the transcendence of Ideas and the immanence of the logical structure of the solution to a dialectical problem within mathematics'.[9]

In a letter to the mathematician Maurice Fréchet, Lautman provides the following example in order to clarify his thought on this point:

> One can envisage abstractly the Idea of knowing whether relations between abstract notions exist, for example the container and the content, but it happens that any effort whatsoever to outline a response to this problem is ipso facto the fashioning of mathematical theories. The question of knowing whether forms of solidarity between space and matter exist is in itself a philosophical problem, which is at the centre of Cartesian metaphysics. But any effort to resolve this problem leads the mind necessarily to construct an analytic mechanics in which a connection between the geometric and dynamic can in fact be asserted.[10]

In order to avoid the charge of naive idealism, Lautman is careful to qualify the transcendence of Ideas as simply the 'possibility' of experiencing concern for a mode of connection between two ideas.[11] The anteriority of Ideas is here rational or logical as opposed to psychological or historical.[12] And this is precisely why Lautman argues that mathematics not only incarnates traditional metaphysical problems, it can also give birth to problems that could not have been previously posed. As we mentioned above, Lautman's particular approach to the philosophy of mathematics does not so much consist in finding a well-established metaphysical problem within a mathematical theory. It is rather a matter of grasping the overall structure of a given theory in order to extract the problem that is at once defined and resolved in it.[13]

Nevertheless, as Lautman goes on to argue, just as, in the very meaning of these terms, 'intention' precedes 'design' and the 'question' the 'response', the existence of established mathematical relations necessarily refers to the prior, positive Idea of the search for such relations.[14] Or to put it another way, because the 'sufficient reason' for the diversity and development of mathematical theories, along with their progressive integrations and interferences, cannot be found within mathematics itself,[15] one is obliged to affirm the prior existence of something like the dialectic of Ideas.

In short, to conceive of the historical development of diverse mathematical theories and their 'mixes' as responses or solutions to problematic Ideas is to give unity and meaning to these theories.[16]

Now, it is of course clear that Badiou's concern is not that of the unity and meaning of mathematics in Lautman's sense. However, it will be the contention of this chapter that there is something like a dialectic of Ideas that traverses *Being and Event*, and that it is precisely this dialectic that allows Badiou to make the claim that 'ontology is set theory'. Or to put it another way, it is only because Badiou shows set theory to be capable of providing a systematic response to a series of dialectically opposed notions which can be found in the history of ontology (and philosophy more generally) that set theory can be said to be ontology. These dialectical couples include: the one and the multiple, Nature as poem and Nature as Idea, the finite and the infinite, and the continuous and the discrete. This chapter shall demonstrate how the Zermelo-Fraenkel axiom system which 'founds' Badiou's set-theory ontology in *Being and Event* resolves these dialectically opposed notions.

The One and the Multiple

Being and Event begins by outlining and then advancing a solution to the problem of 'the one and the multiple'. This is a problem, Badiou argues, with which any possible ontology will have to deal. It can be unpacked in the following way. Firstly, any presented concrete thing must be *one*. A thing is, after all, *this* thing. Secondly, however, presentation itself is *multiple*, which is to say that what can be presented is presentable in multiple and variable ways. When it is asked whether being is one or multiple, therefore, one comes to an impasse. For, on the one hand, if being is one, then the multiple cannot be. On the other hand, if presentation is multiple and there cannot be an access to being outside of all presentation, then the multiple must be. But if the multiple is, then being is not equivalent to the one. And yet there is a presentation of *this* multiple only if what is presented is one. Badiou then says that this deadlock can only be broken by declaring that the one, strictly speaking, is *not*: oneness is rather only a 'result', a multiplicity which has been 'counted for one'. Badiou calls such a multiplicity a 'situation', and every situation must have a 'structure' which is the operator of its count-as-one (BE 23–4).

For Badiou, then, every identifiable being is in situation. In other words, every being is a consistent multiplicity, counted-for-one. What is not in situation, what is not counted-for-one as this or that thing, could only be qualified as 'no-thing'. There is, then, no-thing apart from situations, that is apart from consistent one-multiples, and these situations must all be posterior or subsequent to a structuring or count-as-one operation. However, at the same time, to say as I did above that the one is a result must mean that anterior to any possible count-as-one or consistent multiple there must be, and could only be, inconsistent multiplicity. In the final analysis, therefore, if the one is only ever a result, then inconsistent multiplicity – this no-thing which is outside of any situation – must ultimately be presupposed as the one-less 'stuff' or pure unqualified being of any possible being: that which is included in what any presentation presents (BE 24–5).

But now, what can be said about this pure, unqualified being? More specifically, how can it be presented to thought, not as some specific 'thing' or consistent one-multiple, but qua being? In other words, what could ontology be – the science of being qua being? Ontology, for Badiou, must be a situation, but it clearly cannot present inconsistent multiplicity as a one-multiple. Ontology must rather be a situation capable of presenting inconsistent multiplicity as that from which every presented or in-situation 'thing' is composed, but without thereby giving inconsistent multiplicity any other predicate other than its multiplicity. In other words, ontology will be the situation which 'presents presentation' in general (BE 27–8). And the only way it can do this, following Badiou, is by somehow showing in its very structure that this no-thing or inconsistent multiplicity exists, and that everything in the ontological situation is composed out of it, but without thereby counting this inconsistent multiplicity for one. And for Badiou, it is the axioms of set theory which fulfil this prior structural necessity, since they only give an implicit definition of what it operates on: the pure multiple (BE 28–30, 52–9). In short, then, for Badiou, insofar as set theory alone can respond to the above analysed ontological problematic, it is the only possible ontology.

So how exactly do the ZF axioms fulfil ontology's a priori requirements, the requirements which, it is evident, correspond to nothing internal to set theory? First of all, it reduces the one to the status of a relationship, that of simple *belonging*, written $\in$. In other words, everything will be presented, not according to the one of a concept, but only according to its relation of belonging or counting-for-one: 'something = α' will thus only be presented according to a multiple β, written α ∈ β or 'α is an element of β'. Secondly, the theory has only one type of variable and hence does not distinguish between 'objects' and 'groups of objects', or between 'elements' and 'sets'. In other words, to be an element is not an intrinsic quality in ZF. It is a simple relation: to-be-an-element-of. Thus, by the uniformity of its variables, the theory can indicate without definition that it does not speak of the one, and that all that it presents in the implicitness of its rules are multiples of multiples: multiples belonging to or presented by other multiples. Indeed, and thirdly, via the 'axiom of separation', the system affirms that a property or formula of language does not directly present an existing multiple. Rather, such a presentation could only ever be a 'separation' or subset of an already presented multiplicity. A property only determines a multiple under the supposition that there is already a presented multiple (BE 43–8). Everything thus hinges on the determination of the initial pure multiple. But as was seen above, as a necessary consequence of the decision that the one results – called for by the problematic relationship between the one and the multiple – there must be, anterior to any count, inconsistent multiplicity, and it is this which is ultimately counted. It appears, then, that this inconsistent multiple – the void, the unpresentable of presentative consistency – is the absolutely initial multiple.

How, then, can the void have its existence assured, and in such a way that ontology can weave all of its compositions from it alone? As Badiou says, it is by making this nothing 'be' through the assumption of a pure proper name: ∅ (BE 66–7). That the void is named is not to say, of course, that the void is thereby one. What is named is not the one of the void, but rather its uniqueness or 'unicity'. In what sense is the void unique? Another axiom of ZF tells us this. This is the 'axiom of extensionality' which will fix the rule of difference or sameness for any two multiples whatsoever, that is according to the elements which belong to each. The void set, then, having no elements – being the multiple of nothing – can have no conceivable differentiating mark according to this axiom. But then, if no difference can be attested, this means that there is a unicity of the unpresentable within presentation. There cannot be 'several' voids: the void is unique and this is what is signalled by the proper name, ∅ (BE 67–9).

So how does set-theory ontology weave its compositions out of this proper name? What is crucial to this operation is the 'power-set axiom' or 'axiom of subsets'. This axiom guarantees that if a set exists, another set also exists that counts as one all the subsets of this first set, thereby regulating or counting as one the internal compositions of a given being or situation. It has been seen what belonging means: an element (a multiple) belongs to a situation (a set) if it is directly presented and counted for one by this situation. *Inclusion*, on the other hand, concerns subsets or parts of a situation rather than directly presented elements. In other words, elements directly presented by a set can be re-presented, that is grouped into subsets that are said to be included in the initial set. Inclusion is written $\subset$: $\alpha \subset \beta$ or α is a subset (a part) of β.[17] The power-set axiom gathers together or counts as one all such inclusions, all of the sub-compositions of internal multiples. It says that if a set α exists, there also exists the set of all its subsets: its power set $p(\alpha)$ (BE 81–4). What, then, can be said of the void from the point of view of the difference between belonging and inclusion?

It has already been seen that the void is never presented: it never belongs to another multiple. What is more, since the void is the multiple of nothing, nothing belongs to the void. However, it can be shown both that the void is a subset of any set – it is universally included – and that the void possesses a subset, which is the void itself (BE 86). Indeed, it is impossible for the empty set not to be universally included. For, following the axiom of extensionality, since the set $\varnothing$ has no elements, nothing is marked which could deny its inclusion in any multiple (see also NN 64). Furthermore, then, since the set $\varnothing$ is itself an existent-multiple, $\varnothing$ must be a subset of itself (BE 86–7).

One can now begin to see how the axioms of set theory – which are, for Badiou, the 'laws of being' – weave compositions out of the void. The argument is as follows: since the void admits at least one subset, itself, the power-set axiom can be applied. The set of subsets of the void, $p(\varnothing)$, is the set to which everything included in the void belongs. Thus, since $\varnothing$ is included in $\varnothing$, $\varnothing$ belongs to $p(\varnothing)$. This new set, $p(\varnothing)$, is thus 'our second existent-multiple in the "genealogical" framework of the set-theory axiomatic. It is written $\{\varnothing\}$ and $\varnothing$ is its sole element': $\varnothing \in \{\varnothing\}$ (BE 89). Now, let us consider the set of subsets of $\{\varnothing\}$, that is $p(\{\varnothing\})$. This set exists, since $\{\varnothing\}$ exists. What, then, are the parts of $\{\varnothing\}$? There is $\{\varnothing\}$ itself, which is the total part, and there is $\varnothing$, since the void is universally included in any multiple. The multiple $p(\{\varnothing\})$ is thus a

multiple with *two* elements, $\varnothing$ and $\{\varnothing\}$. Woven from the void, this
is, as Badiou puts it, 'the ontological schema of the Two', which
can be written $\{\varnothing,\{\varnothing\}\}$ (BE 92, 131–2). It becomes clear that this
is where the unlimited production of new multiples begins, woven
from the void in accordance with the laws of being (and particu-
larly the power-set axiom). For, since this set, $\{\varnothing,\{\varnothing\}\}$, exists, one
can consider its power set $p(\{\varnothing,\{\varnothing\}\})$, etc. . . . This process can
obviously be repeated indefinitely and it is in fact in this way that
one can generate our counting numbers, our 'natural' or 'ordinal'
numbers (also called Von Neumann ordinals):

$$0 = \varnothing$$
$$1 = \{\varnothing\} = \{0\}$$
$$2 = \{\varnothing,\{\varnothing\}\} = \{0,1\}$$
$$3 = \{\varnothing,\{\varnothing\},\{\varnothing,\{\varnothing\}\}\} = \{0,1,2\} \ldots {}^{[18]}$$

Nature as Poem and Nature as Idea

Indeed, it is from this generation of 'natural' numbers, all woven
from the void in accordance with the axioms of being, that Badiou
will establish his ontological concept of 'Nature'. Or more precisely, that Badiou understands Nature in this way is the result of
the way in which set-theory ontology provides a resolution of the
tension, highlighted since the work of Heidegger, between Nature
understood poetically as appearance or the poetic coming-to-
presence of Being (the pre-Platonic poem), and Nature interpreted
as Idea, subtracted from all appearance (in the manner of Plato)
(BE 123–9; on Plato see also BE 31–7). In other words, within the
perspective of a set-theoretical ontology, Badiou will be able to find
another arrangement of these two opposed orientations. In short,
following Heidegger, he will maintain that Nature is 'the stability
of maintaining-itself-there' within the opening forth of its immanent coming-to-presence. On the other hand, he will mathematise
the Platonic subtraction of being from appearance. Or again, he
will develop a concept of Nature as a network of multiples which
are interlocking and exhaustive without remainder, but which are
also woven entirely from what is subtracted from all presence: the
void. The point is, of course, that without reference to the opposing conceptions of Nature belonging to Heidegger and Plato, the
assertion that natural or ordinal numbers formalise the being of
natural things would appear somewhat arbitrary or as a play on

words. Certainly, nothing within set theory itself authorises such an ontological appropriation of the generation of ordinals.

Let us follow Badiou as he formulates his concept of Nature in the wake of this dialectical couple. On the one hand, conceding the stability of Nature to Heidegger, a multiple α will be said to be 'natural' (also called normal, ordinal or transitive) if every element β of this set is also a subset or part (that is, if $\beta \in \alpha$ then $\beta \subset \alpha$), and if every element β of α is itself natural in this way (that is, if $\gamma \in \beta$ then $\gamma \subset \beta$). This doubling of belonging and inclusion guarantees that there is nothing uncounted or unsecured in natural multiples which might contradict their internal consistency and concatenation. Just as Nature can never contradict itself, natural multiples remain homogeneous in dissemination. Every natural multiple is here obviously a 'piece' of another, for, by the definition of inclusion, if β is included in the natural multiple α, every element γ that belongs to β must also belong to α, and so on (BE 123–9).

On the other hand, mathematising Platonic subtraction, it can be said that the name of the void founds the series of natural multiples, conceived of in the way that has just been seen, in the double sense of formalising its concept and acting as its indivisible limit or atom. As examined above, an unlimited series of natural multiples can be generated from the void and the laws of ontology. For not only does the element $\{\varnothing\}$ have $\varnothing$ as its unique element, since the void is a universal part, this element $\varnothing$ is also a part. Furthermore, since the element $\varnothing$ does not present any element, nothing belongs to it that is not a part. There is thus no obstacle to declaring it to be natural. As such, the power set of $\{\varnothing\} - p(\{\varnothing\})$ or the Two: $\{\varnothing,\{\varnothing\}\}$ – is natural, and all of its elements are natural, and so on. Ordinal numbers thus both formalise the concept of natural multiples within set theory and are themselves existing natural multiples. And what is more, the name of the void is the ultimate natural element or atom which founds the entire series, in the sense in which the void is the 'smallest' natural multiple. In other words, if every natural multiple is a 'piece' of every other, the void is the only natural multiple to which no further element belongs (BE 130–40).

Needless to say, however, in Badiou's set-theoretical concept of Nature, there can be no possible formulation of Nature-in-itself. For Nature-in-itself would have to be a multiple which makes a one out of all the ordinals. But since this multiple would itself have to be an ordinal to make a one out of all the ordinals that belong to it, it would have to belong to itself. However, since no set can belong to itself, Nature in itself can have no sayable being (BE 140–1). Indeed, that no founded or consistent set can belong to itself is a fundamental presupposition of set theory. The ZF axiom system can even be said to have arisen in response to the paradoxes induced by self-belonging, such as those demonstrated by Russell (BE 40–3). In fact, the ZF 'axiom of foundation' was formulated in order to exclude the introduction of sets which belong to themselves. This axiom says that a set is founded if it has at least one element whose elements are not themselves elements of the initial set, that is, if it contains an element which has no members in common with the initial set. It is thus obvious that no set founded in this way can belong to itself (BE 185–7).

The Finite and the Infinite

This last point leads to a further problem, even if Badiou does not pose it in quite this way. What is crucial here is that this problem corresponds to that of the ontological problem of 'being-in-totality'. It has been seen that there cannot be a set of all sets which would govern the total count. But this does not in any way dispense with the task of examining the operation of the count. For precisely, when one turns to examine it, one notices something strange: because the one is not, because the count-as-one is only an operation, something always escapes the count-as-one and threatens thereby to ruin consistency. This 'something' is nothing other than the count itself, and this is true of natural as much as non-natural situations (BE 93–4). In other words, because the 'one' is only an operational result, if the count-as-one is not itself counted for one, it is impossible to verify that 'there is Oneness' is also valid for the counting operation. 'The consistency of presentation thus requires that all structure be doubled by a metastructure which secures the former against any fixation of the void', that is against any inconsistency (BE 93–4). This metastructure of a structured set – what Badiou also calls the 'state of the situation' (BE 95) – is precisely the power set which counts as one all of the initial set's parts. That is to say that it counts all of the possible internal compositions of the elements of the initial set up to and including the 'total part': the composition of elements that is the initial set. 'The completeness of the initial one-effect is thus definitely, in turn, counted as one by the state in the form of its effective whole' (BE 98).

Be that as it may, one cannot dispense in this way with the problem of the completion of the count of one-results without also dealing with a second historico-philosophical problem, a problem which can be phrased as: what is the relationship between being-in-totality and the finite/infinite couple? Or again: in the shadow of the problem of being-in-totality, what does it mean to say with the moderns that Nature is essentially infinite (BE 143)? Following Badiou's reconstruction of the history of the relationship between being-in-totality and the finite/infinite couple, one observes first of all that Aristotle's ontology was a finite ontology, since he refused to accept the existence of anything actually infinite or 'non-traversable' in nature. Indeed, for Aristotle, infinity could only be 'potential'. Medieval ontology, for its part, kept the finite Aristotelian ontology and supplemented it with an infinite being: God. Being-in-totality was thus here distributed into finite and infinite beings, God representing the 'punctual limit' of what finite beings cannot know (BE 142–3). Now, however, with the moderns, the concept of infinity shifts from God to Nature. But this does not mean that Nature is likened to a de-punctualised God. Indeed, as shown in Kant's antinomies, the one of Nature is illusory. Thus, following Badiou, since the one is not, that Nature is infinite must necessarily mean that presentation itself is infinite, and indeed infinitely infinite. If the one is not, there cannot be any one-infinite-being but only, as will be seen, numerous infinite multiples. The recognition of the infinity of Nature, the infinity of being, is the recognition of the infinity of situations: the count-as-one, even of a finite natural multiple, concerns an infinity of infinite multiples (BE 143–6).

What does it mean exactly when Badiou says that Nature or the count-as-one concerns infinite multiples? To say that situations are essentially infinite must mean that the finite is itself derived from the infinite. For, precisely, would not the succession of finite natural multiples or ordinals have need of the infinite in order to qualify it as the one-multiple that it is, that is in order to form-one out of all of its terms? This is what the 'axiom of infinity' declares: there exists an infinite limit ordinal, ω_0, and for all α, if α belongs to this limit ordinal, and if α is not void, then α is a finite, natural successor ordinal ($\varnothing$ of course is the initial existent multiple, not a successor). One can thus see that infinity counts-as-one all of the successor ordinals insofar as it is the 'support-multiple in which all the ordinals passed through mark themselves, step by step' (BE 155–6).

Strictly speaking, however, infinity is not simply equivalent to the limit ordinal ω_0, for one can also generate infinite successor ordinals for it such that, precisely, $\omega_0 \in S(\omega_0)$ (also written ω_1) (see BE 275–7).[19] So, then, an ordinal is infinite if it is ω_0 or if ω_0 belongs to it. An ordinal is finite if it belongs to ω_0 (BE 158–9).

It is thus in this way that Badiou can affirm, with the moderns but also within his set-theory ontology, that Nature is infinite. Or again, that being qua being is infinite. Or finally, that what can be said of being qua being – the presentation of inconsistent multiplicity or of what would be presentation in itself – essentially concerns infinite multiples and indeed, since one can always generate further infinite successor ordinals, an infinite number of infinite multiples (see BE 275–7). Yet this is not the end of the problem of the distribution of the finite and the infinite within being-in-totality. For it must now be asked: what here becomes of the necessary re-securing relationship between presentation and re-presentation – between the count and the count of the count – with respect to this understanding of the essential infinity of natural presentation? For a finite set of n elements, the power set is obviously equivalent to 2^n, but what could the power set of an infinite set possibly amount to?

The Continuous and the Discrete

In fact, the more precise question that Badiou asks is the following: is the power set $p(\omega_0)$ – that is to say, the count-as-one of all possible subsets of the complete series of finite natural numbers, sufficient for a complete numerical description of the geometrical continuum – equivalent to ω_1, the smallest infinite natural multiple which directly succeeds and counts-as-one ω_0? This is Cantor's famous 'continuum hypothesis' (see BE 295). The importance of this hypothesis is that, if it were true, we would have a 'natural measure' for the geometrical or physical continuum. Or in other words, we would have a quantitative knowledge of being qua being. For, if the continuum could be numerically measured, every discrete multiple could be quantitatively secured therein. The 'great question' of Badiou's set-theory ontology, translating the problematic couple continuous/discrete, is thus: is there an essential 'numerosity' of being (BE 265)? The answer is: we possess a natural measuring scale (the succession of ordinals), but it is impossible to determine where, on this scale, the set of parts of ω_0

is situated (BE 277–8). Or more precisely, following the work of Cohen and Easton, it appears that

> it is deductively acceptable to posit that [$p(\omega_0)$ is equal to] ω_{347}, or $\omega(\omega_0)_{+18}$, or whatever other cardinal as immense as you like . . . Easton's theorem establishes the quasi-total errancy of the excess of the state over the situation. It is as though, between the structure in which the immediacy of belonging is delivered, and the metastructure which counts as one the parts and regulates the inclusions, a chasm opens. (BE 280)

To recap: on the one hand, the One is not and being qua being essentially concerns an infinite number of rigorously defined, infinite, natural multiples, all woven from the void (BE 269: '*being is universally deployed as nature*'). On the other hand, the 'there is Oneness' of the presentation of such multiples – the count of the count – must be completely secured in order to render these discrete 'one'-beings consistent (BE 93–4). But now this means that, if we had a measure for this void-less continuum we would also have a quantitative knowledge of being qua being. This measurement cannot, however, be fixed. This 'un-measure', that is to say this variant on the enduring metaphysical problem of the relationship between the discreet and the continuous – itself the more general expression of the question of the distribution of the finite and the infinite within being-in-totality – is what Badiou calls the 'impasse of ontology' (BE 279).[20] To resolve it, Badiou will be led to a consideration of what, with Cohen's 'ontological' technique of 'forcing', corresponds to the philosophical notions of the event, the subject and truth.

We cannot examine in detail these further developments. Suffice it to say that what Badiou calls an 'event' will be an unfounded multiple (inscribed in ontology by the supplementary signifier ♀) which supplements the situation for which it is an event. It will be a self-founding 'supernumerary' something – named or posited as existent – whose place cannot be recognised in the situation as given, even though it can come to belong to or be counted within that situation, giving thereby the general 'one-truth' of said situation. This supplementation by the event will call for a 'subject' who asserts and then verifies – by examining one by one the connection of the infinite number of in-situation multiples to the event – the existence of the supernumerary event in the situation. This subject 'is' here nothing other than a finite multiple or 'fragment' of an infinite procedure of verification, a finite fragment which maintains a law-like relation to the aforementioned 'one-truth' which can be articulated in ontology (forcing). Finally, the 'truth' of the situation will be the 'indiscernible' or 'generic' multiplicity which will have resulted from the necessarily infinite procedure of verification which groups as 'one' all of the terms of the situation that are positively connected to the name of the self-founding event.[21]

Or again, to put it more 'ontologically', Cohen's technique shows that sets of conditions of a generic subset ♀ can be constructed which force, in a generic extension, the number of parts of ω_0 to surpass an absolutely indeterminate cardinal δ given in advance (see BE 420–6). This is the effective 'ontological proof' of the 'un-measure' of the continuum. But at the same time, as Badiou argues, this proof produces within ontology a 'one' account of inconsistent being qua being. How? In short, it constructs an infinite generic multiple by collecting, starting from the void, series of multiples attached to a supplementary, evental signifier ♀. But because it is not itself 'discerned', this generic multiple sets no limits to what it can rigorously collect as one and is thus, in the final analysis,

> composed of terms which have nothing in common that could be remarked, save belonging to *this* situation; which, strictly speaking, is its being, qua being . . . It is rightfully declared *generic*, because, if one wishes to qualify it, all one can say is that its elements *are* . . . [This is] the truth *of the entire situation*, insofar as the sense of the indiscernible is that of exhibiting as one-multiple the very being of what belongs insofar as it belongs. (BE 338–9)

Conclusion

Ultimately, then, it appears that the ontology outlined in *Being and Event* is grounded insofar as it resolves, in specifically set-theoretical terms, a series of dialectical couples: the one and the multiple, Nature as poem and Nature as Idea, the finite and the infinite, and the discrete and the continuous. This way of establishing set theory's 'ontological identification' constitutes Badiou's debt to Lautman and is fully in line with the former's scattered remarks about the latter examined above. But it also follows from this that while Badiou's ontology fulfils its aim of 'presenting presentation' in set-theoretical terms, it only does so in relation to another, prior and very different presentation of the ontological situation itself: that is, insofar as it must be thought as a response to a series of dialectical couples. But then this is also to say that being is equivocal in Badiou's system. Being is said once for the ontological situation insofar as it is grounded in a Lautmanian dialectic of problematic Ideas, and it is said once again for what the ontological situation, so determined, can say of being in general in a set-theoretical vocabulary.

Of course, Badiou would reply to this that if having an equivocal conception of being is what is required in order to think the particular, generic truth-procedures which collectively condition his philosophy, then he is happy to bear the criticism. As he writes in *Deleuze: The Clamor of Being* (although in relation to a reading of his system that differs from the one presented here, except in relation to the charge of equivocity):

> Deleuze always maintained that . . . I fall back into transcendence and into the equivocity of analogy. But, all in all, if the only way to think a political revolution, an amorous encounter, an invention of the sciences, or a creative work of art as distinct infinities – having as their condition incommensurable events – is by sacrificing immanence (which I do not actually believe is the case, but that is not what matters here) and the univocity of Being, then I would sacrifice them. (D 91–2)

But what disadvantages does such a conception in fact present, if any? The first disadvantage, of course, is that Badiou does not have a single or unified concept of being. It is true that, in the history of ontology, being has often been said in different senses: in Aristotle, for example, but also in the work of various medieval philosophers, for whom God 'is' in a different way from the way in which his creatures 'are' (Duns Scotus here being the notable exception). Nevertheless, Ockham's Razor could apply here, leading one to prefer an ontology in which being is said in a single sense of all there is.

A second disadvantage would be that, because Badiou's ontology presupposes a prior dialectic of problematic Ideas but does not itself think the nature of this dialectics, it cannot think its relation to another philosophical system presenting a different but equally systematic solution to the same problems resolved by Badiou's ontology, except as irreducible subjective conflict pure and simple. Again, this would not concern Badiou, who has a militant conception of the subject. But perhaps it would be of concern for those seeking a more supple approach to thinking the relations between the antagonistic subjectivities – political, scientific and so on – which can fall under different philosophical world views.

Taking these two points together, then, one can ask oneself the following critical question: can we conceive of a univocal conception of being which would be grounded solely on a Lautmanian-style dialectic of problematic Ideas, wherein beings in general could be considered to be 'solutions' to this dialectic, and in such a way that the various antagonistic subjectivities characterising our contemporary world can be thought together without irreducible conflict? I believe that Gilles Deleuze, another follower of Lautman, has developed such an ontology, particularly in his *Difference and Repetition*. As Deleuze writes:

> The problem is at once transcendent and immanent in relation to its solutions. Transcendent because it consists in a system of ideal liaisons or differential relations between genetic elements. Immanent, because these liaisons or relations are incarnated in the actual relations which do not resemble them and are defined by the field of solution. Nowhere better than in the admirable work of Albert Lautman has it been shown how problems are first Platonic Ideas or ideal liaisons between dialectical notions, relative to 'eventual situations of the existent'; but also how they are realized within the real relations constitutive of the desired solution with a *mathematical, physical* or other field.[22]

Indeed, in *Difference and Repetition*, Deleuze shows how entities in diverse domains – physical, biological, psychological, social, linguistic, mathematical – can all be considered to emerge as solutions to Lautmanian 'problematic Ideas'. Moreover, Deleuze shows how the subject who thinks and 'actualises' problematic Ideas is itself merely a provisional 'solution' to these latter, which means that subjective conflict is really only an illusory 'freezing' of the underlying and ever-shifting differential relations constituting the dialectic of Ideas.[23] Such a Lautman-inspired ontology, then, it would appear, might offer a way around some of the difficulties associated with Badiou's fascinating project. Nevertheless, the full justification of this claim cannot be dealt with here.

Notes

1. Lautman's primary thesis was published as *Essai sur les notions de structure et d'existence en mathématiques. I. Les Schémas de structure. II. Les Schémas de genèse* (Paris: Hermann, 1938), and his secondary thesis as *Essai sur l'unité des sciences mathématiques dans leur développement actuel* (Paris: Herman, 1938). The 1977 collected edition was entitled *Essai sur l'unité des mathématiques et divers écrits* (Paris: Union générale d'éditions, 1977). Since then, Lautman's collected works have been republished as *Les mathématiques, les idées et le réel physique* (Paris: Vrin, 2006), and can now be found in English translation as *Mathematics, Ideas and the Physical Real*, trans. Simon Duffy (London: Continuum, 2011). We shall refer to this last text throughout. For an introduction to the work of Lautman in English, see Fernando Zalamea's introduction 'Albert Lautman and the creative dialectic of modern mathematics', in Lautman, *Mathematics*, pp. xxiii–xxxvii. See also Charles Alunni, 'Continental genealogies. Mathematical confrontations in Albert Lautman and Gaston Bachelard', in Simon Duffy (ed.), *Virtual Mathematics – The Logic of Difference* (Manchester: Clinamen Press, 2006), pp. 65–80; and Simon Duffy, 'Deleuze and Lautman', in Graham Jones and Jon Roffe (eds), *Deleuze's Philosophical Lineage* (Edinburgh: Edinburgh University Press, 2009), pp. 356–79.
2. The French reads: 'Comme l'ont montré en particulier, dès les années trente, les travaux d'Albert Lautman, tout fragment significatif et novateur de la mathématique réelle peut et doit susciter, en tant que condition vivante, son identification ontologique.'
3. Emblematic in this regard is Oliver Feltham's excellent 'Translators Preface' to *Being and Event*. See in particular BE (xvii–xviii).
4. Lautman, *Mathematics*, p. 189.
5. Badiou here distinguishes quite sharply between his and Lautman's Platonism on the one hand, and Anglo-analytic mathematical Platonism on the other. Whereas the former can be characterised as a 'dialectical Platonism' which focuses on the question of participation or the intersection between the sensible and the intelligible, the latter is characterised by its ontological commitment to the independent existence of abstract mathematical objects.
6. Lautman, *Mathematics*, p. 183. On the question of the 'meaning' that the dialectic of Ideas imparts to mathematical theories, see in particular Jean Petitot, 'Refaire le "Timée" – Introduction à la

philosophie mathématique d'Albert Lautman', *Revue d'histoire des sciences*, 40: 1 (1987), pp. 79–115.

7. Lautman, *Mathematics*, pp. 189, 204, 221, 240.
8. Ibid., pp. 28, 189, 223.
9. Ibid., p. 206.
10. Ibid., p. 223 – original emphasis removed.
11. Ibid., p. 189.
12. Ibid., pp. 221–2.
13. Ibid., p. 189.
14. Ibid., p. 204.
15. Nor, evidently, can we find this sufficient reason in the theories' greater or lesser abilities to appropriate an already given empirical real. On this point, see Catherine Chevalley, 'Albert Lautman et le souci logique', *Revue d'histoire des sciences*, 40: 1 (1987), p. 61.
16. The term 'mixes' is Lautman's. See *Mathematics*, pp. 157–70.
17. It should here be noted that inclusion is not really another primitive relation, to be added to that of belonging. Rather, inclusion can be defined on the basis of belonging, for $\beta \subset \alpha$ is equivalent to saying $(\forall\gamma)[(\gamma \in \beta) \rightarrow (\gamma \in \alpha)]$, or again, for all γ, if γ belongs to β then γ belongs to α (BE 82).
18. Taken from Peter Hallward, *Badiou: A Subject to Truth* (Minneapolis, MN and London: University of Minnesota Press, 2003), p. 103.
19. And not only infinite successor ordinals, but also infinite limit ordinals. Consider the series: $\omega_0, \omega_1, \omega_2 \ldots \omega_n, \omega_{n+1} \ldots \omega_{(\omega_0)}, \omega_{S(\omega_0)}, \ldots \omega_{(\omega_0)_{(\omega_0)}}, \ldots$ (BE 275–7).
20. On the admitted importance of 'the famous "problem of the continuum"' for Badiou, see BE (5 and 281).
21. The reference here to events in their opposition to structured situations, as well as the reference to processes of transformation of situations, makes it clear that what is in play here is not only the couples continuous-discrete and finite-infinite, but also the couple fixity-change.
22. Gilles Deleuze, *Difference and Repetition*, trans. Paul Patton (London: Athlone, 1994), pp. 163–4.
23. For a detailed discussion of Deleuze, Lautman and problematic Ideas, see Sean Bowden, *The Priority of Events: Deleuze's Logic of Sense* (Edinburgh: Edinburgh University Press, 2011), Ch. 3.

4

Badiou's Platonism: The Mathematical Ideas of Post-Cantorian Set Theory
Simon Duffy

Plato's philosophy is important to Badiou for a number of reasons, chief among which is that Badiou considered Plato to have recognised that mathematics provides the only sound or adequate basis for ontology. The mathematical basis of ontology is central to Badiou's philosophy, and his engagement with Plato is instrumental in determining how he positions his philosophy in relation to those approaches to the philosophy of mathematics that endorse an orthodox Platonic realism, i.e. the independent existence of a realm of mathematical objects. The Platonism that Badiou makes claim to bears little resemblance to this orthodoxy. Like Plato, Badiou insists on the primacy of the eternal and immutable abstraction of the mathematico-ontological Idea; however, Badiou's reconstructed Platonism champions the mathematics of post-Cantorian set theory, which itself affirms the irreducible multiplicity of being. Badiou in this way reconfigures the Platonic notion of the relation between the one and the multiple in terms of the multiple-without-one as represented in the axiom of the void or empty set. Rather than engage with the Plato that is figured in the ontological realism of the orthodox Platonic approach to the philosophy of mathematics, Badiou is intent on characterising the Plato that responds to the demands of a post-Cantorian set theory, and he considers Plato's philosophy to provide a response to such a challenge. In effect, Badiou reorients mathematical Platonism from an epistemological to an ontological problematic, a move that relies on the plausibility of rejecting the empiricist ontology underlying orthodox mathematical Platonism. To draw a connection between these two approaches to Platonism and to determine what sets them radically apart, this paper focuses on the use that they each make of model theory to further their respective arguments.

59

Orthodox Platonism in Mathematics and Its Problems

Orthodox Platonism in mathematics advances an ontological realism according to which mathematical objects, like numbers, functions and sets, exist. These mathematical objects are considered to be abstract, causally inert and eternal. The problem that accompanies orthodox Platonism is an epistemological one. If mathematical objects are causally inert, how do we know anything about them?[1] Any such knowledge would require epistemic access to an acausal, eternal and detached mathematical realm.

The epistemic problem for realism in mathematics presumes something like a causal theory of knowledge, according to which claims to knowledge of particular objects is grounded in some account of the causal link between knower and object known. While this empiricist framework may account for knowledge of ordinary objects in the physical world, this sets up a problem for the orthodox Platonist as it doesn't account for knowledge of mathematical objects.

A further issue that can be raised is the question of the applicability of the abstract mathematical realm to the ordinary physical world. Generally, mathematics is applied when a given area of the physical world is postulated as exemplifying a certain mathematical structure. In nearly all scientific theories, the structures of physical systems are described or modelled in terms of mathematical structures.[2] But this doesn't explain how the eternal, acausal, detached mathematical universe relates to the material world, which is the subject matter of science and everyday language. The challenge to the orthodox mathematical Platonist is to provide an account of how it is that mathematical knowledge is utilised or deployed in scientific discourse, and of how it seems to function as an essential part of it.

One realist approach, which begins with the latter problem of the relation between mathematics and science in order to attempt to provide a response to the epistemic problem, is that presented in the Quine-Putnam indispensability argument. Quine and Putnam considered mathematics to be indispensable for science, and, on the basis of the understanding that the best scientific theories determine what one ought to believe to exist, it follows that one ought to believe that the mathematical entities implicated in these theories exist.[3] While this approach does seem to provide a response to the epistemic problem, it fails to address the issue of exactly how mathematics can be applied to science, that is while noting the indispensability of mathematics for science, it fails to provide an account of the nature of this relation. The response to the epistemic problem provided by the indispensability argument can therefore not be sustained, or at least, from a realist perspective, not until an adequate response is provided to the question of the nature of this relation.[4]

One way of addressing the nature of this relation is to actually attempt to provide a uniform semantics for both mathematical and scientific languages, rather than merely presuming this to be the case which is all that is required for the indispensability argument. This could be achieved by developing a model-theoretic framework according to which the relationship between mathematical language and mathematical reality is modelled on the relationship between a formal language and model-theoretic interpretations of it. The point is that if realism is correct, then model theory provides the picture, or 'model', of how mathematical languages describe mathematical reality.

Model theory is the branch of logic developed to study (or model) mathematical structures by considering first-order sentences which are true of those structures and the sets which are definable in those structures by first-order formulas.[5] In model theory, there are three different languages that are in operation: (1) the mathematical language itself, which is informal; (2) the object language, which is the set of first-order sentences of a formal language that 'models' the first; and (3) the metalanguage, which is the informal or semi-formalised language in which the semantics is carried out, i.e. it is the language used to describe what is happening in the object language. The assumption is that standard first-order sentences of a formal language capture something about real mathematical languages. A first-order sentence is a formula that has well-defined truth values under an interpretation. For example, given the formula $P(x)$, which states that the predicate P is true of x, whether $P(x)$ is true depends on what x represents, and the first-order sentence $\exists x P(x)$ will be either true or false in a given interpretation. An interpretation of the set of sentences of a first-order language assigns a denotation to all non-logical constants in that language, for example what is denoted by P. It also determines a domain of discourse that specifies the range of the universal ($\forall$) and existential ($\exists$) quantifiers, where the domain of discourse generally refers to the set of entities that a model is based on. The result is that each term, x, is assigned an object that it represents, and each sentence, for example $\exists x P(x)$, is assigned a truth value. In this way, a model-theoretic interpretation determines the satisfaction conditions for the formal sentences and thereby provides semantic meaning to the terms and formulas of the language.[6] The metalanguage, which is a 'fully developed language',[7] must contain a faithful representation of the object language and should have the resources to make substantial assertions about the ontology that is attributed to the object language. In this way, the central notion of model theory is 'truth in a model'. The conditions for truth in the proposed model represent truth conditions, and it follows that truth in a model is a model of truth. What this means is that the truth of the existence of mathematical objects in the model, or in the object language, is a model of the truth of the existence of mathematical objects for the mathematical language itself. One criticism of this approach is that the best that can be achieved is that all models of a theory are isomorphic, in which case the ontology is only determined up to isomorphism, i.e. metaphysical realists do not really have any access to the correspondence they postulate.[8]

The structuralist approach to the programme of realism in the philosophy of mathematics, represented in the work of Stewart Shapiro, draws upon Plato to set up a response to this criticism, a response which is an extension of the model-theoretic approach. Shapiro argues that Plato distinguishes between two different approaches to natural numbers: arithmetic and logistic. Arithmetic 'deals with the even and the odd, with reference to how much each happens to be'.[9] According to Plato, if 'one becomes perfect in the arithmetical art', then 'he knows also all of the numbers.'[10] Logistic differs from arithmetic 'in so far as it studies the even and the odd with respect to the multitude they make both with themselves and with each other.'[11] So while arithmetic deals straightforwardly with the natural numbers, Shapiro argues that theoretical logistic concerns 'the relations among the numbers'.[12] Drawing upon the work of Klein, who argues that theoretical logistic 'raises to an explicit science that knowledge of relations among numbers which . . . precedes, and indeed must precede, all calculation',[13] Shapiro argues that 'the structuralist rejects this distinction between Plato's arithmetic and theoretical logistic.' He maintains that 'there is no more to the individual numbers "in themselves" than the relations they bear to each other.'[14] Shapiro turns to the *Republic* to find the ultimate Platonic endorsement of this move. He argues that 'in the *Republic* (525C–D), Plato said that guardians should pursue *logistic* for the sake of knowing. It is through this study of the *relations* among numbers that their soul is able to grasp the nature of numbers as they are in themselves. We structuralists agree.'[15]

In order to overcome the criticism of the problem of isomorphism in the model-theoretic framework, the structuralist program of realism in the philosophy of mathematics deploys the model-theoretic framework in relation to the problem of mathematical structures, which it can more directly address. In this respect, as Shapiro argues, 'Structure is all that matters.'[16] Mathematical objects are defined as structureless points or positions in structures that have no identity or features outside of a structure. And a structure is defined as the abstract form of a system, which highlights the interrelationships among its objects.[17] The aim of Shapiro's structuralist approach is to develop a language in which to interpret the mathematics done by real mathematicians, which can then be used to try to make progress on philosophical questions.

The 'Modern Platonist' Response and Its Reformulation of the Question

Another avowedly Platonic approach that redeploys the model-theoretic framework is that provided by Alain Badiou in *Being and Event*, and subsequently elaborated upon in *Logics of Worlds*. The main point of distinction between the approaches of Badiou and Shapiro that sets their projects apart and at odds with one another is that Badiou rejects the empiricist framework that characterises the epistemic problem for the orthodox Platonist.

Badiou considers himself to be a 'modern Platonist' (TW 54), and draws upon three crucial aspects of Plato's work to set up this transformation.

First, Badiou maintains that 'the independent existence of mathematical structures is entirely relative for Plato' (TW 49), the claim being that Plato's account of anamnesis[18] does not set up the 'criterion of the exteriority (or transcendence) of mathematical structures (or objects)' (TW 49). On the contrary, it designates that 'thought is never confronted with "objectivities" from which it is supposedly separated' (TW 49). Badiou considers a mathematical structure to be an 'Idea' that is 'always already there and would

remain unthinkable were one not able to "activate" it in thought'
(TW 49). He maintains that 'Plato's fundamental concern is to
declare the immanent identity, the co-belonging, of the knowing
mind and the known, their essential ontological commensurability' (TW 49). So the problem for Badiou in this respect is to
provide an account of how these Ideas are activated in thought,
which is facilitated by providing an account of this 'essential ontological commensurability'.

Second, Badiou reinterprets the famous passage in the *Republic*
where Plato opposes mathematics to the dialectic.

> The theorizing concerning being and the intelligible which is sustained
> by the science [*épistémè*] of the dialectic is clearer than that sustained
> by what are known as the sciences [*techné*] ... It seems to me you
> characterize the [latter] procedure of geometers and their ilk as discur-
> sive [*dianoia*], while you do not characterize intellection thus, in so far
> as that discursiveness is established between [*metaxu*] opinion [*doxa*]
> and intellect [*nous*].[19]

In this passage, Plato singles out the procedures of the geometer,
having in mind here the axioms of Euclidian geometry, as operating externally to the norms of thought, i.e. the dialectic. Badiou's
modern move here is to embrace the axiomatic approach specifically because of this externality, which addresses that aspect of the
problem mentioned above of how these Ideas are activated in
thought. Badiou here also reveals his formalist leanings by endorsing the understanding that the theorem follows logically from its
axioms, although it is a formalism without the implicit finitism
that accompanies its usual presentation in the philosophy of mathematics as the manipulation and interpretation of finite sequences
of symbols.

Third, in the *Parmenides* Badiou notes with approval what he
considers to be the formulation, in the account of a speculative
dream, of 'being' as pure or inconsistent multiplicity [*plethos*]
(BE 34). However, he considers Plato to capitulate to the fact
that 'there is no form of object for thought which is capable of
gathering together the pure multiple, the multiple-without-one,
and making it consist' (BE 34). The multiple, in this respect, can
only be thought in terms of the One, and thus as consistent or
structured multiplicity [*polla*]. Plato writes: 'It is necessary that
the entirety of disseminated being [as inconsistent multiplicity]

shatter apart, as soon as it is grasped by discursive thought' (BE 34). Badiou considers this to be where Plato is pre-modern, by which he specifically means pre-Cantorian, because it is Cantor who was the first to 'elucidate the thinking of being as pure multiplicity' (TW 55), an account of which will be given in the next section. In order to maintain the distinction between the two types of multiplicity, *plethos* and *polla*, Badiou suggests transcribing Plato's statement: 'If the one is not, nothing is', to 'If the one is not, (the) nothing is' (BE 35). This then aligns the Platonic text with the 'axiomatic decision' with which Badiou's 'entire discourse originates': 'that of the non-being of the one' (BE 31). According to Badiou, 'under the hypothesis of the non-being of the one, there is a fundamental asymmetry between the analytic of the multiple and the analytic of the one itself' (BE 32). It is only in relation to the 'non-being of the one' that multiplicity as pure or inconsistent, the multiple-without-one, is presentable. In axiomatic set theory, which is the first-order formal language that Badiou deploys in his model theoretic approach, the 'non-being of the one' is characteristic of the void or empty set, $\emptyset$ (BE 69).

In support of these moves, and of the claim that the status of mathematical objects is a secondary problem, Badiou draws upon comments made by Kurt Gödel about axiomatic set theory and Cantor's continuum hypothesis:

> The question of the objective existence of the objects of mathematical intuition (which, incidentally, is an exact replica of the question of the objective existence of the outer world) is not decisive for the problem under discussion here. The mere psychological fact of the existence of an intuition which is sufficiently clear to produce the axioms of set theory and an open series of extensions of them suffices to give meaning to the question of the truth or falsity of propositions like Cantor's continuum hypothesis.[20]

With this, Badiou positions Cantor's continuum hypothesis, and the development of transfinite numbers that underpins it, as of central importance to his approach. Badiou argues that

> With Cantor we move from a restricted ontology, in which the multiple is still tied to the metaphysical theme of the representation of objects, numbers and figures, to a general ontology, in which the cornerstone and goal of all mathematics becomes thought's free apprehension of

multiplicity as such, and the thinkable is definitively untethered from the restricted dimension of the object. (TW 46)

Badiou characterises this 'general ontology', which is nothing other than pure multiplicity, as 'being qua being', and, on the basis of Cantor's account of transfinite numbers, maintains that 'it is legitimate to say that ontology, the science of being qua being, is nothing other than mathematics itself' (BE xiii). Badiou then presents this 'general ontology' as modelled by the Zermelo-Fraenkel axiomatisation of set theory (abbreviated ZF) and the open series of extensions of them, including in particular those by Gödel and Paul Cohen. In response to Quine's famous formula: 'to be is to be the value of a variable',[21] Badiou responds that 'the ZF system postulates that there is only one type of presentation of being: the multiple' (BE 44). He maintains that 'mathematical "objects" and "structures" . . . can *all* be designated as pure multiplicities built, in a regulated manner, on the basis of the void-set alone' (BE 6), and that '[t]he question of the exact nature of the relation of mathematics to being is therefore entirely concentrated – for the epoch in which we find ourselves – in the axiomatic decision which authorizes set theory' (BE 6). In order to characterise this axiomatic decision, an account of the development of transfinite numbers, which Badiou considers 'to prompt us to think being qua being' (NN 98), is required.

Cantor's Account of Transfinite Numbers or Ordinals

To begin with, an ordinal number describes the numerical position or order of an object, for example first, second, third, etc., as opposed to a cardinal number which is used in counting: one, two, three, etc. An ordinal number is defined as 'the order type of a well ordered set'.[22] There are finite ordinals, denoted using Arabic numerals, and transfinite ordinals, denoted using the lower case Greek letter ω (omega). While the ordinality and cardinality of finite sets is the same, this is not the case with transfinite ordinals and cardinals, as will be explained shortly. It was Cantor who developed transfinite ordinals as an extension of the whole numbers, i.e. transfinite ordinals are larger than any whole number. The smallest transfinite ordinal ω, is the set of all finite ordinals $\{0, 1, 2, \ldots\}$, which is the countably infinite set $\mathbf{N}$ of natural numbers.[23] The cardinality of this set is denoted $\aleph_0$

(aleph-o).[24] Note that the cardinality of Z, the integers, and Q, the rational numbers, is also $\aleph_0$, whereas R, the set of real numbers, is uncountably infinite, and its cardinality is denoted by c, which is called the 'continuum' in set theory. Because R is the power set of Z, where the power set of any set is the set of all of its subsets, and because every set of size or cardinality n has a power set of cardinality 2^n, then $c = 2^{\aleph_0}$. While there is only one countably infinite cardinal, $\aleph_0$, there are uncountably many countable transfinite ordinals, because like other kinds of numbers, transfinite ordinals can be added, multiplied and exponentiated:[25]

$$\omega, \omega + 1, \omega + 2, \ldots, \omega \times 2, (\omega \times 2) + 1, \ldots, \omega^2, \omega^2 + 1, \ldots,$$
$$\omega^3, \ldots, \omega^\omega, \ldots, \omega^{\omega^\omega}, \ldots, \varepsilon_0, \ldots$$

The cardinality of the ordinal that succeeds all countable transfinite ordinals, of which there are uncountably many, is denoted $\aleph_1$ (aleph-1).[26] Each ordinal is the well-ordered set of all smaller ordinals, i.e. every element of an ordinal is an ordinal. Any set of ordinals which contains all the predecessors of each of its elements has an ordinal number which is greater than any ordinal in the set, i.e. for any ordinal α, the union $\alpha \cup \{\alpha\}$ is a bigger ordinal $\alpha + 1$. For this reason, there is no largest ordinal. The ordinals therefore 'do not constitute a set: no multiple form can totalise them' (NN 98). What this means for Badiou is that the ordinals are the ontological schema of pure or inconsistent multiplicity.

Badiou argues that '[t]he anchoring of the ordinals in being as such is twofold' (NN 98). (1) The 'absolutely initial point . . . is the empty set', which is an ordinal, and is 'decided axiomatically' as the empty set, $\varnothing$. In ZF, the axiom of the void or empty set states that the empty set exists. As the 'non-being of the one', the empty set provides set theory with its only existential link to being and thereby grounds all the forms constructible from it in existence. Badiou defers here to Zermelo's axiom of separation, which states that 'if the collection is a sub-collection of a given set, then it exists.'[27] Rather than using this axiom to prove the existence of the empty set by specifying a property that all sets do not have, which would be the orthodox Platonist approach since all sets already exist, Badiou argues that in order for the axiom of separation to separate some consistent multiplicity as a sub-collection, some pure multiple, as the multiple of multiples,[28] must already be presented, by which Badiou means the initial multiple, the empty set, which is guaranteed rather by the axiom of the empty set (BE 45). (2) 'The limit-point that "relaunches" the existence of the ordinals beyond . . . the whole natural finite numbers . . . is the first infinite set, ω', which is also 'decided axiomatically'. The axiom that formalises the infinite set representing the natural numbers, N, is the axiom of infinity, which states that there exists an infinite set. These two axiomatic decisions, which Badiou considers to be crucial for modern thought, represent the ordinals as 'the modern scale of measurement' of pure or inconsistent multiplicity. He maintains that these two decisions determine that nothingness, the empty set, 'is a form of . . . numerable being, and that the infinite, far from being found in the One of a God, is omnipresent', as pure or inconsistent multiplicity, 'in every existing-situation' (NN 99). Before clarifying what Badiou means here by 'every existing-situation', which is dependent upon the model-theoretic implications of his approach, the Platonist implications of axiomatic set theory that Badiou is drawing upon require further explication.

The Platonist Implications of Axiomatic Set Theory

ZF and the extensions of it by Gödel and Cohen allow the Cantorian theory to be developed in full while avoiding all known paradoxical constructions, the simplest of which is Russell's paradoxical set of all sets, which Cantor called an inconsistent or absolutely infinite set.[29] The main problem left unanswered by Cantor's theory of transfinite numbers is the hypothesis, which tried to make sense of these inconsistent or absolutely infinite sets, referred to as the continuum hypothesis (abbreviated CH). CH proposes that there is no infinite set with a cardinal number between that of the 'small' countably infinite set of integers, denoted $\aleph_0$, and the 'large' uncountably infinite set of real numbers, denoted $2^{\aleph_0}$. CH therefore asserts that $\aleph_1 = 2^{\aleph_0}$, where $\aleph_1$ is the cardinality of the ordinal that succeeds all countable transfinite ordinals. Cantor believed CH to be true and spent many fruitless years trying to prove it. If CH is true, then $2^{\aleph_0}$ is the first cardinal larger than $\aleph_0$. However, independently of whether or not CH is true, the question remains as to whether such a cardinal $2^{\aleph_0}$ exists. Cantor argues for the existence of $2^{\aleph_0}$ by invoking the well-ordering principle (abbreviated WO), which simply states that a set is said to be well-ordered by a relation < (less than) of ordering between its elements if every non-empty subset has a first element. This argument implies that every set can be well ordered and can therefore be associated with an ordinal number. The problem with Cantor's argument is that it assumes there to be a method for making an unlimited number of successive arbitrary choices for each subset to determine this first member. If the set is the set N, then there is no problem, since the standard ordering of N already provides well-ordering. But if the set is R, there is no known method to make the required choice. The assumption of the existence of such an infinite sequence of choices was considered by many to be unjustified.[30] In response to this problem, Zermelo provided a proof of WO on the basis of the axiom of choice (abbreviated AC, and indicated by the 'C' in ZFC), which proposes a function that provides for 'the *simultaneous choice* from each nonempty subset' of the first element.[31] This axiom 'reduces the construction of a transfinite sequence of successive choices', which in Cantor's argument appear to proceed through time, 'to the assumption of a single simultaneous collection of choices'.[32] The main problem with AC for many mathematicians was that it presupposed the independent existence of the function that it proposes, i.e. it asserts existence without explicitly defining the function as a mathematical object and thus lays the axiomatic grounds for orthodox mathematical Platonism in set theory and the problems outlined above associated with it.

While a committed Platonic realist in the philosophy of mathematics who 'conceives sets to be arbitrary collections of entities existing independently of human consciousness and definitions' would consider AC to be 'immediately intuitively evident',[33] Badiou, on the contrary, considers the acceptance of AC to be solely the result of an axiomatic decision, the reasons for which will become evident once more of the history of dealing with CH is presented. So while both Badiou and the orthodox Platonist accept AC, and therefore that the cardinal $2^{\aleph_0}$ exists, the question that remains to be addressed is whether or not CH is true.

In 1937, Gödel proved that if ZF is consistent then it remains consistent if AC and the generalised continuum hypothesis (abbreviated GCH) are added to it as axioms. The GCH states that if an infinite set's cardinality lies between that of an infinite set and that of its power set, then it either has the same cardinality as the infinite set or the same cardinality as its power set. This is a generalisation of CH because the continuum, R, has the same cardinality as the power set of integers, Z. Gödel also introduced the notion of 'constructible set' to show that when the universe of sets, V, is restricted to the class of constructible sets, L, i.e. when V = L, then all the axioms of ZFC and GCH are proved.[34] What this consistency result showed was that any instance of GCH could not be disproved using ZFC.

The notion of constructible sets is problematic for the orthodox Platonist as the restriction to definable objects is contrary to the conception of an independently existing universe of arbitrary sets. Most Platonists would therefore reject V = L and the proof that relies on it. Badiou, on the contrary, affirms Gödel's notion of constructible sets, i.e. L, as another necessary axiomatic decision and the result that follows. Badiou argues that by 'considering constructible multiples *alone*, one stays within the framework of the Ideas of the multiple' (BE 300) elaborated above.[35]

This result, that GCH could not be disproved using ZFC, did not rule out that some instance of GCH could be proved in ZFC, even CH itself;[36] however, Gödel projected that CH would be independent or could not be derived from ZFC and that 'new axioms' might be required to decide it.[37]

Progress on this problem was not made until 1963 when Paul Cohen[38] proved that if ZF is consistent then: (1) AC is independent or cannot be derived from ZF; (2) CH is independent from ZFC; and (3) V = L is independent of ZFC + GCH.[39] The proof effectively showed that CH does not hold in all models of set theory. The technique he invented and called the method of forcing and generic sets involved building models of set theory. This method takes its point of departure in that used by Gödel. Rather than produce only one model by restricting a presumed model of set theory, V, to obtain that of the constructible sets, L, Cohen extended the model of constructible sets, L, by the adjunction of a variety of generic sets without altering the ordinals.[40] In fact, he adjoined sufficiently many generic subsets of $\omega = \{0, 1, 2, \ldots\}$ that the cardinality of this constructed model of ZFC, $\aleph_1$, was greater than $\aleph_0$ but less than c, thus violating CH.

The procedure of forcing starts with a countable transitive model M for any suitable finite list of axioms of ZFC + V = L.[41] The method of forcing is then used to construct a countable transitive model G, called a *generic extension* of M, for a finite list of axioms of ZFC + V = L, such that M contains G, abbreviated as M[G]. M[G] is 'the set of all sets which can be constructed from G by applying set-theoretic processes definable in M'.[42] As long as M doesn't equal G, G will satisfy V ≠ L. G can also be made to satisfy ¬CH and 'a wide variety of other statements by varying certain details in [the] construction'.[43] While Gödel's method of constructibility established the consistency of statements true in L, specifically GCH, Cohen's method of forcing 'is a general technique for producing a wide variety of models satisfying diverse mathematical properties.'[44] It has since become the main method for showing statements to be independent of ZF or ZFC. Cohen's independence results are the basis of Badiou's claim that AC and V = L are 'axiomatic decisions', as they are undecidable within the framework of ZF or of ZFC + GCH respectively. As for CH, it is 'demonstrable within the constructible universe, and refutable in certain generic extensions. It is therefore undecidable for set theory without restrictions' (BE 504).

Building on Cohen's work, Easton[45] shows that for each regular transfinite cardinality of a set, the cardinality of its power set can be any cardinal provided that it is superior to the first and that 'it is a successor cardinal' (BE 279), where a successor cardinal is the smallest cardinal which is larger than the given cardinal.[46]

Consonant with Gödel's projection, a number of 'new axioms' called strong axioms of infinity, or large cardinal axioms, are candidates or have been newly proposed in the attempt to decide CH. These include the axioms that assert the existence of inaccessible cardinals, or Mahlo cardinals, and stronger axioms for the existence of measurable cardinals, compact cardinals, supercompact cardinals, huge cardinals.[47] What the large cardinal axioms attempt to do is 'to constitute within the infinite an abyss comparable to the one which distinguishes the first infinity, ω_0, from the finite multiples' (BE 311). It is in this way that the large cardinal axioms are considered to be 'strong axioms of infinity'. However, for each of these axioms, if it has been shown to be consistent with ZFC then it remains consistent regardless of whether CH or ¬CH is added. That is, 'CH is consistent with and independent from every large cardinal axiom that has been proposed as at all plausible.'[48] What this means is that 'none of them quite succeed' in deciding CH.

On a purely formal level, Kanamori and Magidor argue that interest in large cardinal axioms lies in the 'aesthetic intricacy of the net of consequences and interrelationships between them'. However, they go further to suggest that the adaptation of large cardinal axioms involves 'basic questions of belief concerning

what is true about the universe', and can therefore be characterised as a 'theological venture'.[49] Badiou endorses this suggestion and incorporates large cardinal axioms into his approach as
approximations of the 'virtual being required by theologies' (BE
284).

The Model-Theoretic Implications of Badiou's 'Modern Platonism'

The definitive statement of Badiou's model-theoretic orientation
in *Being and Event* is in the chapter on the 'Theory of the Pure
Multiple', where he effectively states that 'the object-language (the
formal language) . . . which will be that of the theory in which I
operate' (BE 39) is axiomatic set theory, specifically ZFC, including, as indicated above, Gödel's axiom of constructibility, $V = L$.
What this means is that the object-language that Badiou deploys is
already itself a model of ZFC insofar as the acceptance of $V = L$,
which in Cohen's terminology is the model M, indicates Badiou's
decision to solely accept the existence of constructible sets, or
as Badiou refers to them, 'constructible multiples' (BE 306). So
Badiou's object-language already implicates the model M of ZFC
that is determined in the first stage of the procedure of Cohen's
method of forcing and generic sets.

The metalanguage with which Badiou discusses the object-
language and that has the resources to make substantial assertions
about the ontology attributed to the object language is the 'fully
developed language' of philosophy itself, specifically Badiou's
philosophy, which he refers to as a metaontology. For Badiou,
mathematics doesn't recognise that it is ontology – this is left up to
philosophy itself whose task is to explain how it is that mathematics is ontology.

The model-theoretic interpretations of the object language
are the very generic extensions generated by Cohen's method of
forcing, which constructs a *generic extension* G of M such that
M contains G, i.e. M[G]. Cohen's generic extensions themselves
are unknowable from the model M of which they are extensions,
thus furnishing Badiou with the concept of the indiscernible multiple. This distinction between the indiscernible multiples of the
generic extensions and the constructible multiples of M is also
characteristic of their eventual nature, in so far as 'the event does
not exist' and is not decided (BE 305) in the latter but is decided

and is a condition of the former. Badiou therefore characterises generic sets, indiscernible multiples, as the 'ontological schema of a truth' (BE 510). A procedure of fidelity to the truth of an indiscernible multiple is a *generic procedure* of which Badiou lists four types: artistic, scientific, political and amorous. He characterises these generic procedures as 'the four sources of truth' (BE 510). In addition to the role as metalanguage to the object language is the role of philosophy 'to propose a conceptual framework in which the contemporary compossibility' of these generic procedures 'can be grasped' (BE 4). These generic procedures are therefore characterised by Badiou as the conditions of philosophy. This marks an abrupt shift from talking about the sets of the model M as constructible multiples, to talking about specific constructible multiples, or as Badiou refers to them, 'situations' (BE 178), that are presentable by the model and its generic extensions. This is, however, consonant with Badiou's reorientation of the epistemic problem of the orthodox Platonist in mathematics. By claiming that mathematics is ontology, Badiou reorients the debate from an epistemological question about the nature of the relation between mathematical language and mathematical objects to an ontological question about how being is thought and how mathematics is implicated in this question. Badiou maintains that it 'is nothing new to philosophers – that there must be a link between the existence of mathematics and the question of being' (BE 7), and he singles out 'the Cantor-Gödel-Cohen-Easton symptom' (BE 280) of mathematics as providing the impetus for rethinking the nature of this link.

In regards to the orthodox epistemic problem, Badiou refuses the reduction of the subject matter of mathematics to the status of objects on the model of empirical objects. In *Being and Event*, he maintains that:

> If the argument I present here holds up, the truth is that *there are no* mathematical objects. Strictly speaking, mathematics *presents nothing*, without constituting for all that an empty game, because not having anything to present, besides presentation itself – which is to say the Multiple –, and thereby never adopting the form of the object, this is certainly a condition of all discourse on being *qua being*. (BE 7)

He rather draws upon Plato's account of anamnesis to reinstate mathematical objects to the status of Ideas. He argues that: 'A

mathematical idea is neither subjective ("the activity of the mathematician"), nor objective ("independently existing structures").
In one and the same gesture, it breaks with the sensible and posits
the intelligible. In other words, it is an instance of thinking' (TW
50). Badiou draws upon Cohen's deployment of Gödel's idea of
constructible sets to characterise what he refers to as 'the being
of configurations of knowledge' (BE 284). Badiou argues that the
axiom of constructibility is 'a veritable "Idea" of the multiple' and
that the constructible universe that is a 'model' of the ZFC + V =
L axioms is 'the framework of the Ideas of the multiple' (BE 426).
It is the axioms of 'the Cantor-Gödel-Cohen-Easton symptom' (BE
280) that present this framework, and it is philosophy as metaontology that articulates how this framework should be thought in
relation to the generic procedures. For this reason, Badiou maintains that:

> Mathematical ontology does not constitute, by itself, any orientation
> in thought, but it must be compatible with all of them: it must discern
> and propose the multiple-being which they have need of. (BE 284)

The ontology that Badiou proposes is dependent upon his axiomatic decision to present the empty set as the 'non-being of the
one', which he characterises as the primitive name of being. This
is a metaontological claim that cannot be derived mathematically. The ontology of the hierarchy of constructible sets, which
is obtained by iterating the power-set operation on the empty
set through the transfinite, 'is rooted in it' (TW 57). As Cassou-
Noguès points out:

> Badiou can not found his axioms and establish that they are true
> propositions of the ontology of the multiple. But in the perspective
> that he puts in place, this foundation is not required. It is only neces-
> sary to remain faithful to . . . the event of Cantor's work and pursue a
> process that is thought to be producing truths, without ever being able
> to establish it.[50]

This is of course consonant with Badiou's own characterisation of
philosophy as metaontology, and of ontology as 'a rich, complex,
unfinishable science, submitted to the difficult constraint of a *fidelity* (deductive fidelity in this case)' (BE 8). The coherence of his
approach rests solely upon the fidelity of his philosophy to this

event. The consistency with which Badiou can continue to develop his philosophy in response to the ongoing engagement that mathematics has with the presentation of being qua being is the sole testament to this fidelity.

In this respect, Cohen's method of forcing is also behind the shift in focus that occurs in Badiou's second main text, *Logics of Worlds*, which exhibits an attempt to extend this fidelity by experimenting with the category theoretic extension of set theory, Heyting Algebra and Sheaf Theory. Kanamori points out that 'Forcing has been . . . adapted in a category theory context which is a casting of set theory in intuitionistic logic.'[51] Heyting algebra replaces Boolean algebra in intuitionistic logic, where Boolean algebra has become an important instrument in the interpretation of, and is deployed in an alternative approach to, Cohen's original procedures of the method of forcing. Kanamori also indicates that 'forcing can be interpreted as the construction of a certain topos of sheaves. The internal logic of the topos of presheaves over a partially ordered set is essentially Cohen's forcing . . .'[52] This move on Badiou's part can be seen as an attempt to address the fact of the ongoing engagement that mathematics has with the presentation of being qua being, and the potential limitations of the singular commitment to set theory in *Being and Event* as the definitive statement of this presentation.

It is not at all clear that this requirement of fidelity, which is characteristic of Badiou's metaontology, contributes anything to the debates about the realism of mathematical objects as conducted in the philosophy of mathematics. At best what Badiou is offering is an alternative way of formulating the question of fidelity, which for Badiou is to Cantorian set theory and the non-being of the one, rather than to the indispensability argument for Quine and Putnam, or to the existence of mathematical structures for Shapiro. The significant feature of this difference is that it entails accepting a radical alternative formulation of the relation between philosophy and mathematics that purports to render superfluous the empiricist framework within which these debates have to date been conducted. Whether or not Badiou's philosophy is robust enough to displace the indispensibility argument or the structuralist programme in realism has yet to be demonstrated in any convincing way.

Notes

1. See Paul Benacerraf, 'Mathematical truth', *Journal of Philosophy*, 70: 19 (1973), pp. 661–79.

2. Stewart Shapiro, *Philosophy of Mathematics, Structure and Ontology* (Oxford: Oxford University Press, 2000), p. 17.

3. See Willard V. Quine, *From a Logical Point of View* (Cambridge, MA: Harvard University Press, 1964); *Theories and Things* (Cambridge, MA: Harvard University Press, 1981); Hilary Putnam, 'What is mathematical truth', in *Mathematics Matter and Method: Philosophical Papers, Volume 1*, 2nd edn (Cambridge: Cambridge University Press, 1979).

4. See Shapiro, *Philosophy of Mathematics*, p. 46.

5. David Marker, 'Model theory and exponentiation', *Notices of the American Mathematical Society*, 43 (1996), pp. 753–9, at p. 753.

6. For an account of a model-theoretic framework see Marker, 'Model theory', pp. 754–5; Shapiro, *Philosophy of Mathematics*, pp. 46–8.

7. Shapiro, *Philosophy of Mathematics*, p. 71.

8. Hilary Putnam, *Reason, Truth and History* (Cambridge: Cambridge University Press, 1981), pp. 72–4; Shapiro, *Philosophy of Mathematics*, p. 67

9. Plato, *Plato: Complete Works*, ed. John M. Cooper (Indianapolis, IN: Hackett, 1997), *Gorgias* 451A–C.

10. Ibid., *Theatetus* 198A–B; see also *Republic* VII 522C.

11. Ibid., *Gorgias* 451A–C; see also *Charmides* 165E–166B.

12. Shapiro, *Philosophy of Mathematics*, p. 73.

13. Jacob Klein, *Greek Mathematical Thought and the Origin of Algebra*, trans. Eva Brann (Cambridge, MA: MIT Press, 1968), p. 23.

14. Shapiro, *Philosophy of Mathematics*, p. 73.

15. Ibid.

16. Ibid., p. 56.

17. See ibid., pp. 76–7.

18. The Platonic doctrine of anamnesis holds that all learning is recollection, and that perception and enquiry remind us of what is innate in us (Plato, *Meno* 80A–86C; *Phaedo* 73C–78B).

19. Plato, *Republic* VI 511C–D. Badiou's translation. See TW 44.

20. Kurt Gödel, 'What is Cantor's continuum problem?' [1947, revised and expanded 1964], in Paul Benacerraf and Hilary Putnam (eds), *Philosophy of Mathematics: Selected Readings*, 2nd edn (Cambridge: Cambridge University Press, 1983), p. 485.

21. Quine, *Theories and Things*, p. 15.

22. Joseph W. Dauben, *Georg Cantor: His Mathematics and Philosophy of the Infinite* (Princeton, NJ: Princeton University Press, 1990), p. 199.
23. A countable set is any set that is either finite or the same size as **N**. An uncountable set is any set bigger than **N**.
24. Dauben, *Georg Cantor*, p. 179. Note that **N**, ω and $\aleph_0$ all name the same set, i.e. the set of natural numbers.
25. Ibid., pp. 103–11.
26. Ibid., p. 269.
27. Kenneth Kunen, *Set Theory: An Introduction to Independence Proofs* (Amsterdam: North Holland, 1983), p. 12.
28. That is, the multiple from which all other multiples are constructed.
29. Russell's paradox raises the question of whether the set of all sets which are not members of themselves is a set. If the set exists, then it is included as one of its own sets, i.e. it is both a member and not a member of itself, which is a contradiction.
30. See Solomon Feferman, *In the Light of Logic* (Oxford: Oxford University Press, 1989), p. 37.
31. Ibid., p. 39.
32. Ibid.
33. Ibid., p. 40.
34. Gödel's 'constructible sets' are sets defined solely in terms of the subsets of the previous stage of construction that have already been constructed, rather than the set of all subsets as it is in V.
35. He maintains that 'the constructible universe is a *model* of these axioms [i.e. ZFC + V = L] in that if one applies the constructions and the guarantees of existence supported by the Ideas of the multiple, and if their domain of application is restricted to the constructible universe, then the constructible [universe] is generated in turn' (BE 300).
36. Feferman, *In the Light of Logic*, pp. 66–9.
37. Gödel, 'What is Cantor's continuum problem?', p. 476.
38. Paul. J. Cohen, *Set Theory and the Continuum Hypothesis* (New York: W. A. Benjamin, 1966).
39. The method of showing that a certain statement is not derivable from or is not a logical consequence of given axioms is to exhibit a model in which the axioms are true but the statement is false. This is indicted by the following notation: (1) ZF + ¬AC; (2) ZFC + ¬CH; (3) ZFC + GCH + V ≠ L. See Akihiro Kanamori, 'Cohen and set theory', *Bulletin of Symbolic Logic*, 14: 3 (2008), pp. 351–78, at p. 235.

40. See Ibid., p. 360.

41. According to Kunen, 'Cohen's original treatment made forcing seem very much related to the constructible hierarchy. His M was always a model for V = L' (Kunen, *Set Theory*, p. 235).

42. Kunen, *Set Theory*, p. 188.

43. Ibid., p. 185.

44. Ibid., p. 184.

45. William B. Easton, 'Powers of regular cardinals', *Annals of Mathematical Logic*, 1 (1970), pp. 139–78.

46. See Judith Roitman, *Introduction to Modern Set Theory* (New York: Wiley, 1990), pp. 91–2.

47. See Akihiro Kanamori, *The Higher Infinite. Large Cardinals in Set Theory from Their Beginnings* (New York: Springer, 1994), p. 472.

48. Feferman, *In the Light of Logic*, pp. 72–3.

49. Akihiro Kanamori and Menachem Magidor, 'The evolution of large cardinal axioms in set theory', in *Higher Set Theory: Lecture Notes in Mathematics*, 669 (New York: Springer, 1978), p. 104.

50. Pierre Cassou-Noguès, 'L'excès de l'état par rapport à la situation dans *L'être et l'événement* de A. Badiou', *Methodos*, 6 (2006), http://methodos.revues.org/471, para. 33.

51. Kanamori, 'Cohen and set theory', p. 371.

52. Ibid.

5

Sets, Categories and Topoi: Approaches to Ontology in Badiou's Later Work

Anindya Bhattacharyya

Mathematics is ontology. This is the famous opening declaration of *Being and Event*, Alain Badiou's major work to date, and it serves remarkably well as a three-word summary of the entire book. But despite Badiou's argument that mathematics *in general* is the discourse that expresses being qua being, the book itself concentrates almost exclusively on a *specific region* of mathematics: the theory of pure sets, as developed by Georg Cantor, Gottlob Frege, Ernst Zermelo, John von Neumann, Kurt Gödel, Paul Cohen and others over a roughly hundred-year period starting from the 1870s.

This focus should not come as a surprise to anyone versed in contemporary mathematics. For both the interest in pure sets and the development of their theory was to a large extent driven by the foundational role claimed for them with respect to mathematics in general. Their extreme internal simplicity notwithstanding, sets can be nested within each other and thereby used to model pretty much any other mathematical entity. In other words, sets can be deployed in an ontological role *within* mathematics; they are the 'ontology of ontology', so to speak. From this perspective everything 'is' a set, in that the domain of mathematical discourse can more or less be identified with the universe of all possible sets.

Mathematicians were attracted by such a homogenous and systematic foundation because it seemed to hold out the prospect of finally ironing out the paradoxes and puzzles that have plagued the subject for centuries. Or so it was thought. For the development of set theory in fact uncovered a host of strange and unexpected phenomena that dashed any hopes of securing mathematics on a stable foundational plateau. In particular, Gödel's famous First Incompleteness Theorem demonstrated that for any reasonable axiomatisation of set theory one could concoct statements that were formally 'undecidable', in that they were neither provable nor refutable from the axioms.[1] Cohen later proved that these undecidable statements included certain fairly basic questions about infinite cardinals, such as the continuum hypothesis that Cantor had spent his later years attempting to prove.

While the intellectual achievement of mathematical set theory is beyond doubt, the peculiarly ambiguous results of its programme could not help but give an impetus to those who had always been sceptical of set theory's foundational aspirations. This scepticism took many forms, but typically it admitted that sets could be used to model any other mathematical entity, but denied that these other entities actually *were* sets in any deeper ontological sense. It was rather a case of sets *simulating* other entities, or of other entities being 'implemented' as sets, to use the mathematical jargon. In fact this attitude often went hand in hand with a more general scepticism towards ontological questions in general, and a concomitant 'structuralist' emphasis on the operations and relations between mathematical entities rather than the entities as such. As Quine put it: 'There is no saying absolutely what the numbers are; there is only arithmetic.'[2]

Badiou is, of course, aware of these arguments and takes care in *Being and Event* to put forward a more sophisticated justification for his focus on set theory than merely asserting the ontological credentials of sets. In the book's Introduction he writes:

> I am not pretending in any way that the mathematical domains I mention [that is, set theory and adjacent disciplines] are the most 'interesting' or significant in the current state of mathematics. That ontology has followed its course well beyond them is obvious. Nor am I saying that these domains are in a foundational position for mathematical discursivity, even if they generally occur at the beginning of every systematic treatise. To begin is not to found. My problem is not, as I have said, that of foundations, for that would be to advance within the internal architecture of ontology whereas my task is solely to indicate its site. However, what I do affirm is that historically these domains are *symptoms*, whose interpretation validates the thesis that mathematics is only assured of its truth insofar as it organises what, of being qua being, allows itself to be inscribed. (BE 14)

He immediately adds: 'If other more active symptoms are interpreted then so much the better.' This statement is significant precisely because another 'more active symptom' was indeed rapidly

emerging within mathematics during the latter half of the twentieth century: category theory.

Categories were first developed in the early 1940s by Saunders
Mac Lane and Samuel Eilenberg, two US-based mathematicians working on algebraic topology.[3] Initially little more than
a notational convenience, categories rapidly became formalised
and started to spread to other areas of mathematics. Algebraic
geometry in France was a notable 'early adopter' of categories,
especially under the influence of Alexander Grothendieck. It soon
became clear that categories – along with associated paraphernalia
such as functors, natural transformations and adjunctions – acted
as a kind of universal mathematical language, a lingua franca
illuminating hitherto unsuspected connections between different
areas of mathematics.

We will examine categories in more detail later, but for now
it suffices to think of a category as a collection of 'objects' and
'arrows' between them that satisfy certain laws. Typically – but
not necessarily – the objects will be mathematical structures of a
specified sort, and the arrows will be structure-preserving transformations between them. So, for instance, we could form a category
out of topological spaces and the continuous functions between
them. Or we could collate together all groups and the homomorphisms between them. Or to take a particularly simple but crucial
example, we could consider the category of all sets and all functions between them.

The abstract elegance of categories, together with their seeming
omnipresence and ability to connect disparate mathematical
regions, soon raised the question of whether they could act as
an alternative 'foundation' to sets – and, arguably, a superior
one since categories arose directly out of and were immediately
applicable to general mathematical practice, whereas set theory
was a specialist mathematical sub-discipline whose techniques and
insights were typically of little interest or use to mathematicians in
other fields. The situation is further complicated by the fact that
sets can themselves be considered as forming a category, a special
kind of category known as a topos. It turns out that many of the
key 'foundational' properties of sets are also shared by topoi in
general. This in turn suggests that the foundational role ascribed
to sets is merely an arbitrary metaphysical prejudice on our part,
since we could equally well ascribe the same role to some other
collection of 'set-like' entities inhabiting a topos.

Much of Badiou's work since *Being and Event* has involved getting to grips with these new 'symptoms' and extending his metaontology to take account of them. An early effort to tackle category theory can be found in the essay 'Group, Category, Subject' collected in *Briefings on Existence*. But it is in *Logics of Worlds*, billed as the successor to *Being and Event*, that Badiou provides a thorough examination of topos theory. Roughly speaking, topoi play the equivalent role in *Logics of Worlds* to sets in *Being and Event*. In particular, Badiou argues that topoi encode the ontology of *appearance*. This is a strange kind of phenomenology where objects do not appear 'to a subject', but rather 'in a world'. And the relationship between sets and topoi is thereby recast as the relationship between being-qua-being and being-there, or being-in-a-world.

In this essay I aim to do three things. First, I offer a basic account of sets, categories and topoi, basic enough to be accessible to non-mathematicians, but detailed enough to equip them with the tools to follow the later arguments. Second, I use this account to shed a little light on how the systematic ontology of Badiou's later work interacts with that of *Being and Event*. Third, I raise some tentative questions about the compatibility between the two systems and ask whether the topos-based ontology of *Logics of Worlds* adequately replies to some of the criticisms of his earlier work.

Sets and Functions

Georg Cantor, the founder of set theory, famously sought to define a set as any 'grouping into a totality of quite distinct objects of our intuition or our thought' (cited in BE 38). Badiou ruefully notes that the subsequent development of set theory served to undermine each of these concepts. Nevertheless, Cantor's definition remains a good place to start, since it captures the notion that a set is a *collection* of entities called its *elements*, and that furthermore it is *nothing more* than that collection: it has no further kind of structure, no order, spatiality or arithmetic. In particular we should note that two sets are deemed equal if and only if every element of one is an element of the other and vice versa. It follows from this definition that the *empty set*, the set with no elements, is unique.

What exactly can we do with these minimally structured collections of elements? Very little until we notice that sets can themselves be elements of other sets. The set construction, in other words, can be nested – and it is this feature that imbues sets with the power to model far more complex mathematical entities. For instance, a set of two elements does not have any particular order imposed upon the pair: $\{a, b\}$ is the same thing as $\{b, a\}$. But what if we want an ordered pair $\langle a, b \rangle$, where the a comes first and the b comes second? In fact we can obtain such an entity using a trick discovered by the Polish mathematician Kazimierz Kuratowski: we define $\langle a, b \rangle$ to be the set $\{\{a\}, \{a, b\}\}$. The reader can check that $\langle a, b \rangle$ and $\langle b, a \rangle$ are distinct sets according to this definition, and that given an ordered pair, that is a set of the form $\{\{a\}, \{a, b\}\}$, we can reconstruct a and b respectively.

Given two sets a and b we say b is a *subset* of a if every element of b is also an element of a. It follows from this definition that every set is a subset of itself, and that every set has the empty set as a subset. But in general a set will have many other subsets apart from these two. We denote the set of all subsets of a by Pa – this is called the *power set* of a. It plays a crucial role in Badiou's ontology: he calls Pa the *state* of the situation a.

We can use these constructions of ordered pairs and subsets to create more complex structures. For instance, given two sets A and B we can consider the set of all ordered pairs $\langle a, b \rangle$ where a is an element of A and b is an element of B. This set is called the *Cartesian product* of A and B, denoted $A \times B$. A typical example of such a construction would be an infinite plane, which is precisely the set of all pairs of coordinates $\langle x, y \rangle$ where x and y are both drawn from the set R of real numbers. We can thus denote the plane as $R \times R$, or R^2.

What about a *relation* between two sets A and B? How do we model that using nothing but sets? For instance, A could be the set of all authors and B the set of all books: we might then wish to model the relation 'a is the author of b'. In fact this relation is simply a specified collection of ordered pairs $\langle a, b \rangle$, or equivalently, a specified subset of the product $A \times B$. Conversely, any subset of $A \times B$ defines a unique relation between elements of A and elements of B: a is related to b if and only if $\langle a, b \rangle$ is in the subset under consideration.

Mathematicians are particularly interested in relations between A and B that satisfy a further property: namely, that every element of A is related to exactly one element of B. Such a relation effectively assigns to each element a of A an element $f(a)$ of B. It is called a *function* from A to B and can be informally thought of as a 'recipe' for turning an element of A into an element of B. For instance, the function $f(x) = x^2$ is a function from the real line R to itself. Considered as a relation it comprises the pairs $\langle x, y \rangle$ where $y = x^2$, that is a parabola in the plane.

From Sets to Categories

The mathematics of the above section is compressed but standard. Readers who are unsure of any details should consult any introductory text on set theory, where the same constructions will be spelled out at a more leisurely pace. The material is also covered in Appendix 2 of *Being and Event*, which includes some important comments by Badiou on the 'structuralist illusion' in mathematics and the Heideggerian theme of the forgetting of being. For now it is enough to note that a *function* from one set to another can be treated *as* a set in its own right. Or, as Badiou puts it (discussing relations in general rather than functions):

> Who hasn't spoken, at one time or another, of the relation 'between' the elements of a multiple and therefore supposed that a difference in status opposed the elementary inertia of the multiple to its structuration? Who hasn't said 'take a set with a relation of order . . .', thus giving the impression that this relation was itself something completely different from a set? Each time, however, what is concealed behind this assumption of order is that being knows no other figure of presentation than that of the multiple, and that thus the relation, inasmuch as it is, must be as multiple as the multiple in which it operates. (BE 443)

We should also note in passing two fundamental properties of functions that play a crucial role in the transition to the category theoretic perspective on mathematics. First, functions can be *composed*. If f is a function from A to B and g is a function from B to C, we can define a new function that takes any a in A to $g(f(a))$ in C. This composite function from A to C is denoted $g \circ f$ (or simply gf). Moreover, composition when viewed as a binary operation on functions is *associative*, in that $h \circ (g \circ f) = (h \circ g) \circ f$ for any composable functions f, g and h.

Second, every set is equipped with a special function that sends each of its elements to itself. So for any set A, we can define a function e from A to A that 'leaves everything as it is', that is sends each a in A to that a in A. This function is called the *identity* on A, and it acts as a neutral element in composition: $e \circ f = f$ for any function f to A and $g \circ e = g$ for any function g from A. From an ontological point of view this identity function is simply the 'diagonal' subset of $A \times A$, that is the set of pairs $\langle a, a \rangle$ for each a in A.

It is these two properties of functions – associative composition and the existence of identities – that category theory takes as its starting point. Specifically, a *category* is defined to be a collection of 'objects' and a collection of 'arrows' between them. (We will ignore the troublesome question of what exactly a 'collection' means in this context.) These arrows are subject to certain rules: (1) given any arrows f from A to B and g from B to C, there is a 'composite' arrow $g \circ f$ from A to C; (2) given f from A to B, g from B to C and h from C to D, then $h \circ (g \circ f) = (h \circ g) \circ f$; (3) for any object A there is an 'identity arrow' e from A to A such that $e \circ f = f$ and $g \circ e = g$ for all suitable f and g.

Clearly sets and the functions between them form a category, one typically denoted **Set**. And one can form plenty of other categories by considering sets equipped with a certain structure and functions that preserve that structure. For instance, we could take our objects to be groups (roughly speaking, sets equipped with a type of 'multiplication' operation) and our arrows to be homomorphisms (functions between groups that 'preserve' the multiplication). Or we could take our objects to be topological spaces and our arrows to be continuous functions between them.

However, the abstractive power of categories only comes into its own once we drop the assumption that objects somehow 'ought' to be sets of some sort, and that arrows 'ought' to be functions. For in general an object in a category has no internal structure whatsoever. It is simply a point, a momentary resting place from which arrows arrive or depart. (In fact some presentations of category theory go even further, ditching objects altogether and defining categories solely in terms of their arrows.) And the arrows too have no internal mechanics: all that matters is their source, their target and the composition relationships they enter into with other arrows.

The notion of *isomorphism* provides an indication of just how radical this abstraction is. An arrow f from A to B is called an isomorphism if it has an inverse, that is an arrow g from B to A such that $f \circ g$ and $g \circ f$ are both identity arrows. One can easily show that such an inverse, if it exists, is unique and is itself an isomorphism. Clearly all identity arrows are isomorphisms, and the composition of two isomorphisms yields a third. We say two objects A and B are *isomorphic* if there is an isomorphism between them. Isomorphism acts as an 'equivalence' relationship among objects: roughly speaking, if A and B are isomorphic then any arrows to or from A can be 'translated' into equivalent arrows to or from B.

Now it can be shown that the language of category theory – the apparatus of arrows, composition, identities, sources and targets outlined above – is incapable of distinguishing between isomorphic objects inside a category. Insofar as an object can be specified using the terminology and techniques of category theory, it is specified 'up to isomorphism' only. There could be several or an infinite number of objects that fit the specification, but one can be assured that they will all be mutually isomorphic. From the point of view of categorical abstraction, isomorphic objects are 'the same' – not quite identical, but indistinguishable and thereby admitting the highest degree of similarity appropriate to that abstraction.

The contrast here with sets could not be starker. The question of whether two sets are the same or not is governed by the axiom of extensionality: two sets are the same if and only if they have the same elements. Furthermore, the axiom of foundation ensures that the apparent circularity of this criterion can be dissipated. At the level of ontology, identity is an all-or-nothing affair. But the moment one steps onto the phenomenological level described by categories, identity starts to blur: distinct-but-isomorphic objects can no longer be distinguished.

Before we move on to consider topoi, we should briefly consider how this categorical phenomenology relates to Badiou's comments on the 'structuralist illusion' mentioned above. Badiou's argument here proceeds on more or less Heideggerian lines. The naive attitude of the working mathematician, who takes functions and relations at face value, represents a necessary abdication of the ontological vocation of mathematics. A 'forgetting of being', a 'technical domination', but one that is nevertheless an 'imperative of reason', since mathematical practice would be impossible without it. 'Actual mathematics is thus the metaphysics of the ontology that it is. It is, in its essence, *forgetting of itself*' (BE 446).

Badiou diverges from Heidegger at one point only: mathematics possesses internal resources to 'forget the forgetting' and consequently should not be written off as mere nihilistic technique:

> Even if practical mathematics is necessarily carried out within the forgetting of itself – for this is the price of its victorious advance – the option of de-stratification is always available . . . In this sense, mathematical ontology is not technical, because the unveiling of the origin is not an unfathomable virtuality, it is rather an intrinsically available option, a permanent possibility . . . [Mathematics] is both the forgetting of itself and the critique of that forgetting. (BE 447)

But this account is unsatisfactory. It sets up an unacceptable island of privilege within mathematical praxis: plebeian 'working mathematicians' who labour under their structuralist delusions versus aristocratic set theorists who apprehend the truth of the discipline. More fundamentally, it puts ontological clarity and practical efficacy at loggerheads with each other. It concedes far too much to Heidegger in its acceptance that the accusation of technical nihilism holds water for the vast bulk of mathematical practice. Its response to Heidegger's charge sheet amounts to little more than special pleading for set theory.

Moreover, Badiou's own argument contains the germ of a more robust approach to these issues. For if mathematics can both forget being and forget that forgetting, then by the same token it can *forget the forgetting of the forgetting*. And in fact this fits far better to mathematical practice. Forgetting being corresponds to a naive mathematical approach that does not broach ontological questions; forgetting the forgetting corresponds to grounding that naive discourse on a rigorous ontological foundation; and forgetting the forgetting of the forgetting corresponds to understanding that the precise nature of that ontological foundation is arbitrary: what matters is that one *can* implement general mathematical entities as sets, not *how* that implementation takes place. From this perspective category theory is an extension and deepening of the ontological vocation of mathematics, rather than being a reversion to illusion or a sacrifice of theory on the altar of practice.

The categorical properties of sets

We mentioned above that sets and the functions between them form the category **Set**, and that the properties of objects in categories are cast in terms of the arrows between them rather than through reference to any internal structure of the object. It is worth seeing how this approach works in the case of **Set**, that is, how we can characterise various properties of sets through 'arrows only' definitions.

To begin with let's consider the concept of a *singleton set*, that is a set with exactly one element. Suppose {*t*} is such a singleton and *A* is any other set. How many functions *f* are there from *A* to {*t*}? Exactly one, since *f*(*a*) must be equal to *t* for every element *a* of *A*. In fact one can easily check that this property characterises singleton sets: if for every set *A* there is exactly one function from *A* to *T*, then *T* must be a singleton.

Now since we have characterised singletons purely in terms of functions, we can generalise this approach to any category. We say *T* is a *terminal object* of a category if and only if there is a unique arrow from *A* to *T* for every object *A* of the category. Not every category will have such terminal objects, but in those that do *T* will play a roughly analogous role to that played by singletons in **Set**.

We should note in passing that this arrows-based approach characterises singleton sets but does not and cannot specify *which* particular singleton we are talking about. More generally, we can show that any two terminal objects in any category are isomorphic, and that any object isomorphic to a terminal object is itself terminal. As mentioned above, category theory can only distinguish objects up to isomorphism. All singletons look 'the same' as far as the pattern of arrows in and out of them are concerned. What the set is a singleton *of* is a question that cannot be framed, let alone answered, from a categorical perspective.

Terminal objects are just one example of a family of categorical constructions known as *limits*. Each of these defines a particular object and associated arrows 'up to isomorphism' in terms of the uniqueness of arrows to or from that object. For instance, given any two objects *A* and *B*, we can define a *product* object *A* × *B* equipped with two projection maps from *A* × *B* to *A* and *B* respectively. Readers can consult the standard literature for the details of this construction; for now it will suffice to note that in **Set** the Cartesian product defined above, together with maps sending an ordered pair <*a*, *b*> to *a* and *b* respectively, acts as a product in the categorical sense too.

What about the *subset* construction? Is there a way of casting it in categorical language, or what amounts to the same thing, generalising the construction to that of a *subobject* in an arbitrary category? It turns out that the answer is yes – twice. There are two ways of describing subsets categorically, and the equivalence of the two turns out to be a fundamental property of the category Set – so fundamental that any other category sharing that property can be considered more or less 'Set-like'.

The first approach notes that any subset B of A comes equipped with a natural function j that takes any element of B to the same element considered as an element of A. This inclusion function, as it is known, has the property of being *monic*, or 'left cancel-lable': if $j \circ g = j \circ h$, then $g = h$, for any pair of functions g and h from a common source to B. Moreover, any monic function to a set A defines a unique subset of A, namely the *image* of that function (that is those elements of A that are values of the function).

This approach generalises to an arbitrary category quite straight-forwardly. Given any object A and a monic arrow j to A, we say j is a subobject of A. If j and k are two subobjects and h is an isomorphism such that $j = k \circ h$, we say j and k are isomorphic as subobjects. One can easily check that in Set, a subobject of a set A is simply an injective function to A, and this function is isomorphic as a subobject to the inclusion of its range in A.

The second approach starts from the observation that given any subset of A, every element of A is either in that subset or not. This means we can think of the subset as a function from A to 2, the two-element set {*true*, *false*}. This *characteristic* function, as it is known, returns the value *true* on elements of A that are in the subset and *false* on those that are not. The subset can be recon-structed from the characteristic function as the inverse image of {*true*}, that is the set of all elements in A that are sent to *true* by the function. Conversely, every function from A to 2 defines a unique subset of A in this manner. Thus the subsets of A and the functions from A to 2 are essentially equivalent, in the sense that there is a natural way of converting one into the other and back again, from subset to characteristic function and vice versa.

How do we perform this construction in an arbitrary category? We start with a special object Ω called the *subobject classifier* that plays the same role as 2 does in Set. We also specify an arrow t from T to Ω called the truth arrow, where T is a terminal object in our category. This arrow to Ω plays the same role as the element *true* does in 2. Finally, we want to ensure that the arrows from an arbitrary object A to Ω correspond precisely to the subobjects of A (strictly speaking, to the isomorphic classes of subobjects of

A). This amounts to stating that for any subobject j of A, there is a unique arrow x from A to Ω such that j is the 'pullback' of t along x. A pullback is a special kind of limit, similar to the product construction mentioned earlier. Its precise details need not concern us here – the key point is that it plays a similar role to the inverse image of {*true*} above.

To recap. In **Set** there is a precise and natural correspondence between the subsets of A and the functions from A to 2. Every subset A gives rise to such a function and vice versa. In a general category this translates into a correspondence (up to isomorphism) between subobjects of A and arrows from A to a special object Ω, known as the subobject classifier. Every subobject of A gives rise to an arrow from A to Ω and vice versa.

Of course there is no guarantee that a subobject classifier actually exists in any particular category. But if it does, we know that the objects of that category mimic those of **Set** with respect to the dialectic between wholes and parts. Instead of subsets we have subobjects – but those subobjects are well-behaved, in that they admit being indexed by maps to Ω.

Topoi and the logic of appearance

We are finally in a position to define topoi, the mathematical centrepiece of Badiou's *Logics of Worlds*. A topos is a category with two additional conditions: it is 'cartesian closed' and it has a subobject classifier. The category of sets and functions between them is a topos, with 2 playing the role of subobject classifier. But there are many other kinds of topoi that involve more complex subobject classifiers, which testify to a more complex logic of wholes and parts at work in these alternatives to our familiar set theoretical world.

First a brief word on what 'cartesian closed' means. A category is cartesian closed if it admits a basic 'algebra' whereby objects have 'products' and 'exponents'. We have already seen how in **Set** we can 'multiply' two sets A and B to create their cartesian product $A \times B$. Similarly we can define 'A to the power B' to be the set of functions from B to A. A cartesian closed category is one where similar operations exist on its objects.

The more significant condition is the one about subobject classifiers. The existence of the subobject classifier – what Badiou calls a 'transcendental' – imposes a certain set-like logic of wholes and parts upon the category. The precise nature of that logic is determined by the structure of the subobject classifier. This logic need not necessarily be classical, as it is in the case of **Set**. In fact the internal logic of a topos is typically constructive (or intuitionist) rather than classical.

We have come a long way, so perhaps it is time to retrace our steps. We began with the doctrine of the pure multiple, or set theory. Starting from our ontological axioms we derived a host of secondary constructions on sets: subset, product, relation, function, characteristic. We then noted that the importance of these constructions lay not so much in what they were but in the grammar of relations they embodied. In particular, sets admit an *algebra* whereby they can be combined together through multiplication and exponentiation, together with a *dialectic* of wholes and parts. Neither this algebra nor this dialectic are built into the axiomatic foundation of sets; they arise out of those foundations. But any category that admits such an algebra and dialectic – any topos – can by virtue of this admission play the same foundational role as sets. Set theoretical ontology thus supplements itself in the course of its unfolding and points towards its own generalisation, the theory of topoi.

What then is the articulation between sets and topoi, between the 'ontology of ontology' and the supplement it necessarily produces? What is at stake in this move from a *universe* of sets to a *multiverse* of topoi – each with its own logic, its own dialectic of parts and wholes, the familiar **Set** being merely one of many possible worlds, many foundational choices?

Badiou deploys several terms terms here: logic, relation, appearance, phenomenology. Being is supplemented by being-there or being-in-a-world. Multiples do not just exist, they exist in a web of relations with other multiples. This web of relations constitutes a world where entities appear to one another. And the logic of that appearance is determined by the properties of that world. In particular the logic of wholes and parts – the dialectic alluded to above – is governed by that world's transcendental.

The study of the logic of appearance is traditionally called phenomenology, and Badiou retains this term to describe the supplement to the pure ontology set forth in *Being and Event*. This is an appropriate choice in many ways, but we should note two crucial respects in which Badiou's phenomenology departs from that of the philosophical tradition.

First, phenomenology – certainly since Kant and arguably before – has typically involved appearance *to* a subject. Even Heidegger does not fundamentally depart from this conception: for him being is disclosed *to* a privileged entity that enquires: Dasein. But for Badiou appearance is appearance *in* a world. Entities appear without there being anyone to appear to. In this respect Badiou's phenomenology is a theory of objects without subjects that complements his earlier project of a subject without objects.

Second, phenomenology is *part* of ontology rather than being distinguished from it. Appearance is being-there and thus part of ontology proper. It makes no sense to think of entities as they are on the one hand and as they seem to be on the other. This envelopment of phenomenology within general ontology parallels the mathematisation of logic, a revolution in thought that has unfolded over the past two hundred years. Recall that for Badiou ontology is mathematics – all of mathematics, not just set theory – and if phenomenology has been mathematised then it has been ontologised. Strictly speaking, the articulation is not between ontology and phenomenology as traditionally understood, but between *onto*-logy and onto-*logy*. Where we once had a metaphysical opposition, we now have a difference of emphasis.

The Ontology of the Multiple: Decentred or Dethroned?

We have described in some detail how Badiou's phenomenology of topoi supplements his pure ontology of sets. Yet this supplement comes at a price: it threatens to overwhelm and displace the origin that gave rise to it. One can see this tension at work both within Badiou's corpus and in mathematics more generally.

The contrast between set-theoretical and categorical 'foundations' of mathematics is a stark one. Arguably 'contrast' is too mild a way of putting it: one would better speak of a *rivalry*. Thinking about mathematics in terms of categories involves a wrenching away from familiar set-theoretic assumptions, and requires considerable effort to master. We have seen how topoi act as the appropriate categorical generalisation of sets, and how this generalisation can bridge the gap between sets and categories, opening up a passage from the former to the latter. This is the strategy that Badiou adopts. By putting topoi at the centre of his later work, notably *Logics of Worlds*, Badiou can maintain his earlier pure ontology (characterised by classical decision and a refusal of relativistic sophistry) in an uneasy alliance with his later phenomenology (characterised by a ramification of possible worlds and a descriptive suspension of the decision between them). We see this tension in the following passage from Badiou's essay 'Being and Appearance', which appears in the English language collection *Theoretical Writings*:

> The theory of topoi is descriptive and not really axiomatic. The classical axioms of set theory fix the untotalisable universe of the thinking of the pure multiple. We could say that set theory constitutes an ontological decision. The theory of topoi defines, on the basis of an absolutely minimal concept of relation, the conditions under which it is acceptable to speak of a universe for thinking, and consequently to speak of the localisation of a situation of being. To borrow a Leibnizian metaphor: set theory is the fulminating presentation of a singular universe, in which what there is is thought, according to its pure 'there is'. The theory of topoi describes possible universes and their rules of possibility. It is akin to the inspection of the possible universes which for Leibniz are contained in God's understanding. That is why it is not a mathematics of being, but a mathematical logic. (TW 174)

So while Badiou admits a multiverse of possible universes, there is still a Platonic decision that accords an ontological privilege to *one* particular universe. We *might* be in any topos, but we *are* in **Set**. For many mathematicians this configuration remains a messy compromise. They urge that we go further and replace set-theoretical foundations with ones based on categories and topoi. They are not satisfied with simply decentring the role of sets – they call for sets to be dethroned altogether. F. W. Lawvere, one of the founding figures of category theory, has long polemicised this point of view. At the very least it accords with the direction of mathematical practice, though whether Badiou would be moved by such empirical considerations remains somewhat questionable.

But this question is not merely one confined to mathematics or Badiou's ontological interpretation thereof. It impinges directly on at least two major debates surrounding Badiou's philosophical work. I want to end by briefly sketching these debates and the implications that categories and topoi have upon them. Hopefully this account will at the very least shed light upon the issues and perhaps point to directions for future research.

The first debate concerns the status of relationality in Badiou's work. As noted earlier, relations are a secondary concept in *Being and Event*, ones that arise out of the ontology of the pure multiple rather than being hard-coded into its axiomatic set-up. This has led to criticisms that Badiou's ontology remains impoverished and weak when it comes to grasping the relationality of being, since it does not accept relationality as a fundamental ontological category. In particular, it raises questions over whether Badiou's ontology is of any use in characterising the social and political world where relations are generally considered paramount.

One could counter that the secondary status of relation in mathematical ontology has not had any limitative or deleterious effect on the thinking of relation within mathematics itself. On the contrary, mathematicians are constantly concerned with relations and have been so successfully for centuries. More than that – in recent decades mathematicians have discovered at least one hitherto unthought relation, that of *adjunction*, whose profundity and omnipresence in mathematics is only just beginning to be grasped.

But this rejoinder doesn't quite hit the mark. For the most creative thinking of relation, and the concept of adjunction in particular, has arisen out of category theory through the very gesture of bracketing off 'foundational' ontological questions. Category theory proceeds from ignoring the innards of mathematical entities and tackling them solely from the perspective of the arrows between them. The fact that such an approach leads to theoretical breakthroughs and innovations such as adjunction only fuels the suspicion that the pure ontology of set theory is at the very least dispensable. The possibility arises, therefore, that one can maintain Badiou's subordination of philosophy to its mathematical condition while radically transforming the content of the mathematical ontology that condition prescribes.

The second debate concerns perhaps the most controversial aspect of Badiou's work, his theory of the state. For the Badiou of *Being and Event* at any rate, the state is an ontological fixture. Its existence is guaranteed by an axiom – the power set axiom – in sharp contrast to the status of relation. This is coupled to an explicit critique of the Marx-Engels theory of the state and an implicit critique of the revolutionary political practice it proposes.

This leads to a curious pessimism in Badiou's work. If the state is ontologically inscribed, it is in a sense immovable, and to that extent revolutions are doomed to failure. All they do is replace one kind of state with another, foreclosing the possibility of communism understood as a world without a state. Of course it is undeniable that the great revolutionary sequences of France, Russia and China have failed to dislodge the state, and much of Badiou's pessimism on this score takes its cue from this historical failure. But it is one thing to note the historical record and quite another to elevate it to an ontological principle. In practice Badiou's theory of the state finds itself allied to a sectarian and abstentionist political practice that ironically resembles that of certain Deleuze-influenced autonomist currents that Badiou openly despises and condemns as petit bourgeois romanticism. Even worse, it risks endorsing a certain liberal common sense that views revolution as at best misguided idealism and at worst totalitarian horror.

Yet are things as bleak as they seem? For Badiou's theory of the state is underpinned by an identification of the state of a situation X with the power set of that situation PX (the set of subsets of a particular set). And the machinery he deploys to analyse this relation – presentation, representation and the dialectic between them – is fundamentally tied to the specific configuration of that dialectic at work in classical Zermelo-Fraenkel set theory.

This picture is quite different in an arbitrary topos. Rather than working with sets and power sets, we have objects and power objects. And the relations between the two are governed by the transcendental, the subobject classifier, of that topos. At bottom the question of the state and situation is a question of the dialectic of parts and wholes. And as we have seen, topos theory admits far more variability on this score than classical set theory. So the transition from Set to an arbitrary topos involves a certain loosening of the relations between state and situation. This opens up the possibility that we can hold fast to Badiou's central insight into the mathematical nature of ontology, hold fast to his fidelity to philosophy's mathematical condition and even accept his identification of the state with power objects – while drawing radically different conclusions about the nature of the state and the viability of revolution.

In 1926 the mathematician David Hilbert issued a famous rejoinder to those who criticised Cantor's transfinite set theory as philosophically or theologically unacceptable: 'No one shall expel us from the paradise that Cantor has created for us.'[4] One could say about category theory today that no one shall expel us from the paradise created by Eilenberg, Mac Lane, Lawvere and many others. Taking this injunction seriously, I submit, involves radicalising Badiou's ontology yet further and stripping it of its residual attachment to the classical set theory of Zermelo-Fraenkel – an attachment that despite its undoubted historical grandeur and brilliance can only serve as a conservative brake on thought today.

Notes

1. Kurt Gödel, 'On formally undecidable propositions of *Principia Mathematica* and related systems I' [1931], in Martin Davis (ed.), *The Undecidable* (Mineola, NY: Dover, 1965).
2. W. V. Quine, *Ontological Relativity and Other Essays* (New York: Columbia University Press, 1969), p. 45.
3. Their collaborative research has been collected in the volume Saunders Mac Lane and Samuel Eilenberg, *Eilenberg-MacLane, Collected Works* (New York: Academic Press, 1986).
4. David Hilbert, 'On the infinite', in Jean Van Heijenoort (ed.), *From Frege to Gödel* (Cambridge, MA: Harvard University Press, 1967), p. 376.

II. Philosophical Notions and Orientations

6

The Black Sheep of Materialism:
The Theory of the Subject
Ed Pluth

In an important essay, Adrian Johnston takes Alain Badiou to task for being too dismissive of and ill-informed about the natural sciences – neurobiology in particular. Johnston is consciously echoing Badiou's rejoinder to philosophers for ignoring developments in mathematics for too long – the cost of which ignorance meant a floundering about in ontological matters that could have been resolved with the help of set theory. Johnston's point is that the neurosciences should hold a similar status for philosophers now when it comes to formulating a materialist theory of the subject.

I heard a similar charge recently by a physicist – although the charge was thrown at philosophers and philosophy generally, and had nothing to do with Alain Badiou's work or my take on it. He simply accused philosophers of still being stuck on Plato, while the sciences have moved way past all that. I didn't come up with the right reply to this until later, when I was walking home – perhaps out of fear of seeming impolite. But my silence might also have been due to weariness from hearing such things. We're always having to defend philosophy, if not from the sciences, then either practically, or ethically (we're not all tyrants, and yes, we know it is rude of us to point out, but there is a difference between truth and opinion). And what is everyone always telling us? If it isn't that what we do isn't important anymore, or is of questionable value, it is that we're terribly behind. As if everyone is sure that there have been no philosophical innovations since Plato, and that philosophy really has no history in the strong sense – it just circles around the same, eternal set of problems.

The clever reply that occurred to me was something like – well, at least we've gone as far as Plato; you're still not past Democritus! We philosophers have moved past problems involving matter and cause, and are on to problems involving form, substance, ideas, truth, the subject ... And if you believe Hegel, we're well past Plato too. In other words, can it not be said that the materialism of the contemporary sciences is philosophically not new and not striking, and little different from a Democritean atomism? So, to accuse philosophers of basically not advancing past Democritus would be absurd. It represents a misunderstanding of what philosophy does, and also of what the sciences do.

I know what would have been said in reply – it is the sciences that have moved on, and not philosophy! We know far more now: we know that atoms are hardly the last things. Furthermore, Democritus didn't have the scientific method. But still, formally and philosophically, is it not the case that the natural sciences remain philosophically Democritean? The fact that they have hit on many different kinds of things, and even non-things, does not suggest otherwise. Can it not be said that the contemporary sciences differ from Democritus – again, philosophically – only on the nature of the what, and not on anything else?

I was reminded of this incident when reading Johnston's excellent essay, 'What Matter(s) in Ontology'. It is not the case that Johnston is dismissive of philosophy at all, of course, and he is definitely not a Democritean. Nor does he think the sciences – neurobiology in particular – are somehow ahead of philosophers. Philosophers, Badiou in particular, are just ignorant of how much the sciences have changed, and of how little they embrace a vulgar, simplistic materialism.

But when Badiou told philosophers that they had, to their detriment, lost sight of mathematics and what it was doing, this was because he could point to an innovation in mathematics that leads (arguably, but that's for another place) to a new philosophical view: that being is multiple *and* that there are truths. The contrast to other philosophies is important here. Plato was able to affirm that there are truths, but not that being is multiple. Nietzsche could affirm that being is multiple, but there are no truths. Set theory helped Badiou with the articulation of a new philosophical position – what Badiou has called a Platonism of the multiple (MP 104). With respect to Johnston's point: what would be the similar innovation that contemporary neuroscience (or any science) would introduce into philosophy?

Johnston suggests that it would help us with developing a theory of the subject within a materialist framework. What neurobiology is showing us, in the wake of work by Donald Hebb and others, is that 'mental phenomena literally sculpt and re-sculpt the brain, which itself . . . must be thought of as plastic . . . The plastic brain is simultaneously constituting (i.e., it shapes the mental life arising from it) and, as Hebb shows, constituted (i.e., it is shaped by the mental life arising from it.'[1] This is very good. But this is certainly not news to philosophers, although it may be to neuroscientists and the general public. Indeed, Hebb's claim was anticipated by some insights about learning from William James.[2] And, had Hebb read his Marx, he would have already found the claim that 'thinking and being are thus certainly *distinct*, but at the same time they are in unity with each other' (Marx, quoted in TS 193).

Maybe what is supposed to be news to philosophers is that there is empirical confirmation for a view some of them were already inclined to hold. Johnston does write that

a plethora of consequences crucial to a scientifically informed materialist model of the subject flow from the Hebb-event, including: the collapse of standard versions of the nature-nurture distinction; the invalidation of reductively mechanistic/eliminative materialisms; and, the debunking of vulgar genetic determinism in relation to human beings. These consequences make possible a new materialism and correlative conception of subjectivity.[3]

Again, this is all very good, although it sounds like Johnston is claiming that a theory of the subject within philosophical materialism is justified now because of discoveries from neurobiology. Johnston says he does not intend to suture philosophy to science: 'Fidelity to the Hebb-event is no more of a suturing of philosophy to science than is Badiou's fidelity to the Cantor-event (if anything, Badiou tries to tie philosophical meta-ontology to one sub-discipline of one formal science with a suture-like rigidity and inflexibility).'[4] The suggestion, in a parenthetical *tu quoque*, is that Badiou actually sutures philosophy (at least one branch of it, metaontology) to set theory. However, there is a difference between suturing one branch of philosophy to a science (mathematics in this case) and suturing philosophy itself to science. The old branch of natural philosophy has been sutured to – or better, surrendered to – the hard sciences for a long time, and rightly so. In fact, it is no longer really considered a branch of philosophy at all. Isn't this what Badiou wants to see happen with ontology in the wake of set theory? Philosophers need not bother with it anymore. What is Johnston doing with philosophy and its relation to the sciences?

My point is that the status of the neurosciences for philosophy within Johnston's position needs to be clarified. If they are not just providing empirical confirmation for insights philosophers have already been inclined to defend, it is not clear what they are doing for philosophy. And if their role is to give empirical confirmation, then it is difficult to see how Johnston is not suturing philosophy to science: the value of philosophical claims would depend on the value of empirical claims from the natural sciences. Johnston is indeed claiming that insights from the neurosciences 'make possible a new materialism and correlative conception of subjectivity'.[5] And if they did not make this possible, what would that status of a materialist theory of the subject be?

But there is another important line of argumentation in Johnston's essay that will lead us to the reason why he wants to see some sort of alliance between philosophy and the neurosciences. He and others are right to point to some potentially fatal peculiarities in Alain Badiou's materialism, and are right to question what qualifies it as such. It is entirely correct to observe, as they do, that Badiou's is a materialism that is not only anti-naturalist, but also one that has very little to do with any notion of matter. Nor does it seem to be any sort of physicalism at all. So, what is it about the category of materialism that Badiou thinks is so important to keep for his philosophy, and what, if anything, justifies his use of it?

I will argue here that there are multiple senses of materialism at work in Badiou's philosophy, and only some of them are really justified – the crucial one being materialism's equalisation or levelling down of what might otherwise be construed as distinct regions and orders of being. However, if this were all there were to Badiou's materialism, his philosophy might be accused of being a monism. We'll see that Badiou's attempt to use matter as a name for being in *Theory of the Subject* is in fact a monistic stumbling block for his position at the time, and goes against another, more promising, line of reasoning put forth in the same book: that a materialism needs as its primary category not matter but the 'conceptual black sheep' of materialism, the subject itself (TS 189).

To gain an understanding of Badiou's take on materialism his discussion of the historical sequence of idealisms and materialisms in *Theory of the Subject* still deserves pride of place as it remains his most sustained treatment of the topic. One thing Badiou emphasises there is the manner in which materialisms have always been organised around a category demeaned by the dominant philosophical idealisms against which they emerge. Thus the category of nature, as developed in Cartesian dualism, and even the Christian world view generally was embraced and promoted by what we could call the first-wave materialism of the bourgeoisie of the French eighteenth century (excluding from consideration the Ancient schools) (TS 186). And it is important to observe that this first-wave materialism essentially endorsed the conception of nature (mechanistic) that was developed within the idealism it rose against (TS 186). In the next phase of the sequence, dialectical and historical materialism, it is history that is embraced – a category that was problematic for the bourgeoisie with its affirmation of an ahistorical human nature. And here too, it is worth noting that this second-wave materialism essentially preserves the conception of history (as progressive, teleological, eschatological) that was developed within the idealism it contested. So, one of Badiou's guiding ideas concerning materialism is that within the categories minimised or diminished by idealism itself are to be found the sources of the materialism that will rival it.

The idealism targeted by Badiou's third-wave materialism is what he calls the linguistic idealism of structuralist anti-humanism, primarily found in the works of Althusser, Foucault and Lacan. He writes that 'there are three materialisms, for the excellent reason that there are three idealisms: religious idealism, humanist idealism, and then . . . linguistic idealism' (TS 188). The 'axiom of all our best thinkers' is that the central, organising figure of Man is dead, due to the fact that language 'is that of which experience is the effect, and . . . is . . . that which makes his speech possible' (TS 187–8). Language is structure; discourse, in some sense, is constitutive, and this amounts to saying that 'language precedes the world' – an idealist thesis if there ever was one, Badiou notes (TS 189). And if there is any status for the subject within this 'idea-linguisterie' it is only as excluded, decentred, eclipsed or subjected (TS 188).

So it seems as if there is a simple pattern: from idealisms built around God, then Man, then Language, to materialisms that will be developed around Nature, then History, then, it might seem, a theory of the subject, since this is the category rejected by 'idea-linguisterie'. Yet it is not clear that the subject is supposed to be a basis for Badiou's materialism, as nature and history were for the previous ones. And this question is still the critical issue facing Badiou's materialism.

But before continuing this study of the subject in the materialism of Badiou, I want to consider a further aspect of how any idealism is being portrayed here: it is primarily understood as ideology, as the way in which a dominant class articulates and justifies its hold over a situation – idealism 'being the obligatory language of conservation' (TS 184). So, Badiou considers materialisms as the modes in which oppositional movements articulate themselves – at least in the period from the French Revolution to May 1968. What this means is that there is a strategic and formal definition of both idealism and materialism in *Theory of the Subject*, and therefore it need not be the particular ingredients or elements of idealism or materialism that are definitive for either of them. This way, materialism need not be defined by its position on matter (and if historically it has been this is accidental, just because of the positions that had been taken by idealisms), and idealism need not be defined by its position on the immaterial, the ideal, the conceptual, the soul or language either. If this is kept in mind, one can see why Badiou thinks it is justifiable for the materialism of *Logics of Worlds* to endorse obviously non-material notions like those of an 'incorporeal' body, ideas, events, truths and even subjects; and it also makes sense that what he calls the dominant ideology of our day, democratic materialism, will in fact bear the essential traits of an idealism and not a materialism.

Yet Badiou does insist that matter is a primary category for materialism in *Theory of the Subject*. And this is why the discussion of materialism in *Theory of the Subject* is ultimately confused, though still important to consider. The use of the word matter in it cannot really be defended, we'll see, but the use of the category of materialism can be – again, on the basis of a positional or strategic definition of both materialism and idealism.

The problem with the account of materialism in *Theory of the Subject* emerges clearly when two key theses for materialism are given that are directly, as Badiou himself observes, contradictory. They deviate from the strategic and formal definition of materialism *Theory of the Subject* is implicitly proposing, insofar as both are framed as assertions about the nature of what is. The first thesis is 'there is the one' and the other is that 'the One precedes the Other' which, Badiou notes, amounts to a concession that there are in fact two: 'there is the two' (TS 190). Materialism thus seems to be both a monism and a dualism! (It is significant, of course, that Badiou had not yet developed the thesis that 'the one is not' – certainly, this thesis would have helped out . . . but the sense in which it might be a materialist thesis is not at all clear either.) For materialism, the name of being, of the 'one', is matter: 'il y a l'un' is treated as a 'thesis of identity: being is exclusively matter' (TS 193). (Earlier, Badiou explains that 'every material-ism posits the primitive unicity of being, with the implication that its intimate constitution requires only one name. Matter is this name' (TS 190).) Yet materialism is also led to 'abdicate its essen-tial axiom, which is monism, and to posit the thesis of all major idealisms, namely that there are indeed two regions of being. However, it does so only with the aim of annulling this thesis. For in truth there is only one region of being for materialism' (TS 192–3).

Badiou is making it sound as if it is the status of the second thesis that is shaky for materialism. But it is actually the first thesis that is the problem, and it is materialism's need to abdicate its monism, expressed by the second thesis, that is ultimately more important than its need to annul the claim that there are two regions of being. For the second thesis, seemingly dualist, is taken to be just an assertion of the primacy of matter: matter precedes whatever its others are taken to be – thought, in particular. Badiou tries to resolve the contradiction among the two theses, then, by stipulat-ing that while the first thesis is indeed about the name of being, the other should be read as a description of its ordering (TS 193). So, materialism says being is one, yet there are two (or should it read, echoing Lacan's famous 'y a d'l'un', something like y'a du deux? There is something of the two, or there is a two-effect?). There is one name for being, it is matter, and yet there seems to be some-thing (many things!) other than matter, but . . . really all that too is matter; matter is all there is.

And for precisely these reasons, Badiou stipulates that material-ism's assertion of the primacy of matter in its second thesis 'does not mean ontological hierarchy, or pre-eminence' – one of matter over anything else (TS 209). Because 'there exists *only* matter' there is no hierarchy of matter over thinking, or whatever you like, only because matter is, again, all there is (TS 193). Thinking is as much material as anything else, and thus has as much of an ontological status as anything else. There is, thus, no question of any subordination of thought to matter here. If matter is all there is, what is there to be subordinated?

But the monism Badiou associates with materialism in the first thesis may seem to be reconfirmed in the second thesis. The intuition Badiou is trying to preserve here comes from the quote from Marx mentioned above, no doubt a reworking of a famous thesis from Parmenides: 'Thinking and being are thus certainly *distinct*, but at the same time they are in unity with each other' (TS 193). Accounting for the manner in which the two 'are in unity with each other' is the important point, and this is why I think Badiou's claim about matter as the name for being and the potential monism of this view in the first thesis is the real problem, and is actually less important and more dispensable than it seems. (Ultimately, we know, it is abandoned altogether, in the famous thesis from *Being and Event* that 'the one is not' (BE 23).) The second thesis highlights another key feature of materialism, one that is worth preserving and will be preserved, which is not that being is material, nor is it any thesis about the name of being at all. Rather, it is the claim that materialism embraces a levelling down of apparent differences between orders of being. Call this the egalitarian thesis. Thus I want to say the key thesis of materialism in *Theory of the Subject* – and beyond, as we shall see – is really the second one, the apparently dualistic one, which is actually not dualistic but an ontological equaliser.

So what a reading of *Theory of the Subject* shows us about the difference between idealism and materialism is that the former ranks and orders the two (or more), while materialism levels them. Idealism can be considered then something like a philosophy of difference – it is not really adequate to say it is a dualism, although this is how Badiou tends to describe it in *Theory of the Subject*. One has an idealism when there is some kind of two-worlds view, or at least some kind of ranking among worlds.

The reason why this is important is that on these terms even an apparent materialism, a potential ally, a philosophy that names being 'matter', can in fact be a secret idealism. An eliminative or reductive materialism, insofar as it institutes a hierarchy between matter and thinking, would by this rationale qualify as an idealism insofar as it subordinates thinking to matter, or insofar as it somehow degrades the status of thought and language. Thus such a philosophy could effectively be a philosophy 'of the two' – although it would be just a starved dualism, in which one of the traditional substances is vaporised into a philosophical illusion, an odd emanation or after-effect of what is primary, of what there is. Given this, it can be observed that Badiou gets something else wrong in *Theory of the Subject*: the dominant form of idealism would turn out to be different from what Badiou was saying it was at the time. It would not be structuralist anti-humanism or a discursive idealism, but a version of materialism itself, as *Logics of Worlds* in fact argues.

This requires a further specification concerning the strategy of materialism. Badiou is trying to break with two of the main strategic features of prior materialisms. He observes that prior materialisms worked by inverting the terms of the then dominant idealisms. In the case of the third-wave materialism Badiou is developing, since the idealism to be combated is supposed to be a linguistic idealism that debases or decentres the category of the subject (in Althusser, Foucault, Lacan), the inversion strategy might go one of two ways. One would be to suggest that the world should be placed before language. But wouldn't this be a naive empiricism? The other way would be to suggest that since the subject is what is excluded by the linguistic or discursive idealism of high structuralist anti-humanism, a rehabilitation of the subject ought to occur. Badiou will do something like this, but not without questioning whether one can get at a theory of the subject by a typical materialist inversion, precisely because this would amount to promoting the subject over the real, which would obviously itself be an idealist move (TS 189). So, the dilemma is that any classical materialist strategy against the structuralist anti-humanism of the 1960s threatens to be retrograde: either it will be a naive empiricism or a bad idealism. Badiou does affirm that 'the essence of active materialism, by a Copernican inversion, demands the position of a theory of the subject, which previously it had the function of foreclosing' (TS 188). But what stance on the subject should be taken, and what kind of Copernican reversal can this really be? And to repeat my earlier question: can the subject serve at all as a basis for materialism, as nature and history did previously?

It is difficult to situate the rest of the discussion in the section of *Theory of the Subject* entitled 'A Materialist Reversal of Materialism' without keeping this dilemma for materialist strategy in mind. For the text veers off into a discussion of what seem to be primarily epistemological matters, and then, even more oddly, it concludes with a discussion of algebra and topology – which seem to be quite far from typical materialist concerns. But what emerges from the discussion is that there are already materialisms that have developed in the wake of the 'linguistic idealism' Badiou critiques, and he wants to establish that these materialisms are 'heretical' – versions of the naive empiricism or bad idealism mentioned above. One is represented by Deleuze (the 'gauchiste' deviation) and the other by Lévi-Strauss (the 'rightist' deviation). In Deleuze, the difference between thinking and being is rendered too 'asymptotic' while in Lévi-Strauss a possible full match between thinking and being, one that is an 'adequation without remainder', is promised (TS 206). (My aim here is not to consider whether these readings of Deleuze and Lévi-Strauss are in any way justified, but simply to follow the argument being made for materialism and the subject within it in *Theory of the Subject*.) These materialisms, Badiou considers, do manage to contest the primary thesis of 'linguistic idealism' – which is the thesis that discourse, not the subject, and not anything else, is constitutive of the world and/or experience (TS 188). Yet where they fail is in getting the relation between thinking and being correct: one places them too far apart (as asymptotes), the other too close together (as mimetic), to put it simply.

In place of the models (metaphors, Badiou also calls them) of the asymptotic relation between thinking to being on the one hand, and the potential reflective or mirroring relation they might have on the other, Badiou's materialism embraces a model that he describes as a 'topological algebra' in which the subject itself represents the 'torsion' of thinking and being with each other (TS 209). What does this tell us about the place of the subject in materialism? We've seen that, on the one hand, Badiou in *Theory of the Subject* wishes to continue to use 'matter' as the name for being. But we have also seen that such a naming is not sufficient to qualify as a materialism. The second thesis, I argued, is more important: it equalises apparently distinct regions of being without collapsing them into a monistic unity. It seems to me that sticking to this is more important for following the rest of the argument in *Theory of the Subject*, and for Badiou's subsequent development, than is sticking to matter – or anything else – as the name of being.

Again, what the desired materialist theory of the subject needs to do is level down two different regions – here, let's say, thought, languages and formal codes, on the one hand, and bodies and organisms on the other – without risking monism. This is a line of reasoning about the subject that is continued in *Logics of Worlds*, a text that also sheds light on why it is important for a materialist philosophy to be clear about the nature of idealism. For what has happened is that some version of materialism has itself become idealist.

In *Logics of Worlds* the dominant ideology today is portrayed not explicitly as an idealism but as a bio-materialism, a materialism 'of life', which is joined to another kind of materialism – a democratic materialism. This pervasive ideology is a materialism of life because of its interest in and valorisation of bodies; it is also a democratic materialism because of its view of the equality of languages for worlds (opinions and points of view) (LW 2). These sound like versions of the materialist theses from *Theory of the Subject* – one of them promoting something material and the other promoting an egalitarianism. But Badiou notes that there is something excluded from this ideology: it suppresses 'a language that does not recognize the universal juridical and normative equality of languages' (LW 2). In other words, what it suppresses is the very stuff of a truth procedure. And so, what the ideology of democratic materialism excludes is any exception to being, understood as material/corporeal and/or linguistic. And so, because the stuff of truth procedures is relegated, excluded and subordinated, this ideology qualifies, paradoxically, in the terms of *Theory of the Subject*, as an idealism.

Therefore, and again quite paradoxically, the requisite materialism to rival this 'materialist idealism' is one that affirms that there are truths that are 'not bodies, languages, or combinations of the two' (LW 4). And Badiou can defend this affirmation as a materialism mainly because 'it does not require any splitting of worlds, any intelligible place, any "height". In our worlds, such as they are, truths advance' (LW 4). What is found here again is a materialism that emphasises not a position on matter but an equalising, a levelling down. When Badiou goes on to write that truths are 'incorporeal bodies, languages devoid of meaning, generic infinities, unconditioned supplement' suspended 'between the void and the pure event' the language he uses is manifestly not that of the dominant democratic, but also scientistic, materialisms today (LW 4). It sounds more like mysticism and religion, and perhaps obscurantism. But Badiou's position must be that this is necessary to avoid a worse and more pervasive form of idealism – the ideology of contemporary democratic materialism itself.

The reason why a theory of the subject is the conceptual black sheep of materialism should now be clear: the subject is overtly an exception to the order of being, and the philosophical challenge is to come up with a way to describe that. A subject is 'the active (or corporeal, or organic) bearer of the dialectical overcoming of simple materialism' (LW 45). A subject is corporeal, embodied, organic, material and yet an exception to all that as well. While still, necessarily, incorporated in a body or bodies, the subject is also not reducible to a material locale. In *Logics of Worlds*, Badiou observes:

> So I was not mistaken, more than twenty years ago, in my *Theory of the Subject*, to organize – in my jargon of the time – the dialectic of 'splace' [*esplace*] (or, in more sober terms, of worlds) and the 'out-place' [*horlieu*] (or of the subjects that truths induce as the form of a body). Except that I cut straight to the dialectic, without drawing – in a Greater Logic – all the consequences of the obligatory materialism, of which I declared at the time, obscurely conscious of its compactness, that it was like the black sheep in the herd of ideas. That truths are required to appear bodily [*en-corps*] and to do so over again [*encore*]: that was the problem whose breadth I was yet unable to gauge. It is now clear to me that the dialectical thinking of a singular subject pre-supposes the knowledge of what an efficacious body is, and of what a logical and material excess with regard to the bodies-languages system might be. In short, it presupposes mastery not only of the ontology of truths, but of what makes truths appear in a world: the style of their deployment; the starkness of their imposition on the laws of what locally surrounds them; everything whose existence is summed up by the term 'subject', once its syntax is that of exception. (LW 45–6)

What is clarified now is that the theory of the subject must not in itself be materialist in any typical sense, but is instead better characterised as formalist or 'meta-physical', Badiou even writes. While *Theory of the Subject* gave the impression that the subject might somehow serve as the basis of materialism, Badiou's position in *Logics of Worlds* seems to be that this is no longer the case. He can in fact remain agnostic about the basis of materialism – saying nothing other than that it is the multiple – and develop a theory of being and a theory of appearing in such a manner that the subject takes place within this theory as, precisely, an exception to what is.

So what a materialism needs to defend, in order to contest contemporary 'materialist idealism', are precisely these para-beings such as the subject and truths – precisely the stuff which typically constitutes, not a materialism, but rather an idealism, if not a religion, as Johnston rightly points out when he expresses concerns about the religious language of Badiou's philosophy. Johnston hopes that being more attentive to developments in the natural sciences, in a 'philosophically guided coordination between psychoanalytic metapsychology and cognitive neuroscience' would enable us to avoid an 'ideologically dangerous recourse to religious rhetoric (i.e., grace, transubstantiation, Christ-Paul, etc.) opening the door to and encouraging idealist hijackings of materialism to the benefit of theologies'.[6] Such things may happen, and no doubt already have. Yet to want a philosophical language for materialism and the theory of the subject that would have one foot in scientific clarity instead of 'notions and terminology flirting with blatant, shameless religiosity', as Johnston describes Badiou's language, itself runs the greater ideological risk of suturing philosophy to the sciences.[7] To return to some of my earlier points: either the support from the natural sciences for the theory of the subject Johnston wants to defend – which is not at all unlike Badiou's theory – is important for Johnston's materialism or it isn't. If it is, it is hard to see how Johnston has not become a verificationist. Perhaps then such support is not really important and Johnston is proposing only a strategic alliance. Where Badiou is comfortable flirting with obscure religious terminology, Johnston prefers what he describes as the clarity of the sciences.[8] But what makes the language of the sciences any more clear than Badiou's, or that of any philosophy? Is it because the sciences are referring to facts? That their claims are verifiable? Again, then, the question would be – is Johnston not just reinventing the twentieth century here, subordinating the value of philosophical claims to the value of scientific claims? If one wants to avoid monism and dualism, still be a materialist, and develop a theory of the subject, the challenge Badiou is presenting us with is that we need to persist in thinking the subject as an exception to what is – an exception to bodies and to languages, which are indeed all there are (for this is still a materialism). Johnston is on board with such a project, but not with the language in which it is developed. But can a philosophical language be developed without relying on the sciences for guidance that would not risk sounding religious? Would a philosophical language not be equally ideological for relying on the natural sciences for support? What this is about, ultimately, is the independence of philosophy itself.

I hope to have shown that there is a way to defend the materialism of Badiou's philosophy, provided materialism is understood primarily as a strategy, one of whose most important moves is not a reference to anything like matter, but rather an egalitarian move against an idealism that segregates regions of being – eliminating one or some altogether, or reducing one to another. Badiou sees this occurring in democratic materialism. I've suggested that a reductive/eliminative materialism would be doing the same thing. Johnston is arguing, however that, understood correctly, the neurosciences are not reductively materialist and that they can enable exactly the same theory that Badiou is developing. But, especially given the ideological force the sciences have for us today, it is hard to see how this would not make philosophy dependent on claims from the natural sciences. No doubt Badiou's philosophy runs the risk of enabling theological, perhaps even 'theosophist', adventures.[9] But this is quite different: better to see a philosophy influencing other domains than to see philosophy itself fall victim to another suturing.

Notes

1. Adrian Johnston, 'What matter(s) in ontology: Alain Badiou, the Hebb-event, and materialism split from within', *Angelaki*, 13: 1 (2008), p. 41.
2. Phillip Winn (ed.), *Dictionary of Biological Psychology* (London: Routledge, 2001), p. 345.
3. Johnston, 'What matter(s) in ontology', p. 41.
4. Ibid., p. 44.
5. Ibid.
6. Ibid., p. 38.
7. Ibid.
8. Ibid.
9. Ibid., p. 39.

A Critique of Alain Badiou's Denial of Time in His Philosophy of Events

James Williams

Then we shall be stronger than Time. (SM 130)

I will call this organised control of time fidelity. (BE 211)

But Does Badiou Deny Time?

The first exergue to this chapter is the last line of Alain Badiou's *Second Manifesto for Philosophy*, first published in French in 2009. I have quoted his sign off and slogan as evidence for the main premise of my argument: Badiou seeks to deny time. The denial is not my sole concern, though. It is rather that it is the condition for a series of philosophical and practical consequences through the affirmation of a different kind of time. This is why I have added the second statement, from *Being and Event*. Badiou advocates a control over time through the affirmation of a special kind of time and through the denial of another, perhaps more familiar, sense of time. The implications of Badiou's denial of a time and construction of another are far-reaching and, in my view, violent and negative. Badiou's denial of time is an antecedent to a violence taking the form of negations of real modes of existence in time. These modes follow from the time he seeks to obliterate – to be 'stronger than' through the 'control' of another time. I view the negated modes as valuable and worthy of a defence.

In his second main work, *Logics of Worlds*, Badiou has categorised this kind of resistance within time as reactionary. According to his division of active subjects into three main categories of faithful, reactive and obscure, my defence of time positions me in the second, a reactive subject clinging to a reactionary definition of time and seeking to repress the event (LW 50–61). The second manifesto is a coda and distillation of *Logics of Worlds* in the same way as his first manifesto for philosophy sought to draw out the fundamental lessons of his earlier *Being and Event*. The characterisation and definition of reactionary forces is not new to Badiou's work; a version of it can be found in the definition of the normalisation of the event in *Being and Event* (BE 185, 196), itself related back to his work on history and communism and the struggle against reaction in *Theory of the Subject* (TS 315–16). However, reaction is given in a more clear form in relation to time in *Logics of Worlds*. I will argue against this formal account in relation to time because it is dependent on false alternatives, deduced from a restricted binary ontology dividing event and situation, or truth and world, or infinite and finite. We shall see below that this binary structure is mitigated by dialectics crossing the division. This never overrides the setting of action and value according to the prior ontological split.

If Badiou defines reaction in politics, art, love and science *in relation to time*, how can I contend that he denies time? There are discussions of time and of history throughout Badiou's work, from his study of history and mathematics in the early *The Concept of Model* (CM 48–9), to the methodological reflection on epochs in *Century* (TC 1–10), through time as determined by fidelity and dependent on 'the Two' and on eventual sites and history in *Being and Event* (BE 201–2 and 173–7), up to the study of time and the present in *Logics of Worlds* (LW 49–78). Antony Calcagno has written insightfully on time, Badiou and Derrida.[1] There is a perceptive and suggestive essay by Alex Düttmann that shows time not only to be important for Badiou but also as presenting risks for him: 'An anticipatory fidelity relates to an event as if it belonged to a past and future at the same time, as if it had already taken place precisely because it has not already taken place. The temporal structure of such fidelity exposes it to confusion.'[2] There is deep work on Badiou, Deleuze and time.[3] Is it not perverse, then, to claim that all of this equates to a denial of time?

In response to these indications for Badiou's reflection on time, I will first consider the last line of the second manifesto with its implicit desire and aim to be stronger than time. First, I want to distinguish between different senses of denial. To deny can be understood as merely to negate something, that is to make a claim for non-existence, such as the denial in the proposition 'There is no planet named Lachesis in our solar system.' There is also a denial accepting the existence of something but then attaching it to a value system which denies its importance. There, the denial is really of a subsequent claim, for instance in the proposition and its sub-clause 'I deny the nation state, as legitimately defining individual identity.' The denial bears on the definition of identity rather than on the nation state. Finally, there are forms of denial betraying a deeper unconscious affirmation. The most famous of these is perhaps the patient's claim, under psychoanalysis, '. . . it was not my mother'; this is negation as studied by Freud in his work on the wolf man and in his 'Negation' article.[4] However, I wish to consider a less obviously psychologically unconscious type, where the denial allows for an explanation of a set of consequent positions, aims and drives. These consequences are at odds with an initial proposition, yet are not made apparent when it is stated.

I am not claiming that Badiou denies time in the first sense of denial. He does not simply deny the existence of time in all its forms. It is the other three ways of negating time that are of concern here. Badiou attaches a value system to time by denying importance to some of its forms and by giving too much importance to others. In fact, my argument will be stronger than this, since I want to claim that the forms he gives weight to are fictions – claims to non-existent eternal forms. The violence of his denial follows in part from the imposition of these fictions and from the debasing of other forms of time. In a more practical rather than ideological sense, violence also follows from the types of action and of categorisation allowed by these illusions and rejections. Practically, the value system leads to two types of consequences: positive ones, from Badiou's point of view, such as fidelity to the event in relation to eternal truths, and negative ones, from the point of view of alternative and debased accounts of time, which suffer from a violent eclipse. The denial of time is therefore an imposition of a value system, the concealment of an account of time beneath a fiction, and a series of consequences following from this imposition and concealment.

The two fictions about time we find in Badiou both involve eternity. They are eternal presents and eternal truths. The two are related and the former is never really eternal except through its participation in or disposition to the latter. The present is then a struggle for eternity through the real eternity of truth. In the *Second Manifesto for Philosophy*, Badiou is explicit about the Platonic form of this philosophy, as he is in *The Communist Hypothesis* when defending the communist 'Idea' (CH 229–60).

Badiou speaks of replacing the Platonic Idea of the Good with his own conception of the True. In *The Communist Hypothesis* it is a matter of replacing the Idea of the State with the Idea of communism (CH 254–5).

Once Truth replaces the Good, Badiou sets it within the attribute of the eternal: 'Plato's problem – which is still ours – is how our experience of a particular world (that which we are given to know, the "knowable") can open up access to eternal, universal and, in this sense, transmundane truths' (SM 106). Badiou departs from Plato, or at least from traditional readings of the Platonic transcendence of the Idea,[5] in insisting on the immanence of a truly known object of experience to an eternal truth. He then adds to this by also insisting that truth is material rather than ideal. Badiou's philosophy is a 'materialism' of the idea through the incorporation of a life to a material trace of an event of truth, in a dialectical relation to mere 'worlds of appearance' (SM 107).

Eternal truths occur with events, but these events are themselves outside known worlds, or worlds of appearance. The paradox of this externality yet also presence of the event in worlds is resolved through the concept of the evental site; events are manifested in worlds at evental sites which cannot be equated to the event yet depend on it. Such worlds have set logics of relation which assign intensities to these relations throughout the worlds, with no exception. We can understand such logics of relations as assigning importance and place in a world, for instance in terms of a map of relational hierarchies in a company (*x reports to y, y earns more than x, x must obey y, but z can sack y, so x must also obey z, though z earns less than y, all can be sacked by z and z is therefore the most intense meeting of relations in the company*).

An event of truth, say of Badiou's eternal political truth of equality, has no place in the logic of the world and yet can occur at an evental site where the world's logic is broken (*we became equals when the company's ship was trapped in the tempest*). Incorporation to the trace of the event is then in the struggle of a subject, of a body of committed activity (*organise for the equality we once knew in the tempest*). This activity seeks to make that event material and to be faithful to the truth associated with the event, as manifested at the evental site, against the logic of a world (*we shall struggle for a company of equals*). One of the key problems of Badiou's philosophy lies in the compromises and assaults implied by the mismatch between the logic of a world and the activity of faithful subjects. If this activity has to work in a world, it will constantly be drawn into compromises with the world's logic and hence towards a betrayal of the truth and the event. If the subject opposes the logic of the world, it will come under assault either from those who wish to deny the exception of the event (*there never was, nor can be real equality*), reactionary subjects, or from those who wish to turn this exception into a general rule based on a part of the logic of the past world (*the only equality is in a society of strong men*), obscure subjects.

The struggle of a subject, following the trace of an event and for an eternal truth, is where the two eternities in Badiou meet. A world is never eternal; its logic of relations is always shifting and passing into other worlds. An individual is never eternal but rather passing and mortal:

> It sometimes happens (event, or, for Plato, 'conversion') that we are able to enter into the setting-out of a truth. Admittedly, this process for us is neither an ascension nor linked to the death of a body and the immortality of a soul. It is, as Plato also knew, a dialectic – that of the incorporation of our individual life within the new body constituted around the primordial statement, that trace of the event. (SM 108)

A subject – not to be confused with individuals or individual humans – is incorporation, the making of an active body. This becomes eternal to the extent that it enters into the truth through the trace of the event and a primordial statement: *we were equal once; we can make a world of equals*.

I will argue that the work of the faithful subject, disposed to an eternal truth, yet faced by the danger of compromises and assaults, is the locus for the denial of time in Badiou's philosophy. This gives the denial a twofold structure: a positive side, in the fidelity within a world to an eternal truth (I view as fictional); a negative side, in the denial of the time of the world as true in relation to the eternal truth. These are formal accounts of the denial, but they can be given an informal and therefore somewhat imprecise character. The positive side of the denial of time is a denial of the passing quality of truths themselves and of why they pass. This then leads to fidelity to eternal truths. The negative side of the denial is the active dismissal of the passing quality of the world as all there is, as the only universal. This is the denial of fleeting time through the strength of the subject's control over it. I am critical of the positive and negative sides of Badiou's approach to time. This commits me to a position in relation to time summed up in the following statement: nothing is eternal, except the passing of things in time. Perhaps this is the paradigm of reaction, viewed from Badiou's philosophy.

Being and Event: Time and Intervention

My introduction to Badiou's denial of time has deliberately referred across his work, making loose connections between ideas, themes and concepts from different books belonging to different epochs spanning forty years. This is to show the pervasiveness and consistency of his denial. It is important, though, to pay attention to his arguments as set out in detail in specific works. I will focus on two, *Being and Event* and *Logics of Worlds*. These are the central works of his philosophy of the event, towards which others either build or develop from. They are related yet also make use of different forms of mathematics and different concepts to articulate events and being, or events and worlds. In this section, I will analyse a short but important reference to time from *Being and Event*. This will then be traced to his account of fidelity in the later parts of the book. The reference to fidelity from the earlier work will then allow a transition to the work on time and on the present in the later *Logics of Worlds*. In the conclusion, I will return to the question of violence and to distinctions between different periods of Badiou's work through a critical reading of Alberto Toscano's seminal essay on Badiou and violence, 'Can Violence Be Thought? Notes on Badiou and on the Possibility of (Marxist) Politics'.[6]

The discussion of time in Meditation XX of *Being and Event* bears important resemblances to the work on time in *Logics of Worlds* and to the definition of different types of subject and action in relation to truth and to the event in the later book. The title of the meditation is helpful in understanding the context of this discussion of time. It bears the same clarity of presentation and grasp of his concepts found throughout Badiou's work, a testament to the rigour and robustness of this work. The concepts of the title are 'intervention' (the overarching theme), 'the illegal choice of the name for the event' (the problem), 'the logic of the Two' (the ontological frame for the problem) and 'the foundation of time' (the foundation of time on intervention and the mathematical ontology of the Two).

The passage on time to be studied here occurs in this last concept of foundation, but it is related to the other ones in the way I have indicated briefly in brackets above. Time and distinctions between different types of time, as well as the acts of subjects in relation to events and to truth, arise within the intervention around an event (or more properly between two events, as we shall see). The deepest problem, though, is that the naming of the event or any representation of it within a given situation is either illegal or para-doxical, since if any name from the situation is selected, then we do not have an event external to it. Similarly, the event cannot be identified with the evental site, because this too belongs to the situation (BE 202–4). To give the event a name from the situation is then to force it into the order of a pre-established state that cannot recognise the event as such.

Broadly, this problem can be seen in debates around historical events where different names carry different weights and politi-cal significations (*It is not a revolution, since private property remains in force*). For Badiou, a situation is ordered and regu-lated such that none of its elements are independent of an order-ing, a state. This means that no external event, that is no event outside the ordered situation, can occur within it. Yes, there are events. They are indicated at evental sites. Yet since these sites and their elements are elements of the situation there is either an illegality, something outside the order of the state, or a paradoxical entity, something in and outside the situation at the evental site.

Nonetheless, any subject seeking to be faithful to an event must intervene for the event within a situation. Fidelity begins with an intervention, which itself must be a naming: 'The intervention has as initial operation to make a name of an un-presented element of the site in order to qualify the site's event' (BE 204 – translation modified). The name is therefore taken from the external event, from 'the void at the edge of' the evental site, but it is also taken from the evental site. Badiou draws seven connected consequences from this problematic demand. These consequences determine his study of time. They are striking in their range, from formal logical deductions to political distinctions, and in their language, from logical formalism to theological and social tropes. This reach and style give Badiou's work much of its expressive power. They also contribute to its difficulty and scent of danger or hopeful possibility, or perhaps both.

The seven consequences are:

1. The element of the site in the naming of the event does not exist solely for the situation and its state law. It is not at one with the situation but rather two: element and event. (BE 204–5)
2. The element cannot be distinguished from the site as name, but it is 'projected' into the two of the designation of the event through the intervention. (BE 205)
3. The naming is illegal because the state law governing the situation cannot represent it under law. The choice made by an intervention is then not a choice for the situation. (BE 205–6)
4. The event always remains two, always beyond representation and law, always an 'originary Two' even when it is named, a 'divided effect of a decision'. (BE 206–7)
5. The event is a matter of chance in the situation. Therefore no intervention can claim to be decisive because every intervention answers only to its event. Intervention is therefore a matter of discipline and not origination. (BE 207)
6. The name for the event becomes a problem and struggle for the state of a situation. As 'Two' it resists inclusion because the state must include the event (which would disrupt the ordering). (BE 207–8)
7. In order to avoid a vicious circle for the intervention around the externality of the event, the possibility of the intervention must be assigned to 'the consequences of another event'. (BE 209–11)

I want to stress the essential roles of choice and action in the above consequences. I also want to draw attention to the conditions for such choice and action. The intervention is essential for the presentation of the event through a naming. The illegality and paradox of the naming are the locus for a struggle between intervention and state. However, since the intervention cannot grasp or represent the event, it acts for a second event as a consequence of the first. The second event is defined as a consequence of the first by the intervention. The intervention therefore acts for a relation between the two events and is itself placed between them. The struggle around the event is therefore twofold: on one side, there is a struggle against the event, through the state-sponsored attempt either to deny it or to bring it within order through the name; on the other side, there is the intervention's struggle between two events, faithful to the first through the second. This second struggle is opposed to the first, not in some kind of sterile remove, but in a dynamic opposition. They clash over the event.

There is a complicated and deeply original dialectics in this clash. This is because state and faithful subject each have their dialectics separately with the event, with the 'Two' in the name of the event. But these dialectics meet in another constituted by their clash over the event. The state seeks to repress or suppress the event. Intervention seeks a faithful disposition towards the event, through another event that is a consequence of the first. Ontology becomes essentially political here, a matter of intervention, choice, action and struggle. This struggle is the source of political violence and of the denial of time. As we shall see in the conclusion, it is also the locus for a debate around the necessity of violence in Badiou's work. Though it is not a central part of my argument, it is important to note why Badiou's position is so original. Instead of either a world of will or a world of being, we have a world of being (situation and state), of non-being or the void (the event), and a twofold series of choices and acts, the conflict of the faithful subject and the state, articulating being and non-being, or being and event.

The dynamic nature of Badiou's account can be seen in the following statement: 'At the state-governed surface of a situation, every event is therefore given by an excrescence whose structure is a Two without concept' (BE 209 – translation modified). The event grows out of the state and constitutes a counter presence that the state itself seeks to resist or reject. The intervention is a necessary part of this dynamic, since without an intervention there would be no excrescence. This role depends on another event: 'The intervention presents the event for the coming of another. It is an evental between [*entre-deux*]' (BE 209 – translation modified). Crucially, though, each of the sides in this dynamic struggle implies different relations to time. The struggle is a struggle over time, not in the sense of a struggle within one and the same unfolding time, but rather a struggle between and for different times.

The essential role of intervention in relation to the event and the struggle with state order in a situation therefore also determine the definition of times and distinctions between them. This explains why Badiou follows his consideration of the seven consequences of the problematic demand of the event with a sweeping claim about time: '. . . the theory of intervention is the crux of any theory of time' ('. . . *la théorie de l'intervention est le nœud de toute théorie du temps*' (BE 210 – translation modified)). The translation of the French '*nœud*' is difficult yet pivotal here. The most literal sense is 'knot', but as in English this can either mean bind or crux (the current translation gives it as 'kernel'), where the former is a more straightforward connecting and the latter expresses difficulty and tension. So does the intervention constitute a knotty problem or a seamless binding? The evidence points towards difficulty and tension rather than unification. First, this is because Badiou maintains a distinction between different definitions of time within a theory of intervention. Second, even within the different sides of the distinction, there is still effort and tension.

In fact, the definition of time as tense and difficult mirrors the two sides of the struggle around intervention and the event, and their internal problems and efforts. The distinction first shows up in two definitions of time: in relation to law and in relation to events. On the one hand, time is 'the sensible form of the Law' (BE 210 – emphasis removed). On the other, it is 'intervention itself, thought as the interval (*écart*) between two events' (BE 210 – translation modified). Badiou favours the second definition, in relation to intervention and in-between, or interval. Yet he also registers that this definition is in conflict with the first. To understand this conflict and the differences it is built around we need to be clearer about the two definitions.

The first characteristic of the distinction is that it turns on two approaches to history. This is a constant theme in Badiou's work. He studies time in relation to history (at greatest length in *Theory of the Subject*) and he studies history in relation to political revolt and repression. These terms are used loosely here for want of space, but the distinction is in fact much more complex, since his discussion of intervention and fidelity in relation to events allows for subtle distinctions between different kinds of political action – as we have already seen, briefly, in terms of distinctions between kinds of political subject. Fidelity to the event and its repression, as the attempt to deny the event, are embodied in different definitions of history and in relation to different views of time. They are not distinguished within a single account of history and of historical time. Instead, the struggle between fidelity and repression is more elemental, more essential. It is a struggle about time before it is a struggle about history. It is a struggle about history before it is a struggle between different politics. As intervention between two events, though, it is a political act before anything else.

Historical time of Law is governed by common measure, that is it is homogeneous since all its terms are related through an order and can therefore be treated in terms of general relational comparisons (closeness to the centre, essential and dispensable, for instance). It can also be treated in terms of comparisons of intensity (the strength of something at a given time, for instance). The 'between' time of intervention is by definition without measure because it is defined in terms of the event and hence as outside law as uniformly applicable, hence as illegal, as defined above. Badiou characterises this further by associating the time of intervention with non-being, with evental multiplicity and with that which is not presentable. This notion of time leads to a conception of a history of faithful subjects disposed towards events that cannot be presented, that cannot be reduced to a final unity and that are external or outside being (defined as that which all elements of a situation share).

More importantly the historical time of intervention is therefore not measurable in terms of the distance or degrees between two 'points' or situations. There is no erosion, or duration, or lapse of time between points of an intervention in relation to its two events. This explains the importance of Badiou's choice of the word 'consequences' to define the relation between the two events of an intervention. It is a necessary relation rather than one of loose influence or 'diffusion' (see Blackburn for a distinction between causal consequences and Hume's idea of diffusion).[7] Similarly, it is not subject to general laws. Furthermore, because the time of intervention is between two events, where the intervention is at an event posited as the consequence of another event, the intervention is not at an origin, but rather at a consequence of another chance-driven event. Badiou therefore claims that the intervention is a 'diagonal' of a situation, a projection out of the situation to an external event that the new event is a consequence of. This follows from the definition of the time of intervention as requiring the 'Two': 'Time here is once again the requirement of the 'Two': for there to be an event, it is required that we should be at the point of consequences of another [event]' (BE 210 – translation modified).

Why should these definitions and distinctions be interpreted as a denial of time? The denial is the result of three steps. First, Badiou's account maintains two definitions of time, where the time of intervention must be faithful to an event that has to yield to the time of law in a situation: 'The real difficulty is that the consequences of an event, having to yield to structure, are not discernible as such' (BE 211 – translation modified). Second, the fact those events cannot be decided – cannot be discerned within the situation except as yielding to law – means that fidelity to the event in intervention requires enacting that the consequences of an event are themselves event-like. So, third, since the event cannot be decided as part of the situation, there is a demand for a primary and disciplinary disposition in relation to time: 'That is why it can only be founded on a discipline of time, controlling the consequences of the circulation of the paradoxical multiple from end to end, and knowing how to discern its connection to chance at any time' (BE 211 – translation modified). This control, discipline and discernment form the basis of the denial of the time of the situation: 'I will call this organised control of time *fidelity*' (BE 211). This fidelity is committed to the denial, in an ongoing struggle, of the time of the situation and of its internal erosion and multiplicity, in the name of the controlled time between two events.

To gauge the importance of the short treatment of time in *Being and Event*, we can trace its effect through to the concluding passages of the book. There, Badiou returns to the themes of naming, fidelity and chance with the addition of three concepts that bridge to his later work in *Logics of Worlds*: subjects, truth and forcing. I will turn to the first two in the next section. The latter concept is of mathematical origin, but it is also used in relation to the subject, truth and time. I refer to it because it allows for two further counters to my reading of Badiou. In the closing sections of *Being and Event* he explicitly denounces some kinds of violence as based on a mistaken view of time. My accusation that his denial of time has violent consequences could therefore be perceived to be a misrepresentation that does not take account of Badiou's fullest theory of time and in particular of his understanding of the future. To counter this impression I will now develop my point as it applies to Badiou's definition of the future perfect.

Towards the end of *Being and Event*, Badiou analyses the subject in relation to truth through the idea of the future. He states a fundamental law of the subject and of the 'future perfect' thus: 'If a statement of the language-subject is such that it will have been truthful for a situation where a truth has come to being, then there exists *a* term of the situation that both belongs to that truth ... and that has a particular relation to the names set in play in the statement' (BE 401 – translation modified). I have deliberately skipped the proofs and definitions of Badiou's work on forcing, inspired by the mathematician Paul Cohen's work in set theory, in order to focus on the time aspect of Badiou's statement. For the subject, a truthful statement and its verification can short-circuit the lapse of time and uncertainty between two situations. A statement will have been truthful for a situation, so long as there exists a term that belongs to the situation and to the statement that can be verified in the later situation.

Badiou seeks a form of knowledge that erases the lapse of time, duration and uncertainty between two situations and events: 'Forcing is a relation that can be verified by knowledge, since it applies to a term of the situation . . . and to a statement of the language subject . . .' (BE 403 – translation modified). It is important to note that this does not mean that knowledge about an event becomes certain in the present: 'What cannot be verified by knowledge is whether the term that does or does not force a statement can be discerned' (BE 403 – translation modified). The present is not guaranteed for Badiou. That's the point of his use of the future perfect. What is guaranteed is that we can choose terms that will allow us to verify the truth of a statement in the future, such that they will have been true. The point of intervention, between two events, is to work for such truths, following events, in the search for such terms. There is always uncertainty at the time of the intervention.

Given this continued uncertainty, why do I claim that Badiou denies time? It is because the forcing of a decision by a subject according to the fundamental law depends on the identity through time of truth and of a term between situations. A term retains its identity and a truth remains eternal in relation to a statement, even if the event also remains impossible to discern. I will return to this impossibility and its relation to a subtraction from a state in my conclusion. Here, though, I want to underline that this is a denial of time because it rests on eternal truths and identities independent of the becoming and passing of durational time. How does this conclusion also confirm my claims about the violence of his denial? This question is important because one of the consequences of his work on forcing is a critique of destruction that reaches its strongest point in this powerful claim: 'Killing someone is always a matter of the (old) state of things. It can never be a requisite of novelty' (BE 408 – translation modified). The event never requires a killing, whereas reasons of state can and often do. Where then is the violence?

The answer is that if killing is taken as violence, or indeed when any other example of physical or mental violence is taken as such, then Badiou's position is not necessarily violent. More powerfully, his argument is convincing in its claim that, given the role of the event and the impossibility of discerning it in a given situation in the present, his philosophy is indeed opposed to state sanctioned or legal violence within a situation, since it questions that legality in the name of the event and of truth. There can be no certainty about the rightness of a killing based on an event. The violence of the denial of time lies elsewhere, in the shift in values allowed by the eternity of truths in relation to enduring identities. This shift might allow for distinctions in terms of how far physical and mental forms of violence follow from different positions on time, but this would always be indirect and is not a worry here. Instead, I am concerned with violence as the consequence of a selection between eternity and duration. I will now turn to this aspect of Badiou's denial of time in a reading of *Logics of Worlds*.

Logics of Worlds: An Eternal Present

The work on truth and the subject that closes *Being and Event* is followed closely in *Logics of Worlds*: 'Before engaging and crossing new and dense philosophical stages, let us point to what touches on typical procedures of truth for a subject. Through which we connect again to conceptions established already, in particular in *Being and Event*' (LW 68–9 – translation modified). This connection is deceptive, however, in relation to time. This is because the account in terms of the future perfect becomes a treatment in terms of the present and eternity. In *Being and Event*, future verification under the aegis of a search retained uncertainty in relation to verification, even where there was certainty as to what to seek to verify (see Pluth and Hoens for an account of the roots of this tentative and 'anticipatory' relation to time, and its roots in Badiou's reading of Lacan on 'haste' and logical time in *Theory of the Subject*, TS 254–8).[8] In *Logics of Worlds* the relation through time becomes secure – free of durational terms (such as haste). The vocabulary of that which can and cannot be discernable according to what 'will have been', a future relation, is replaced by a reliable projection of the present into the future thanks to a relation to eternity.

It is important to register that this is not a shift in the definition of truth for Badiou. It is rather a shift in the relation of truth to time, where a new vocabulary of eternity in the present, of resurrection of truths and of immortality, supplements the earlier relation of statement to truth in the future perfect. The task of relating to truth is still that of the faithful subject: 'We shall therefore say that every faithful subject can thus reincorporate to the eventual present the fragment of truth that the old present passed under the bar of occultation' (LW 66 – translation modified). Truths can become hidden and deliberately concealed or erased by obscure or reactionary subjects, with their interest in an order that must reject the event. However, this historical erosion is not final because the subject can resurrect the earlier truth: 'It is this reincorporation that we call resurrection' (LW 66). Where some distance was maintained between theological language in *Being and Event* in terms of time and history, with *Logics of Worlds* the language is much closer to a theological account of a human time touched and salvaged by resurrection.

This language is at its strongest and most influential around the idea of immortality used both in *Logics of Worlds* and the *Second Manifesto for Philosophy*. The concept of immortality is set within an account of a passage beyond the human and an experience of the inhuman: 'In fact, a truth is that by which "we" of the human species are engaged in a trans-species process, one that opens us on to the possibility of being Immortals. Such that a truth is certainly an experience of the inhuman' (LW 71 – translation modified). In relation to time, the key terms here are possibility and experience. For Badiou, there is not a necessary split between a human time of unfolding and loss and the eternal. Instead there is a possibility of the passage from one to the other, in the direction of eternity. Moreover, this is revealed in an experience, a phenomenon of the unfolding of time now associated with an eternal stasis in truth.

The terminology of possibility and experience is then expanded in the direction of the universal and the eternal and away from duration and historical erosion, novelty and loss through two further concepts: the 'absolute' and 'power'. The tension between these two concepts is indicative of the problems of Badiou's account of time, since on the one hand there is the duration and degree of effort in the idea of power, but these arrive at untimely eternity in the idea of the absolute: '. . . "we", of the human species, have the power to be Immortals' (LW 71). 'Such that our relation to truths is absolute, even if typical expressions of the true escape us' (LW 71 – translation modified). The problem for Badiou is then how to reconcile duration and eternity in an account of time which includes both and sets them into relation in a quasi-theological or perhaps even fully theological mode.

The solution given by Badiou is at the core of my argument for his denial of time as it is rendered stronger in *Logics of Worlds*. The problem of eternity *in* duration is resolved by extending the present by making the present eternal under some aspect. Here is the key definition: 'We will call *present*, and write π, the set of consequences of the evental trace, as realised by the successive treatment of points' (LW 52). The present here is extended into the future, as shown in the reference to 'trace', 'consequences' and 'successive treatment'. It is neither a changing duration, nor an instant, nor an unfolding process, but instead a set of points in time. These points are brought together through the actions of the subject, in similar manner to the intervention described in *Being and Event*, but with the important distinction that the barriers to the extension of an event in a situation have now fallen thanks to the introduction of the evental trace and incorporation of points.

This extension of the present takes place through the body of the subject as part of a wider body that is not brought under the present: 'Since the body is only subjectivated insofar as it treats points decision by decision, we must indicate that a body is never entirely in the present. It is divided into an efficacious region, an organ appropriate to the treated point, and a vast inert or even negative component as to this point' (LW 52 – translation modified). Bodies are then both eternally present and in a time of duration, with the distinction dependent upon action in relation to an evental trace and truths. The denial of time through the extension of the present is then also the introduction of a split in bodies, in actual things in time according to the trace and truth.

Conclusion: Which Violence?

In a comprehensive and thoughtful essay on violence and Badiou, Alberto Toscano argues for a 'periodisation' of Badiou's works in relation to violence. According to this division, the main works I have considered come after Badiou's espousal of 'organised, systematic, and importantly *inegalitarian* destruction of the reactionary adversary' of Badiou's Maoist period.[9] This analysis is confirmed in the critique of destruction in *Logics of Worlds*, a book Toscano had seen in draft form when writing his essay. Toscano sums up the new position thus: '. . . rather than an inherent condition of egalitarian novelty, *destruction* is seen as a false attempt to dominate a fundamental unbinding [*déliaison*] *and* to do so through the lethal fiction of the bond provided by the State, nation, party and/or class of agents of a real equality whose only signs can be given in the destruction of the old.'[10]

For Toscano, the key question is whether Badiou's later work escapes the dialectic between power and violence (rendered as *Gewalt* – a term taken from Balibar, whose philosophy has a strong guiding role in Toscano's study).[11] This dialectic is described and espoused in Badiou's works prior to *Being and Event*.[12] Toscano frames his preliminary and tentative response through five 'key points':

1. Badiou views egalitarian politics as corrupted by 'the military or martial referent'.[13] Nonetheless this martial referent remains as a positive source in Badiou's latest works, notably in *Logics of Worlds*.
2. Badiou seeks to resist state violence, but through organisation that does not 'translate into a legal, bureaucratic or military power'.[14]
3. We must distinguish between force, as direct and violent antagonism with the State, and forcing as 'subtraction' from the State in terms of intervention and truth.[15]
4. Badiou develops a critique of terror, but claims that only a critique 'from the side of emancipation' can serve a new politics.[16] This point is supported by the insistence on equality as a principle for intervention in Badiou's later work.
5. Only formalisation can avoid the intrinsically violent nature of dialectical antagonism in the 'Two'. This point joins the extension of the present through truth and points as set out in *Logics of Worlds*, as outlined above.

Toscano draws two important conclusions from these points. In turn, these make useful clarifications. First, a subtractive political intervention may have violence as its consequence but should not have it as an intrinsic part of its constitution. Second, political transformation towards an egalitarian outcome should be kept at a remove from the subject and the event as the '"agent" of conversion'.[17] Importantly, though, Toscano also raises doubts about the promise for avoidance of violence in these points and conclusions. The direction of the critique, though, is not towards the avoidance of violence but rather of its necessity if there is to be a confrontation with State violence: '. . . it is not clear how a politics of prescription that seeks to measure and halt the obscure superpower, the immeasurable excess of what Badiou calls the State of a situation can do without the "tragic" task of assuming some of that power, and some of that violence into its own transformative trajectory.'[18]

It is my view that, in his denial of time, Badiou does not avoid the 'corruption' of violence Toscano suspects must be retained in radical politics. This is because 'lethal fictions' remain in, and indeed underpin, Badiou's account of time in his philosophy of the event. I have traced them through the distinctions and negations necessary for the construction of either an intervention independent of a time governed by the law of the state in *Being and Event*, or through the eternal present of the event and of truth in *Logics of Worlds*. In both cases, the multiple times of duration, of fatigue, of ongoing change, of erosion, but also of delight, renewal and burgeoning are to be sacrificed to the eternity of truths. Toscano is right when he distinguishes this from a direct violence and instead associates it with a violence of 'consequences'. This distinction only matters if the consequences do not come to pass. Against the doubts and reservations of perpetual variation in time, the imposition of the fiction of eternal truths through a philosophy of time applied to the formal framing of political action is always potential violence.

Notes

1. Antonio Calcagnio, *Badiou and Derrida: Politics, Events and their Time* (New York: Continuum, 2007).
2. Alex García Düttmann, 'What remains of fidelity after serious thought?', in Peter Hallward (ed.), *Think Again: Alain Badiou and the Future of Philosophy* (London: Continuum, 2004), p. 204.
3. See Jon Roffe, *Badiou's Deleuze* (Durham, NC: Acumen, 2011).
4. Sigmund Freud, 'From the history of an infantile neurosis', in *The Standard Edition of the Complete Psychological Work of Sigmund Freud*, Vol. XVII, trans. James Strachey (London: Hogarth Press,

1955); Sigmund Freud, 'Negation', in *The Standard Edition of the Complete Psychological Work of Sigmund Freud*, Vol. XIX, trans. James Strachey (London: Hogarth Press, 1961); André Green, *The Work of Negative*, trans. Andrew Weller (London: Free Association Books, 1999).

5. Martin Heidegger, *The Metaphysical Foundations of Logic*, trans. M. Heim (Bloomington, IN: Indiana University Press, 1984), p. 184.

6. Alberto Toscano, 'Can violence be thought? Notes on Badiou and on the possibility of (Marxist) politics', *Identities: Journal for Politics, Gender and Culture*, 5: 1 (2006), pp. 9–38.

7. Simon Blackburn, 'Hume's diffuse effects cannot be reduced to Hefce narrow vision', *Times Higher Education Supplement*, 21 April 2011, http://www.timeshighereducation.co.uk/story.asp?storyCode=415873&sectioncode=26.

8. Ed Pluth and Dominiek Hoens, 'What if the Other is stupid? Badiou and Lacan on "logical time"', in Peter Hallward (ed.), *Think Again: Alain Badiou and the Future of Philosophy* (London: Continuum, 2004), pp. 184–6.

9. Toscano, 'Can violence be thought?', p. 14.

10. Ibid., p 15.

11. Étienne Balibar, 'Gewalt', in Wolfgang Fritz Haug (ed.), *Historisch-Kritisches Wörterbuch des Marxismus*, Vol. 5 (Hamburg: Argument Verlag, 2001).

12. Toscano, 'Can violence be thought?', p. 22.

13. Ibid.

14. Ibid., p 23.

15. Ibid., p. 24.

16. Ibid.

17. Ibid., p. 28.

18. Ibid., pp. 29–30.

8

Doing Without Ontology: A Quinean Pragmatist Approach to Badiou

Talia Morag[1]

In *Being and Event* Badiou declared his 'radical thesis' (BE 5, 15) that ontology *is* mathematics, in particular set theory after Cantor:

> Only there is it finally declared that, no matter how phenomenally diverse are mathematical 'objects' and 'structures', they can *all* be designated as pure multiplicities, constructed in a regulated manner from the empty set alone. The question of the exact nature of the relation between mathematics and being is thus entirely focused – for the era in which we are – in the axiomatic decision authorized by set theory. (BE 6 – translation modified)

Some years earlier, Quine too was engaged in questions about what there is. After much philosophical work he ends up saying something that, on the face of it, sounds very similar: 'We are left with just the ontology of pure set theory [. . .] It is common practice in set theory nowadays to start merely with the null class, form its unit class, and so on, thus generating an infinite lot of classes, from which all the usual luxuriance of further infinities can be generated.'[2]

In this paper I clarify what Badiou means and aims to achieve by his thesis that identifies ontology with mathematics and what philosophical work it actually does and does not do. I will show that, effectively, set theory plays two different and mutually exclusive roles in Badiou's philosophy. One is straightforwardly metaphysical and the second is implicitly pragmatic. It is the second role that can be made more explicit through the comparison of Badiou and Quine.[3]

Through the criticism of Badiou's metaphysics and by drawing on both Quine and Badiou's later work, *Logics of Worlds*, I shall articulate a pragmatist method to answer questions about what there is. By 'pragmatist method' I mean, by and large, what William James called 'an attitude of orientation': '*The attitude of looking away from first things, principles, "categories", supposed necessities; and of looking towards last things, fruits, consequences, facts*',[4] that is the attitude of looking to our explanatory practices and taking those practices seriously.

Badiou's Ontology

Badiou distinguishes between what there is or what kinds of objects there are, and the creation of new kinds of objects. Except for a few short comments, I will only concern myself with the former part of Badiou's philosophical enterprise, which he normally calls 'the order of Being'. In this section, I shall rely on the first half of Badiou's first vast opus *Being and Event*.

Badiou announces the thesis that ontology is mathematics in the introduction to *Being and Event*. He does not attest to his motivation for this thesis, neither does he justify it. Instead, he testifies to the context of its discovery, and then investigates the consequences of this thesis on philosophy, thereby offering a philosophical system. It is the entire book, regarded as articulating the consequences of the thesis, that comprises the context of justification.

Judging a thesis by its consequences is in fact a pragmatist attitude. But as I shall demonstrate in this section, the pragmatically significant part of the consequences Badiou wants cannot, in effect, be drawn from his understanding of his thesis.

But why should we buy into Badiou's thesis in the first place, and why should we care about his philosophical system before we even begin reading about it? Those familiar with Badiou's work will recognise in this structure the retroactive announcement of an Event that claims its revolutionary consequences on the situation in which it occurs – before those consequences can be verified.

Pragmatists, however, will not identify with a claim that seems to drop out of nowhere, and fidelity to unmotivated promises of a true rupture in the philosophical scene will not drive them to push through the next 500 pages. Pragmatists need a contextualised motivation, and the declaration of an answer promising further answers with no respective questions will not do. As Trinity tells Neo in *The Matrix*: 'It is the question that drives us.' I therefore insist to detect in Badiou's description of the context of discovery of his thesis (described in BE 5) the question that drives him.

Badiou describes his interest in the famous 'problem of continuity' in the history of mathematics from Zeno to Dedekind and Cantor. A very general reminder: after we deconstruct a continuous line, say, to discrete extensionless points and then try to reconstruct that line from those points, we arrive at all kinds of paradoxes. Other paradoxes occur if that line is to represent the axis of the real numbers, where its discrete constituents are the real numbers themselves.

In effect, Badiou generalises the history of the problem of continuity and treats the paradoxes that arise from it as expressing some basic reality that underlies them. In each reincarnation of this problem, there is *one* continuous entity understood to comprise *many* discrete entities, which cannot in turn reconstruct that one continuous entity. Badiou blames the discrete entities that figure in the history of the problem of continuity for the various paradoxes involved.

This generalisation implicit in Badiou's testimony regarding the context of the discovery of his thesis turns the couple continuity/discrete in its various well-defined mathematical domains into the obscure couple one/many. Indeed, Badiou names all these discrete entities by the same word, 'the Multiple', since there are *many* of those within their respective continuities. This verbal trick allows him to proceed and make claims about that Multiple, as if it were not abstracted from the various mathematical examples but rather existed prior to all mathematical attempts to give specific articulations for it.

And so Badiou claims that although the Multiple is a concept that belongs to mathematics, it is not constructed by mathematics in the way continuities are. That is why the Multiple is such a troublemaker. Badiou thinks that the Multiple *must* come from outside the mathematical formal discourse and it is what mathematics studies. The Multiple is the Given of mathematics, it is what mathematics is 'stuck with' and aims to theorise. The Multiple, claims Badiou, is Given by Being itself.

In other words, Badiou basically identifies the problem of continuity as a specific and well-defined manifestation of the problem of the One and the Many. In the realm of mathematics, he can indeed know exactly what kinds of ones and manys he is talking about. By the verbal slippage from the specific manys to the generalised 'Multiple', Badiou sees the problem of continuity as indicating the solution to the old metaphysical debate over the One and the Many – not in some particular field of mathematics – but *in general*, in the vague realm of Being as such.

The question that drives Badiou is thus the old metaphysical debate about the One and the Many. The title of the first meditation of the book 'The One and the Multiple: *A Priori* Conditions of any Possible Ontology' echoes just that. Badiou's 'Multiple', then, is no other than the old Many, and that is how I shall refer to it in the rest of this paper.

In passing, I will mention that the second question that drives Badiou is the metaphysical problem of Fixity and Change, with which I do not engage in this paper. He says that it is the question of change within a stable situation that interests him the most. And that is why he has to give an account of stability in order to then give an account of change.[5] Badiou's metaphysical solution to the problem of Fixity and Change through the concept of the Event depends on and stems from his solution to the problem of the One and the Many.

Badiou turns the verbal slippage from mathematics to Being described above into the thesis that mathematics 'pronounces that which is sayable of Being *qua* Being' (BE 8 – translation modified). Mathematics is thus the science of Being qua Being or traditional Ontology with a Capital O, as Putnam would call it.[6]

For Badiou, then, mathematics is not about real numbers or sets or other mathematical objects. Indeed he claims that these are not objects at all! They are a manner of speaking about Being as such, a manner of speaking that evolves over time. This manner of speaking bears the mark of the Many and so all these objects mathematics seems to be talking about are just the articulable aspect of the Many.

Mathematicians are in the business of articulating Being qua Being and they don't even know it. They are the ones doing Ontology. But to recognise the true job description of mathematicians we need philosophers. The identification of Ontology with mathematics is done on what Badiou calls the 'metaontological' level (BE 13, 14, 19), which is basically metaphysics. To see what the mathematical discourse is *really* talking about, the metaphysician has to translate the mathematical discourse into a metaphysical discourse using the One/Many vocabulary.

The mathematical Many, so to speak, that interests Badiou the most is the notion of set. According to set theory, all mathematical objects are reducible to sets, to specific and well-defined Manys.

Badiou's thesis allows him to extract metaphysical conclusions from the very specific mathematical domain of set theory and claim that all objects *in general* are reducible to a 'pure many' (BE 14).[7] If mathematics is Ontology then the debate on the One and the Many is decided. The Many reigns over the realm of Being as such, and 'the one is not' (this formula appears all throughout the book – see, for example, BE 23, 24). Whereas past metaphysicians had a taste for unity, Badiou prefers the Many.[8]

All that remains for the metaphysician to do is to translate set theory into a metaphysical theory with One/Many vocabulary. And this translation project engages Badiou for about two-thirds of *Being and Event*. I now turn to some basic notions of Badiou's metaphysical translation of set theory.[9]

The primacy of the Many in the order of Being is not meant to deny the existence of individuated objects. Yet the individuation of an object means that we can talk about *an* object, about a 'one'. How, then, can an object be one object when 'the one is not'?

Instead of accepting 'one' as an existing unit into his metaphysics, Badiou admits an operation of unification. Every individual object counts-as-one, but is not intrinsically one. In other words, every object or entity is retroactively understood as composed of many, as a result of the operation 'count-as-one'.

Sometimes the many of which the counted-as-one is composed are identifiable as many 'ones'. Each of those 'ones' is also the result of the operation count-as-one. When this is the case, that is when a 'one' is retroactively understood as unification of many other 'ones', the 'one' in question is retroactively understood as a 'consistent many'.[10] Consistent manys are the metaphysical translation of sets that have other sets as members.

Other times, the 'one' under consideration is not composed of identifiable units. In cases like this, our 'one' is retroactively understood as the result of an operation that counted-as-one an 'inconsistent many'.[11] Inconsistent manys are the metaphysical translation of sets that are not composed of other sets. These are nevertheless sets and not an individual, say, since set is the primitive concept of set theory. This is how a 'one' without identifiable composing units is nevertheless a many, but an inconsistent many.

Badiou's metaphysics thus admits two kinds of manys: the consistent many that is composed of many 'ones' and the inconsistent many that is not composed of 'ones'. What exists, what there is, what objects there are, are of the first kind – the many 'ones'.

Badiou calls each such consistent many a *situation*. What exists are situations, and each situation has its own count-as-one operator, which determines what the units are that comprise that situation.[12]

So after all this metaphysical work, what are the ones and the manys Badiou is talking about? One *what*? Many *what*? These questions are particularly disturbing when it comes to inconsistent manys. Those are supposed to be many without having any individuals recognisable as many. Simply many! Maybe even infinitely many. In set theory this can make sense. The sign A can designate a set with no need to specify individual members. But once extracted from mathematical discourse, we talk about sets as classes that have members. We cannot make sense of a many without specifying many what. The words of William James about the metaphysical taste for unity or for 'one' are just as relevant in connection to Badiou's taste for the Many, or for infinity, countable or uncountable. James wrote:

> 'The world is One!' – the formula may become a sort of number-worship. 'Three' and 'seven' have, it is true, been reckoned sacred numbers; but, abstractly taken, why is 'one' more excellent than 'forty-three', or than 'two million and ten'? In this first vague conviction of the world's unity, there is so little to take hold of that we hardly know what we mean by it ... The only way to get forward with our notion is to treat it pragmatically. Granting the oneness to exist, what facts will be different in consequence? What will the unity be known-as? The world is one – yes, but *how* one? What is the practical value of the oneness for US?[13]

Ontology matters to us insofar as it tells us something about the division of what exists into kinds. In Badiou's terminology, a kind is a consistent many or a set of individuated objects. The count-as-one operator of the consistent many is supposed to designate the individuals that comprise the extension of that consistent many and turn them into members of a kind.

So what does it mean to 'count-as-one'? What are the criteria for this count? *Being and Event* offers no such criteria and thus offers no constraints as to what may count as a kind and what not. Indeed, there appears to be no reason to reject a situation whose operator counts-as-one any chunk of space shaped like my cat. Moreover, nothing prevents the count-as-one as being merely extensional. Any set of objects, such as the set of my glasses, the breakfast I had this morning and the song now playing on the radio can be a consistent many with its own count-as-one operator.

As David Lewis said:

> Any class of things, be it ever so gerrymandered and miscellaneous and indescribable in thought and language, and be it ever so super-fluous in characterizing the world, is nevertheless a property [. . .] Because properties are so abundant, they are undiscriminating. Any two things share infinitely many properties, and fail to share infinitely many others. That is so whether the two things are perfect duplicates or utterly dissimilar. Thus properties do nothing to capture facts of resemblance [. . .] Properties carve reality at the joints – and every-where else as well.[14]

In the examples described in *Being and Event*, it becomes clear that Badiou uses consistent manys as the kinds our explanatory practices care about. The poor inconsistent manys have individu-als as members but are unrecognised as consistent and are unjustly ignored by our practices. It seems that Badiou wants to talk about the merely extensional sets as inconsistent manys. His metaphysi-cal apparatus, however, does not do the job he wants it to do.

Firstly, inconsistent manys are not supposed to be composed of many 'ones'. That is what made them inconsistent in the first place. Secondly, without clarifying the criteria for what can count-as-one, merely extensional sets are just as consistent as kinds, whose intension should do justice to the salient similarity between their members. Badiou's distinction between inconsistent and con-sistent sets is empty. We cannot say what inconsistency means and consistent sets are undiscriminating.

As Lewis explains in the above quote, sets in general will not give us kinds. In that paper, Lewis proceeds to talk about what he calls 'elite sets'. Those would be the sets that carve reality at the joints. Lewis calls the properties of his elite sets 'natural'. By and large, Lewis's elite sets would be natural kinds, the ones the natural sciences study (and for Lewis those should be reduced to only one science, namely physics).

What about the tables and chairs of ordinary language? What about social kinds such as married couples and university stu-dents? We have a plurality of explanatory discourses and most (neo-)pragmatists would want to consider their subject matter too as kinds. I will not try here to find criteria that would decide which discourses deserve to be ontologically significant. Instead I just want to enlarge, in principle, Lewis's concept of 'elite sets' into those which would carve not just the reality studied by physics, but the reality studied by the plurality of the natural and social sciences, the reality explained by ordinary language and the reality of whatever explanatory discourses we shall eventually decide upon. From now on I shall use the term 'elite sets' in this generalised sense.

To sum up: Badiou's thesis that mathematics is ontology amounts to the translation of set theory into a metaphysical theory of Being qua Being. Although Badiou's examples pick out elite sets as if as a consequence of his metaphysics his identifications of these elite sets are borrowed from our explanatory practices and do not actually stem from the definition of consistent manys. Effectively, Badiou's metaphysics gives us an unsatisfactory and inflated Ontology with a capital O that includes all possible sets.

But what if we begin our ontological enquiry not with mathematics but with our explanatory practices instead? What ontology would we have then? And what role could set theory have? To explore this route, I turn to Quine.

Quine and Badiou: From Ontology to Ontological Commitments

For pragmatists, enquiry happens on the background of accumulated knowledge, most of which is believed to be true. Enquiry begins not 'from scratch', but in the middle of things, and ontological enquiry is no different. Although Badiou may be said to begin his enquiry in the middle of mathematical enquiry, his thesis about the identity of Ontology with mathematics is nevertheless an a priori principle. As shown in the previous section, this principle leads Badiou to other a priori conditions about the One and the Many but do not serve to identify the kinds of objects there are.

The (neo-)pragmatists, conversely, do not enquire into what there is from the armchair, concentrating their thought on Being qua Being, pretending to ignore the accumulated empirical knowledge about the world. Quine is such a (neo-)pragmatist, and he begins his ontological enquiry in the middle of scientific enquiry.

Badiou, together with the ancient Greeks, asks in an a priori manner about the nature of Being qua Being, which is somehow supposed to condition everything that exists and thus teach us about what is *really* there to know something about. Quine turns the question around and asks pragmatically: given our contemporary scientific theories that successfully explain the world,[15] what objects do these theories commit us to acknowledge as existent? In other words, we do not make ontological enquiries 'in order to know what there is, but in order to know what a given remark or doctrine, ours someone else's, *says* there is'.[16] So, if we want to know what there is we should enquire into the theories we take as true and see what kinds of objects these theories presuppose. The objects resulting from that enquiry will comprise our ontology, or rather, these will be the objects that we are *ontologically committed* to.

Note that ontological commitment is no longer a metaphysical Ontology. As David Macarthur writes:

> [...] it is important to see that the idea of *having an ontology* is ambiguous between endorsing an ontological theory (Ontology) and having such and such ontological commitments. Pragmatic naturalists will not endorse any metaphysical theory, including Ontology [...]. But they will, of course, have what philosophers call ontological commitments in the sense of beliefs about what there is. These will simply reflect best explanatory practice: if our best explanations call for commitment to certain entities then so be it.[17]

Quine's ontological commitments arise not from a priori considerations but from contemporary science and they are thus not metaphysical in the traditional sense. Nevertheless, Quine says that ontological commitments are claims about the true and general 'limning of reality'.[18] Quine is both anti-metaphysical and anti-sceptical about ontological commitments. This twofold attitude to ontology comes from the twofold attitude of pragmatists toward science, namely the attitude that is both fallibalistic and anti-sceptical about science.

Fallibalism about scientific theories is basically the acknowledgement that their status as true of the world may change or be qualified in the future. This could happen if doubt arises about certain beliefs of contemporary science. Such doubt would be very specific and justified and would motivate further enquiry in the particular area of science in which it appeared. But until such real doubt occurs, the pragmatists believe scientific theories to be true and are committed to that belief, as is evident from their everyday reliance on scientific predictions. Fallibalism is an attitude that is open to the possibility of doubt; it is not doubt in itself.[19]

That is to say, although fallibalism rejects claims for absolute unchangeable Truths, it does not imply scepticism in any strong sense and does not diminish the seriousness of the pragmatists' belief in the truths of contemporary science.

According to Quine, a scientific theory presupposes the existence of certain objects or entities. Such a theory is fallibalistic and so the ontology that it implies does not rest on fundamental unchangeable grounds like the old metaphysical Ontology. On the other hand, the anti-sceptical commitment to the truth of a theory carries with it an ontological commitment to the kinds of objects that the theory presupposes. In other words, ontological commitments are as serious as claims about the truth of the theory from which they arise.

Quine's ontological enquiry thus begins with the consideration of our scientific theories and of natural language, which is in effect one such primitive and unsophisticated theory of the world. These theories incorporate and generate observation sentences that provide the contact of those theories with experience. The theories' structure, which links those observation sentences to one another, does not explicitly reveal, according to Quine, the kinds of objects theorised about. But doesn't natural language talk about tables and chairs? Doesn't geography talk about mountains and clouds?

Tables and chairs, mountains and clouds are only vaguely individuated and do not merit full-blown objecthood, according to Quine. Being an object that is identified as a member of a kind that carves reality at the joints demands more. A (natural) kind is defined by the necessary and sufficient conditions that must apply in order for an individuated thing to be an object of that kind.[20] In other words, to be considered as an object, identity conditions must apply. This is what Quine means in his famous slogan that 'there is no entity without identity'.[21]

In order to discover what entities our theories presuppose we have to *logically regiment* them. Only logical regimentation of the theories we hold to be true will provide the kinds of objects with their respective identity conditions to which we are ontologically committed. In other words, only after regimentation of the vaguely individuated things natural language and the sciences talk about can we talk about objects in Quine's demanding sense.[22] Logical regimentation thus involves the operation of *reification*.

Quine often says that there is more than one way to regiment the notation of a theory. The choice between alternative notations would determine which objects are ontologically committed to. But it would not affect the structure of the theory under regimentation nor the observation statements that theory incorporates and generates. When there is such a choice, the ontologist can formulate what Quine calls a proxy function, which would translate one notation to another. Quine calls this phenomenon 'ontological relativity'.[23]

Quine gives quite a few examples of this phenomenon. Sometimes he comments on the choice between two regimentations, that is between two ontological commitments, with expressions such as 'no big deal'[24] or 'no one could tell the difference'.[25] With these comments Quine reminds us of the artificiality of ontological enquiry. Since the conclusions about what objects there are leave intact the theories they came from, they do not have pragmatic meaning. And whatever ontological commitments philosophers have rely on and stem from scientific theories, which are at the end of the day indifferent to their regimentation.

For those who care to commit ontologically to certain entities, Quine offers some guidance as to the choice they have in cases of ontological relativity. He talks about virtues such as simplicity and clarity. Reduction, for example, is one of Quine's favourite mechanisms to achieve such clarity and simplicity. Quine has a taste for 'desert landscapes'[26] and would choose reduction whenever possible, so as to minimise the kinds of objects to which he is ontologically committed. Another guide for choice would be pragmatic. Certain ontologies or notations (those would be synonyms for Quine) would be better for some purposes and other notations for other purposes.

Here is one of Quine's favourite regimentations of ordinary language. Instead of talking about bodies, substances and properties, Quine proposes to talk about all of them as objects, defined as the material content of any portion of space and time.[27] Once we reify these spatio-temporal portions as physical objects we have an ontology of such objects as well of numbers and classes – numbers since they are useful in everyday measurement and in quantitative laws in the sciences, and sets since counting is effectively the measurement of a set.

In order to have less entities in his ontology, Quine proposes to translate the spatio-temporal physical objects into quadruples of numbers which signify their spatio-temporal coordinates in some system of reference or other. In other words, Quine proposes a proxy function that takes any spatio-temporal portion and turns it into a quadruple. And so:

> We are left with just the ontology of pure set theory, since the numbers and their quadruples can be modelled within it. There are no longer any physical objects to serve as individuals at the base of the hierarchy of classes, but there is no harm in that.[28]

But even if physical objects are not officially admitted to this ontology of pure sets, they played a role in its construction. The quadruples in question are far from arbitrary. They are a result of the logical regimentation of spatio-temporal portions. And those resulted from regimentation and reification of bodies, substances and properties, originally individuated by the categories of ordinary language.

Unlike Badiou's count-as-one operation, Quine's reification is discriminating. Not anything can be reified, only what results from the regimentation of our ordinary and scientific categories that individuate what is then regimented and reified. Individuation by theories may be vague, but it is nevertheless discriminatory, and that discrimination is preserved in later regimentations, even if thinned down. In other words, ordinary and scientific categories provide the rough carving of reality, which rules out useless categories like the chunks of space shaped like my cat.

If we put aside Badiou's metaphysical project of translating set theory into a theory of Being qua Being, can we turn Badiou into the French Quine? After all, Badiou does seem to apply set theory to scientific theories by identifying kinds of objects within them and regarding those kinds as sets. Although he offers no principle of regimentation in *Being and Event*, he does seem to use set theory to structure certain discourses. Badiou even briefly acknowledges a sort of ontological relativity. He says clearly that his choice of set theory is not the only possible choice. Other mathematical theories can also be used in a similar way (BE 14). The thesis that mathematics is ontology can be restated as the Quinean conclusion that logico-mathematical regimentations expose ontological commitments.

But even if we disregard Badiou's Ontology and replace it with Quinean ontological commitments, there is still one important difference between Quine and Badiou that a (neo-)pragmatist would want to preserve. Badiou is not concerned only with the sciences and does not have a taste for reduction like Quine. Badiou, like most (neo-)pragmatists, is pluralistic about our explanatory practices. As explained above, Quine's regimentation into sets does not give us the kinds of objects to which we want to ontologically commit, such as cups or people, since they are too vague to allow for identity conditions.

In the previous section I showed that Badiou's Ontology, which begins from set theory, gives us an overly populated world that includes sets that play no role in our discourses. Quine's ontological commitments, which begin from the categories of our discourses and end in sets, give us the 'desert landscapes' that Quine wants, but not the categories that most (neo-)pragmatists want. Badiou's undiscriminating sets and Quine's intensionally defined sets (through necessary and sufficient conditions of membership) do not give us the ontological commitments we are looking for.

At this point, (neo-)pragmatists may ask – why do we need sets at all? Why not just ontologically commit to tables and chairs, clouds and dogs, and whatever categories we use in our explanatory practices? How does talking about these kinds of objects as sets matter to *us*?

Two reasons to retain the talk of sets come immediately to mind. The first is the frequent use our explanatory practices make of taxonomy, namely the inclusion of one category in another.[29] Effectively, we use our categories as sets, and talk about them as including other more specific categories and as being included under more general categories. The way we classify people or animals, for example, and their status in the hierarchy of various taxonomies affects how we treat them. The way we classify certain chemicals affects what we do and try to do with them – and so forth.

The second reason has to do with the vagueness that permeates our ordinary language and many of our theoretical discourses. Although we usually do not think about vagueness, it sometimes confronts us as a problem. In practice, we sometimes have to classify an object but hesitate how, exactly because most of our categories do not come with necessary and sufficient conditions of membership. Yet we do draw the line somewhere, according to the details of the case and the interests and purposes embedded in it. That is, we do treat our categories effectively as sets, demanding them to be definite in number.

Categories are not sets in a straightforward manner, since they do not come ready-made with clear extensional or intensional definitions. Yet we are nonetheless ontologically committed to them as sets, that is as elite sets, in the generalised sense I suggested in the previous section.

A crude way to turn categories such as cups and clouds into sets is simply to impose on them necessary and sufficient conditions for category membership. But this seems arbitrary and artificial. This imposition of identity conditions does not give us a method of how to decide on the classification of borderline cases but rather excuses their classification after the fact. So how can we make these ontological commitments to categories as sets, if not intensionally (through necessary and sufficient conditions) nor extensionally (through arbitrary decisions on what objects are to belong to the category)?

We need some way to structure the categories of our explanatory practices if we want to account for these ontological commitments that turn our categories into the desired elite sets. Such a structure should provide a method for the classification of borderline cases and for the identification of category inclusions.

Badiou does not recognise the difficulty of turning categories into sets, since he simply presupposes that they are sets. Indeed, nowhere in his work can we find reference to the issue of vagueness and the question of how to determine the extension of categories. Nevertheless, his later work *Logics of Worlds* is suggestive of a solution. This is the topic of the next and last section.

What Structures Categories Such That They Can Be Regarded as Elite Sets?

The kinds of entities to which most (neo-)pragmatists want to ontologically commit group objects that are not identical but similar to one another. The notion of kind and similarity are intertwined, as Quine said (with disdain).[30] However, when we regiment a category into a set, we effectively equalise the otherwise unequal members of the category, since they either belong or do not belong to the set.

In the 1970s, the cognitive scientist Eleanor Rosch challenged this equalising feature of the set-theoretical picture.[31] According to Rosch, category-belonging is not equalised, but rather is 'internally structured into a prototype (clearest cases, best examples of the category) and nonprototype members, with nonproto-type members tending toward an order from better to poorer examples.'[32]

The poorest examples are those traditionally thought of as borderline cases. Without the ontological commitment to turning categories into sets, this prototypical picture would not admit any borders in the first place. Without borders there would be no borderline cases, only poor examples of categories.

Rosch says we should simply admit that some dogs like retriev-ers or German shepherds are more 'doggy' than others like Pekinese or Great Danes. Some reds are 'redder' than others, and an office chair is more typical than a bean-bag.

This prototypical picture manifests, according to Rosch, a Wittgensteinian *family resemblance* between the members of the category. She proposes a resemblance principle for the internal structure of a category, according to which 'each item has at least one, and probably several, elements in common with one or more other items, but no, or few, elements are common to all items.'[33]

The difference between the equalising model and the prototypi-cal model can be described pictorially. The members of an equal-ised set would be represented linearly in one horizontal line. In the prototypical model each category looks like a radiating 'sun', with a prototype or a few prototypes at its centre while surrounding it are the non-prototypes, whose varying distance from the centre stands for their degree of family resemblance to the prototype or prototypes.

So what is a prototype? Rosch's answer to that question changes from paper to paper. Since her motivation is to explicate language learning and cognitive processes of concept-application, her defini-tions of a prototype relate to the judgements of the participants in her experiments.

Now, is the German shepherd *ontologically* more doggy than the chihuahua when it comes to the categorisation of ordinary language? Says who, and why? What are the criteria for being a prototype? Judgements of prototypicality for categories may seem just as problematic as identity conditions are for sets.

When it comes to our scientific discourses, however, prototypes are much more easily recognised, for the simple reason that those discourses constructed them as such. That is how Roland Giere, inspired by Rosch's work, identifies the simple harmonic oscilla-tor as a prototype for other more complicated mechanical systems such as the damped oscillator.[34] And that is how Ian Hacking, also inspired by Rosch, identifies certain famous cases of multiple personality as prototypes for other less obvious cases.[35]

The Rosch story has the benefit of doing justice to the similarities and differences between members of a category and can account for some scientific practices and maybe even language learning. But it has two serious problems. One is how to determine prototypes for categories of ordinary language. The second is the danger of stereotypes. The prototypical model would force us to say that some women, for example, are more 'womanly' than others.

Logics of Worlds is suggestive of a way to deal with these problems while retaining Rosch's general method of structuring a category according to the similarities and differences among its members. The new model for the structure of categories can also provide a method for the regimentation of categories into sets to which we can ontologically commit.

I use the weakening expression 'is suggestive of' rather than the straightforward 'suggests' since *Logics of Worlds* is also *Being and Event 2*. That is, Badiou insists on retaining his set-theoretical Ontology, while adding to it the phenomenological order of appearances. His attempt to connect the appearances of categories with their supposed underlying deep structure of a set-theoretical Being suffers problems that arise from the same problem discussed in the first section – namely the obscurity of the count-as-one and the untenable distinction between consistent and inconsistent manys. Nevertheless, *Logics of Worlds* offers important insights that contribute to a new model for the structure of categories.

My purpose for the rest of this section is to read out of *Logics of Worlds* the metaphysical weight it inherits from *Being and Event*, and thus to force a deflated description of the new model for structuring categories.[36] In doing so, I will try and keep track of the differences of my description to Badiou's text in the endnotes. I will then show how this new model can provide a method for making ontological commitments to elite sets. Finally I will describe Badiou's way of turning the internally structured categories into sets and show how it is problematic, again due to the same problem regarding his lack of criteria as to what counts-as-one in his theory of Being qua Being.

Badiou uses category-theory in order to describe the internal structure of each category, as well as the relations between the categories of a given explanatory or descriptive context (that context would be what he calls a 'world').[37] The context determines the significant similarities and differences among the individuals that are categorised. Indeed, it is that network of similarities and differences that accounts for the individuation of objects in the first place.[38] Individuation *is* differentiation and it is the network of similarities and differences that gives rise to it.[39]

In other words, the network of similarities and differences reflects the salience of individuals as such.[40] The particularly salient individuals are those that share some similarities with others but are at the same time greatly differentiated. The noticeable differences and similarities are differences and similarities in certain conceptual respects, which are effectively the categories that classify individuals in that particular context.

Similarly to Rosch's views, each category is internally structured according to comparative degrees of similarity. Unlike Rosch's model, the similarity is not to a prototype, but to a *type*.[41] In other words, no member of the category belongs to it more than others or merits the label of the category more than others. Badiou rather identifies types within the category such that each of its members is characterised by degrees of similarity to each of those types. That degree does not have a fixed value, only a comparative value – a member can be similar to one of the types more or less than another member.

The types can be identified in two ways:

1. Any member of a category can be considered as defining a type, and thus gives rise to an internal comparative structure centred around it. Call this the object-type.
2. A type can also be a list of characterisations that no object fully manifests. Call this the concept-type.

This type-model for the structure of categories is 'democratic' without equalising. One belongs more or less to a type rather than to a category. There is a type of woman that does not work and comes with certain stereotypical intensional features, and women can belong more or less to that type, but they are all women just the same. Indeed, some women who do not work may not fit that stereotype at all. Furthermore, each and every woman can, in certain contexts, define her own type of which she will be the clearest example. And other contexts may give rise to new concept-types to which women will be similar and different.

How exactly the various types of one category interrelate with types of other categories and how they correlate with the conceptual respects that structure the network of similarities and differences of a given context is beyond the scope of this paper.[42] What is important for the purposes of this paper is that this type-model provides a method to determine whether or not an individual belongs to a category.

To belong to a category, an individual needs to be similar enough to one of the types of the category. And it is our explanatory practices that make those similarity judgements all the time and make explicit what 'similar enough' means for each case. This is how categories turn into sets, even in the absence of necessary and sufficient conditions. Our explanatory practices ontologically commit us to the existence of their categories and respective types, as well as to their similarity judgements that decide on the definite extensions of these categories, according to relevant interests and purposes.

In a certain sense, we can still talk like Quine of 'reifying regimentation' of categories as determining our ontological commitments. The regimentation is the identification of the types that structure the categories of a certain explanatory context.

The type-structure of a category is its intension. As was the case for Quine, intensions of categories are revealed through regimentation. To distinguish it from Quine's intensions that were given in terms of necessary and sufficient conditions, call these 'type-intensions'.

Reification of these categories into sets is continuously maintained by the similarity judgements of our practices, which take into account the relevant types and the network of differences and similarities of the relevant explanatory context. The type-model for the structure of categories thus gives the (neo-)pragmatists the elite sets of their ontological commitments. Once we have those sets we can reorganise them into taxonomies as needed.

Badiou wants the phenomenological order of appearing categories to be reconciled with his Ontology of sets. That is, categories should somehow be considered as sets. Badiou does not mention the issue of vagueness. Neither does he talk in pragmatic terms of similarity judgements made by explanatory practices. How, then, coming from metaphysical considerations, does he fix the extension of a category-set?

For Badiou, the extension of a category is doubly determined.

Most categories of a given context are simply the appearance of a consistent many defined in the Ontological order. The consistent many has its own count-as-one operator, which determines the extension of the set in the Ontological level. So the extension of the category-set is usually predetermined by the count-as-one of the being qua being aspect of each context or 'world'. There is no question of borderline cases, since borders are Ontologically predetermined.

The second manner a category is determined as a set goes the other way around, that is from the phenomenological order of appearances to the Ontology of consistent manys, of sets. In other words, Badiou makes a reifying 'decision' to consider each type and thereby each category of a given explanatory context as corresponding to a consistent many that in turn counts-as-one every member of the type and thereby of the category in question (since all members of a category belong more or less to each of its types). That is he makes the decision that every category with all its various types is in fact a set with a definite extension. He calls this decision 'the postulate of materialism' (LW 218).

I said above that the extensions of categories are usually predetermined by the count-as-one operator of their corresponding consistent many in the order of Being qua Being. Sometimes, however, Badiou allows for a category to be created in the phenomenological order of appearances, without having a corresponding consistent many in the respective Ontology.

The new category would effectively be an inconsistent many in the Ontological order but the above 'decision' takes care of that. The new category, although not predetermined by a consistent many, nevertheless corresponds to a consistent many. As the category is being created with its various new types, it collects and recruits, so to speak, its members. The new evolving category is determining its own extension, thus creating in the Ontological order a consistent many with its own count-as-one operator.

There are insights to extract from the Badiouian account of the evolution of new categories.[43] But the claim about the Ontological counterpart of these categories as ensuring their reality is meant to tell more than that. Namely, it is supposed to demonstrate how an inconsistent many can struggle for and win consistency and the elite status that comes with it. But the charm of this metaphor is not enough to make it viable, given that it relies on the distinction between consistent and inconsistent manys. And that distinction, as I showed in the first section of this paper, is empty.

The sets that we can conceive of outside of the domains of pure mathematics all have members. They are all comprised of many 'ones' and thus are all consistent manys. The only useful distinction would be between sets whose members are determined extensionally and sets whose members are determined intensionally. Badiou's count-as-one operator of the Ontological order does not provide that distinction. And so, as I showed in the first section, the only consequence we can consistently draw from Badiou's story about Being qua Being is that all sets exist.

To say that each category, whether old or new, corresponds to a set with a fixed extension is simply to say that one of the sets that exist – and they all do – corresponds to the category in question, even if we cannot know which set it is. In other words, most sets are merely extensional and only some are also intensional (or rather type-intensional) and comprise the categories of our explanatory practices.

But those are precisely the elite sets that we wanted! Who needs all the rest of the sets? The only function the over-proliferation of sets actually has in Badiou's framework is to define the extension of the categories. But that is not a good enough reason to retain them. As I showed above, there is no need for this massively inflated Ontology. Our elite sets, whether old or new, are determined by the ontological commitments to categories, their types and the similarity judgements of our explanatory practices that fix their extension.

A few concluding words. The aspect of Badiou's work that I engaged with in this paper, even if it comprises basically half of his two major philosophical works, is often neglected. Badiou scholars usually discuss the Event and use the terminology Badiou offers to articulate change in contemporary situations, in particular political or social situations. This is where set theory as a theory with its axioms and theorems and so forth, rather than simply the assumption of sets and their inclusion in one another, is supposed to have descriptive benefits. This is where, Badiou's scholars may say, the thesis that Ontology is mathematics manifests its strength.

Dropping Badiou's Ontology in favour of ontological commitments to elite sets should not dismiss, per se, Badiou's use of set theory on those sets. One would have to carefully read out of Badiou's account of the Event and its consequences their metaphysical aspect and retain relevant insights that matter to *us*. Pragmatism, as considered in this paper, is a philosophical method. And that method is not about ruling out metaphysics as unworthy of discussion. Pragmatism is a method not only for careful criticism of metaphysics but also a method to recover its insights that are useful for the understanding of our practices.

Notes

1. I want to thank David Macarthur for the extensive conversations and helpful advice before and during the writing of the first draft of this paper. I also want to thank the members of SHAPE at the University of Sydney for their insightful comments on the first draft of this paper, in particular Paul Redding, Paul Thom, Robert Dunn, David Macarthur and Simon Duffy.
2. W. V. Quine, 'Things and their place in theories', in *Theories and Things* (Cambridge, MA: Harvard University Press, 1981), pp. 17–18. This was not the first time Quine talked of set theory as ontology. The possible reduction of all there is to sets was an idea developed all throughout his philosophy.
3. Badiou unfortunately hardly engages directly with Quine, except in a few paragraphs in *The Concept of Model* (CM 6–7). It is probably due to the unfamiliarity of Quine in 'continental' circles that this connection has been overlooked. Exceptions can nevertheless be found: see Brassier's comparison of Badiou and Quine in regard to Quine's renouncement of the analytic synthetic distinction and its metaphysicalised version in Badiou's writings as the blurring of the ideal and the real in Ray Brassier, 'Badiou's materialist epistemology of mathematics', *Angelaki: Journal of the Theoretical Humanities*, 10: 2 (2005), pp. 135–50.
4. William James, 'What pragmatism means', in *Pragmatism (A New Name for Some Old Ways of Thinking) A Series of Lectures* [1906–7] (Rockville, MD: Arc Manor, 2008), p. 30. Italics in original text.
5. See the quote of Badiou in an interview with Bruno Bosteels in the introduction by Zachary Luke Fraser of *The Concept of Model* (CM xiii).
6. Hilary Putnam, *Ethics without Ontology* (Cambridge, MA: Harvard University Press, 2004), Lecture 1, pp. 17, 21.
7. Badiou says 'pure multiplicity'.
8. This unusual metaphysical taste is often taken as provocative and

original. See, for example, Paul Livingston, 'Review of *Being and Event*', *Inquiry*, 51: 2 (2008), pp. 217–38, at p. 221.

9. I base the following mainly on *Being and Event*, Meditations 1, 3–5 and 8.

10. Badiou uses the term 'consistent multiplicity', but I wish to use consistent terminology that keeps track of the fact that we are dealing here with a metaphysics of Many, with a solution to the old debate about the One and the Many.

11. Badiou uses the term 'inconsistent multiplicity'.

12. I will not discuss in this paper what Badiou calls 'the state of the situation', which is the metaphysical counterpart of the notion of the power set (the set of subsets). I will just hint in passing that through the discussion of the state of situation Badiou engages with the second metaphysical debate that motivates him – the debate on Fixity and Change.

13. William James, 'The One and the Many', in *Pragmatism (A New Name for Some Old Ways of Thinking) A Series of Lectures* [1906–7] (Rockville, MD: Arc Manor, 2008), p. 60.

14. David Lewis, 'New work for a theory of universals', *Australasian Journal of Philosophy*, 61: 4 (1983), p. 346.

15. As is evident from their capacity to reveal 'hidden mysteries', make successful predictions and work 'technological wonders'. W. V. Quine, 'Natural kinds', in *Ontological Relativity & Other Essays* (New York: Columbia University Press, 1969), p. 133.

16. W. V. Quine, 'On what there is', in *From a Logical Point of View* (Cambridge, MA: Harvard University Press, 1964), p. 15. Italics in original text.

17. David Macarthur, 'Pragmatism, metaphysical quietism & the problem of normativity', *Philosophical Topics*, 36: 1 (2009).

18. See, for, example W. V. Quine, *Word and Object* (Cambridge, MA: MIT, 1960), p. 161.

19. An attitude to science as a whole, such as fallibalism, cannot be sceptical in any significant sense. Doubt is an attitude whose object and circumstances are much more specific. See the discussion by Charles Peirce about real doubt vs. self-deceptive or make-belief doubt in 'Some consequences of four incapacities', *Journal of Speculative Philosophy*, 2 (1868), pp. 140–57, and also in 'What pragmatism is', *The Monist* (1905), pp. 161–81.

20. I use the word 'kind' for the sorts of objects Quine aspires to be ontologically committed to, although Quine does not. Quine explains how the notion of kind is intertwined with the notion of

similarity that does not imply the strict identity conditions he wants (see his discussion in 'Natural kinds'). I use the word 'kind' simply to connote the objects we end up being ontologically committed to and I treat separately the question of whether or not it is similarity or identity that ultimately characterises kinds. Quine clearly votes against similarity and for identity. Badiou has a different view in *Logics of Worlds*, as I will show later.

21. This slogan appears in many of Quine's writings. See, for example, *From Stimulus to Science* (Cambridge, MA: Harvard University Press [1995] reprint 1998), p. 40; and 'On the individuation of attributes', in *Theories and Things* (Cambridge, MA: Harvard University Press, 1981), p. 102.

22. Physics, Quine's favourite science, is exceptional inasmuch as its objects are usually well regimented and have clear and strict identity conditions.

23. Ontological relativity is in fact a wider phenomenon. As Quine explains: 'What makes sense is to say not what the objects of a theory are, absolutely speaking, but how one theory of objects is interpretable or reinterpretable in another.' See his 'Ontological relativity' in *Ontological Relativity and Other Essays* (New York: Columbia University Press, 1969), p. 50. Our unregimented background natural language is also one such theory, which we can also use to interpret the objects of another given theory. And this is so even if its objects are hopelessly vague and thus do not imply ontological commitments in Quine's demanding sense.

24. Quine, *From Stimulus to Science*, p. 72.

25. Quine, 'Things and their place in theories', p. 17.

26. See, for example, Quine, 'On what there is', p. 4.

27. Quine notes the reasons for that way of talking in *Word and Object*, p. 170.

28. Quine, 'Things and their place in theories', pp. 17–18.

29. Badiou calls taxonomies 'the language of the situation'.

30. See Quine, 'Natural kinds'. For example: 'The notion of a kind and the notion of similarity or resemblance seem to be variants or adaptations of a single notion' (p. 117); and: 'The notion of kind, or similarity, is [. . .] disreputable' (p. 133).

31. I base the following on the papers: Eleanor Rosch, 'Principles of categorization', in Eleanor Rosch and Barbara B. Lloyd (eds), *Cognition and Categorization* (Hillsdale, NJ: Lawrence Erlbaum Associates, 1978); Eleanor Rosch, 'Natural categories', *Cognitive Psychology* (1973), pp. 328–50; Eleanor Rosch, 'On the internal structure of

perceptual and semantic categories', in Timothy E. Moore (ed.), *Cognitive Development and the Acquisition of Language* (New York, San Francisco, London: Academic Press, 1973); Eleanor Rosch and Carolyn B. Mervis, 'Family resemblances: studies in the internal structure of categories', *Cognitive Psychology*, 7 (1975), pp. 573–605; Eleanor Rosch et al., 'Basic object in natural categories', *Cognitive Psychology*, 8 (1976), pp. 382–439.

32. Rosch and Mervis, 'Family resemblances', p. 574.

33. By 'elements' she means 'attributes'. Rosch and Mervis, 'Family resemblances', p. 575.

34. Ronald N. Giere, *Science Without Laws* (Chicago: University of Chicago Press, 1999), pp. 111–12.

35. Ian Hacking, *Rewriting the Soul: Multiple Personality and the Sciences of Memory* (Princeton, NJ: Princeton University Press, 1995), pp. 24–5.

36. In the following, I rely mostly on the second and third books of *Logics of Worlds*.

37. For Badiou, the concept of 'world' is heavier than merely the indication of a certain context. It is supposed to be the phenomenological aspect of what he called 'situation' in *Being and Event*. One only needs to read Badiou's examples to see how this heaviness inherits the problem of *Being and Event* described in the first section of this paper. For instance, Badiou introduces an example of a typical demonstration day in *Place de la République* (see LW 199–201). He distinguishes the 'Ontological eye' that sees men, women and discussions, and the 'phenomenological eye' that sees other 'significant differences' that belong to the context of the demonstration or to the 'world-demonstration', such as anarchists and Kurds. But why do certain objects like men and women and discussions count-as-one Ontologically and anarchists do not? This is not at all clear, and Badiou offers no criteria for the distinction between what belongs to Ontology and what belongs to phenomenology. How could there be criteria for such a distinction if counting-as-one in the order of Ontology is as obscure as it was in *Being and Event*? The concept of 'world' does not entail such a distinction either. It merely points to certain 'significant differences', just as any talk of context would. In the context of a demonstration, for example, it is relevant to make distinctions between anarchists and Kurds. But their being people or men and women is also implicit in that context (who else would engage in demonstrations? Cats? Or maybe spatio-temporal chunks of matter?). In what follows I thus equate 'world' and 'explanatory or descriptive context'.

38. I use the term 'object' in the ordinary sense of an individuated thing, and not in Badiou's sense in *Logics of Worlds* (which is basically the reification of a category as a set with a definite extension).

39. Badiou uses the (oxymoronic) term 'degrees of identity' whereas I use here 'similarities and differences'.

40. Badiou calls this salience 'intensity of apparition' and often defines it as the degree of similarity that an appearing thing has to its Ontological self, to its being qua being. But again, this way of describing salience is highly problematic, since the being qua being of an individual object is still obscure. Wasn't it supposed to be just the thing insofar as it is *one* thing and has a certain label? How can one be similar to a label? If the label and oneness come with identificatory necessary intensional features, by what criteria would those be determined? The only helpful notion of salience or 'intensity of apparition' would be derived from the comparative network of similarities and differences in a certain context that differentiates things from one another.

41. I use the term 'type' whereas Badiou uses the term 'atomic component'.

42. For a more detailed account of types (or 'atomic components', to use Badiou's terminology of category-theory), see my 'Alain Badiou within neo-pragmatism: objectivity and change', *Cardozo Law Review*, 29: 5 (2008), pp. 2239–67.

43. This is basically Badiou's category-theory version of the Event and its consequences. See my 'Alain Badiou within neo-pragmatism: objectivity and change', where I offer a pragmatist reading of that version.

9

Towards a New Political Subject?
Badiou between Marx and Althusser

Nina Power

The work of Alain Badiou has been at the heart of a strong revival of Communist thought in recent decades. But Badiou's relationship to Marxism as a tradition within Communism is a matter of some uncertainty: between his calls for a 'Communist Hypothesis', communist 'invariants' and the 'Idea' of Communism, we are put in mind of a strangely pure conceptual political project, one that reaches both before and after Marx, going right the way back to Plato and wholly avoiding some of the 'muddy' historical work that comprises much of Marx's reception, particularly the historical tradition of E. P. Thompson and Eric Hobsbawm, for example. Indeed, Badiou himself states quite clearly his lack of faith in any Marxist lineage or tradition: 'I believe, to put it quite bluntly, that *Marxism doesn't exist*' (M 58). Marxism as such is for Badiou 'the (void) name of an absolutely inconsistent set' (M 58). 'Communism', on the other hand, is at least 'a *space of possible failures*' (CH 40). Badiou might just be, as Bruno Bosteels puts it (in the words of a friend): 'a philosopher who is first and foremost a communist before being, or perhaps even without being, a Marxist'.[1] But why might 'Communism' contain a more useful set of concepts and problems than 'Marxism'?

Negri very recently posed and answered the question in the following way: 'Is it possible to be communist without Marx? Obviously.' Yet, ultimately, Negri does 'not believe that it is possible to speak about communism without Marx'.[2] For others, the disjunction between Marxism and Communism appears as something of a problem, possibly insurmountable, in Badiou's work. As Hewlett argues, 'there is a lack of coherence between two major influences on his writings: the Platonic and idealist on the one hand and the materialist and activist on the other.'[3] This paper attempts to understand Badiou's location between Marxism/

Communism particularly in relation to the idea of the political subject. The centrality of a concept of the subject for Badiou's work cannot be underestimated: it ties him to a Sartrean lineage of thinking politics and causes a central tension with his otherwise strong indebtedness to Althusser, for whom the term 'subject' could only ever be ideological. Nevertheless, Badiou's communist post-Althusserian theory of the subject will be found to be strangely insubstantial, despite his later reliance on terms such as 'generic humanity' and 'the body'. Badiou's desire to retain a notion of the political subject comes at the price of a certain emptying out of the concept. A brief comparison of Badiou's notion of communism and recent work on 'the commons' will be flagged in the final section, that points in a different direction to the tension between Badiou's and Althusser's disagreements over the ideological nature (or otherwise) of concepts of the subject.

The major crux of the paper's comparison between Badiou and Althusser stems from the following point: Badiou is clear that 'there is no theory of the subject in Althusser, nor could there ever be one' (M 59). Yet for Badiou, the question of the subject is central, and the political subject arguably most central. As he states: 'The infinite comes into play in every truth procedure, but only in politics does it take first place. This is because only in politics is deliberation about the possible (and hence about the infinity of the situation) constitutive of the process itself' (M 143). In other words, politics is both a space of political failures, as Badiou described communism above, but also of immediate possibilities. But what is the relationship between the political subject and the *space* of its possible successes or failures? Communism's 'space' of 'particular failures' indicates that Badiou sees Communism as a kind of meta-structure, a hypothesis, rather than, say, a historical tendency. If Badiou is not a historical materialist thinker in the Marxist sense, then does he replace time with space (as his later theory of 'points' might suggest) in a bid to make communism as such an 'invariant'? Certainly, Badiou's notion of the communist invariant appears to operate transhistorically:

> As soon as mass action opposes state coercion in the name of egalitarian justice, rudiments or fragments of the hypothesis start to appear. Popular revolts – the slaves led by Spartacus, the peasants led by Müntzer – might be identified as practical examples of this 'communist invariant'.[4]

If we can identify 'practical examples' of the communist invariant, can we then also identify transhistorical elements of the political subject that would be 'invariant' in the same way? This would seem to lead us back to the difficulty Althusser had in conceptualising the subject – how to describe a subject without recourse to ideological clichés such as 'man', 'humanity', etc. – which leads Badiou to argue for the impossibility of a non-ideological subject in Althusser. But if there is no 'subject' as such that would be the logical partner of the invariant qualities of communism, what name can we give to those who revolt? Are we doomed to endlessly circulate around words that pass in and out of life and historical relevance – proletariat, masses, working class? Can we instead generate new names as a result of new political scenarios? As Bosteels puts it:

> We should not forget, though, that the communist invariants are the work of the masses in a broad sense. There is as yet no specific class determination to the logic of revolt in which slaves, plebeians, serfs, peasants, or workers rise up against the powers that be.[5]

And further:

> Where do we stand today with regard to the dialectics between masses, classes, and the state, between the people and the proletariat, or between the dispersed elements of an invariant and generic communism and the organized forms of knowledge concentrated in the writings of Marxism?[6]

In other words, how does Badiou's understanding of communism marry concepts with content, and invariance with history? It is around this constellation of questions that this paper will circle, addressing the question of Badiou's relationship to Marxism (part one) before turning to the relationship between Badiou and Althusser via the humanism–anti-humanism debate as a way of examining the relationship between the political subject and its 'historicity' (part two) and concluding with some speculative remarks on the question of a contemporary theory of the political subject (part three).

Badiou's 'Marxism'

Badiou's relationship to Marx can only be fully understood through the prism of Mao, or at least through the prism of Badiou's 'Maoist period'.[7] Bruno Bosteels even speaks of Badiou's 'post-Maoism' ('Badiou's relation to Maoism . . . amounts to a form of post-Maoism . . . Mao's own role for Badiou will largely have consisted in introducing an interior divide into the legacy of Marxism-Leninism'[8]). Nevertheless, Badiou's relationship to Mao relates primarily to the question of the relationship between the status of philosophy and a conception of the class struggle in theory, and perhaps less to an understanding of Marxism as such.[9] What I want to do in this section is to cut across the Maoist Badiou, and even across the 'Communist hypothesis'-period Badiou towards a clearer picture of Badiou's relationship to Marxism as a tradition, even bearing in mind Badiou's claim that Marxism as such does not exist. My focus here will be less on the earlier Maoist works and 'transitional' works such as *Peut-on penser la politique?* (1985) which have been interrogated at length for their relationship to Marxism by Bosteels, Toscano and others, and more on the more recent comments Badiou has made with regard to Marx and communism, the better to determine what Badiou's current relation to the tradition of Marxism might be.

It is important to note from the outset that there are some thinkers who take Badiou's entire project to be completely antithetical to Marxism: 'The truth is that Badiou's "communism" is deeply anti-Marxist' argues Chris Cutrone, claiming that Badiou's commitment to communism before, during and after Marx misses the key contribution of Marx's analysis: 'Marx's thought and politics are not continuous with the Spartacus slave revolt against Rome or the teachings of the Apostles – or with the radical egalitarianism of the Protestants or the Jacobins.'[10] Similarly, in terms of historical materialism's economic dimensions, it has also been argued that Badiou's analysis of politics does not commence or really engage with any fleshed-out description of capital; indeed, the category of the economic as an analytic lens is largely absent from his work.[11] So who (or what) is Marx for Badiou?

In the conclusion to his *Second Manifesto for Philosophy* (published in France in 2009 and translated into English in 2011), Badiou explicitly acknowledges his debt to Marx's idea of politics:

In politics, the expansion (foreseen by Marx) into the global market modifies the transcendental (the world, the active arena) of emancipatory action, with it being perhaps only today that the conditions are assembled for a Communist International that is neither state controlled nor bureaucratic. (SM 122)

It appears here that the historical conditions – specifically the global reach of the market – identified by Marx in the *Communist Manifesto* are represented by Badiou as the conditions for the possibility of a 'Communist International' that avoids statism and bureaucratic ossification. In the footnote to the above quote Badiou continues:

The words 'Communism' and 'Communists' must be taken in the generic sense they have in the work of the young Marx. For historical reasons, this sense was, to a great extent, overlaid in the twentieth century by the resonance imparted to the word in expressions such as 'Communist Party' or 'International Communist movement' ... 'Communism' must no longer be thought as the adjective attached to 'party' but, quite to the contrary, as a regulatory hypothesis enveloping the variable fields and new organisations of emancipatory politics. (SM 155)

Taking these two citations together we seem to be faced with the fundamental impasse of Badiou's understanding of Communism and his reading of Marx: the phrase 'perhaps only today' indicates that capitalism has inaugurated a historical shift, yet 'Communist' and 'Communism' can only be used ahistorically. It seems that only the expansion of the global market can generate the conditions necessary for communism to be similarly 'global' or international, and yet communism pre-exists capitalist modernity. Badiou's position here is perhaps surprisingly close to that of Paolo Virno who, in an essay from 2004 entitled 'Natural-Historical Diagrams: The "New Global" Movement and the Biological Invariant', argues that

We are therefore dealing with a historically determinate subversive movement, which has emerged in quite peculiar, or rather unrepeatable, circumstances, but which is intimately concerned with that which has remained unaltered from the Cro-Magnons onwards. Its distinguishing trait is the extremely tight entanglement between 'always already' (human nature) and 'just now' (the bio-linguistic capitalism which has followed Fordism and Taylorism).[12]

From 'perhaps only today' to 'always already just now': although Virno is responding to an entirely different lineage than Badiou – an anthropological, biological, linguistic genealogy rather than a Platonic, structuralist, mathematical framework – we nevertheless see a curious agreement here: it is only now, whatever *now* this is (the globalised market, bio-linguistic capitalism) that communism can be 'generic', that is 'an idea regarding the destiny of the human species', as Badiou puts it in 2007 (MS 98). While Virno tackles this question through the prism of work, as befits someone who participated in *Potere Operaio*, Badiou in general says very little about labour.

Badiou's return to the early Marx in his more recent work is thus predicated on a latent notion of substantive humanity: 'In its generic sense, "communist" means first of all, in a negative sense . . . that the logic of classes, of the fundamental subordination of people who actually work for a dominant class, can be overcome' (MS 98). Similarly in *The Century*, Badiou is primarily interested in the Marx that describes the proletariat in negative, empty terms:

> Marx . . . underscored that the universal singularity of the proletariat derives from its bearing no predicate, possessing nothing . . . This anti-predicative, negative and universal conception of the new man traverses the century. (TC 66)

So this subject has a strange double life as absent and underlying – returning us to a ghostly version of Aristotle's original understanding of subject as substance (*hypokeimenon*). It is no surprise, then, that Badiou has a serious problem in the *naming* of this subject, especially if we are talking about the subject of communism as Badiou would have it rather than the classical subject of Marxism, for which we can assume that 'proletariat' would suffice. If Marxism is simply 'the discourse through which the proletariat supports itself as subject', as Badiou says in *Theory of the Subject* (TS 62), then Marxism has perhaps exhausted its capacity to name anew. Nevertheless, it is from within an exhausted Marxism that we must begin for Badiou: 'To stand for Marxism means to occupy a place that is destroyed and, thus, uninhabitable. I posit that there exists a Marxist subjectivity that inhabits the uninhabitable.'[13]

Badiou's reiteration of his commitment to communist invariants may perhaps indicate, however, that inhabiting the uninhabitable has not been as productive as he might have liked. We are perhaps faced with the classical philosophical desire to begin again, to raze to the ground whatever previously exists and come up with new foundations. In more recent work Badiou reiterates instead the idea that we need to go back to the 1840s in order to rethink the relationship between thought and practice: 'This was the great question of the revolutionaries of the nineteenth century: first of all, to make the hypotheses exist' (MS 117). The beginning of a certain kind of political-philosophical thinking that follows Hegel is thus resurrected by Badiou as a way of beginning again, but historically.

Badiou's relation to Marx in his latest writings places us right back at the beginning of Marx's endeavour, as if to rewind communism back in time and release it from its association with states, parties and historical failure. But does Badiou eliminate too much of the history of that project, and lead us back into the realms of theory and the related absence of a political subject that characterised much of Althusser's work? Negri, for one, is highly sceptical of Badiou's purified vision of communism and the concomitant difficulties of naming the subject of this politics, given the hypothetical approach that Badiou takes:

> [T]he object will never eventuate, and the subject will remain indefinable – that is, unless it is produced by theory, unless it is disciplined, unless it is adjusted to truth and made worthy of the event . . . beyond political practice, beyond history.[14]

Do the roots of Badiou's complicated relation to Marxism and Communism in part stem from his admiration for Althusser?

Badiou and Althusser

One cannot begin with man, because that would be to begin with a bourgeois idea of 'man' . . . Marxism-Leninism cannot start from 'man'. It starts 'from the economically given social period'; and at the end of its analysis, when it 'arrives', it may find real men. These men are thus the point of arrival of an analysis which starts from the social relations of the existing mode of production, from class relations, and from the class struggle – Louis Althusser, 'Reply to John Lewis'.[15]

If Badiou returns to Marx's humanist period while simultaneously positioning Marx as merely one discourse within a much more significant history of communism, then what of Badiou's relationship to Louis Althusser, who explicitly defined his project as a theoretical *anti*-humanism? Badiou is clearly and explicitly indebted to Althusser's thought: 'Althusser's sole purpose was to redefine a genuinely emancipatory politics' (E 6–7), yet it is clear that Badiou does not and cannot give up on a notion of humanity as a substrate, however hard it is to name this substrate. This section examines some of Althusser's main claims against humanism and asks whether Badiou can count himself the heir to Althusser in any meaningful way.

Louis Althusser is often presented as the key 'anti-humanist' figure in the polarised humanism–anti-humanism debate of the mid-twentieth century. His concept of 'theoretical anti-humanism' was received in some quarters (in E. P. Thompson's *The Poverty of Theory* in particular) as the heralding of a new and reprehensible kind of inhumanism, a denial of agency and a dismissal of the role of the human subject in the making of its own history:

> Structuralism (this terminus of the absurd) is the ultimate product of self-alienated reason – 'reflecting' the common-sense of the times – in which all human projects, endeavours, institutions, and even culture itself, appear to stand *outside* of men, to stand *against* men, as objective things, as the 'Other' which, in its own turn, moves men around as things.[16]

Althusser's criticisms of humanism in the shadow of Stalin could not be clearer, though their polemical force has often been misinterpreted. In 'Marxism and Humanism' from 1963 he states that '*in ideology*, we see the themes of class humanism give way before the themes of a socialist humanism of the person.'[17] This 'humanism of the person' or 'personal humanism', in the wake of the discovery of Marx's early texts and the declarations of 'All for Man' under Stalin, is understood by Althusser to usher in nothing but a return to idealism and pre-Marxist ideology.

In the 1963 essay 'Marxism and Humanism', Althusser seeks to downplay the 'essentialising' claims made on behalf of 'class humanism' (which he later describes as 'a bit of theoretical mischief'[18]) by both Marx in his early writings, and those who would turn to those texts to extract a universalising form of humanism.

This 'essentialist' class humanism would involve the overcoming of the alienation of the human essence itself through revolution, in a way that Althusser describes as 'religious'. What Althusser does in 'Marxism and Humanism' is to argue that the subject can only be the individuated atomised subject of law and nothing collective; similarly, a class humanism can only be 'essentialist', religious and anti-revolutionary. What Althusser's move does is conflate the critique of the polemical, political abuse of the terms 'humanism', 'man' and 'subject' and to claim that the same problems adhere to the conceptual uses of the term. Thus there can be no positive use of the terms 'humanism', 'subject' and 'man' because they are already really 'religious idealism', 'ideology effect' and 'bourgeois man'. Althusser sums up his position by conflating all strands of humanism: 'Humanity's millenarian dreams, prefigured in the drafts of past humanisms, Christian and bourgeois, will at last find realization . . . in man and between men, the reign of Man will at last begin.'[19]

Althusser reiterates that he thinks that all discussion of alienation must presuppose a 'definite pre-existing essence',[20] and that 'at the end of history', man 'merely has to re-grasp as subject his own essence alienated in property, religion and the State to become total man, true man.'[21] Althusser's claim with regard to Marx is summed up in his famous 'radical break' thesis: 'In 1845, Marx broke radically with every theory that based history and politics on an essence of man.'[22]

Humanism is defined after 'the break' by Althusser as both theoretically pretentious and ideological. The rejection of humanism is accompanied by the rejection of the subject: as *homo economicus*, as legal subject, as ethico-political, as socially atomised and, most importantly, as philosophical: 'For Marx's materialism excludes the empiricism of the subject (and its inverse: the transcendental subject) and the idealism of the concept (and its inverse: the empiricism of the concept).'[23] For every idealism, there is a concomitant empiricism and vice versa. On the basis of Althusser's claim, there is no possibility of a definition of the subject that doesn't extend itself either theoretically or practically into excesses of idealism or concretisation. Simultaneously the alternative, 'real humanism' (proposed by Jorge Semprun), as discussed in the addendum 'A Complementary Note on "Real Humanism"' from 1965, is 'gestural', meaningless and unscientific. The 'real' for Althusser is instead 'the very object of Marxist theory', not the predicate of a revised humanism.[24] So, humanism is ideology, and can never attain the level of a theory or a science.

Althusser's professed anti-historicism in his reading of Marx has often been understood as involving a profound ahistoricism at the heart of his own Marxist project. As Alfred Schmidt asks in his anti-Althusserian text *History and Structure*: does structuralism (by which he means Althusserian structuralism) add its voice to the conservative claim that the present has no historical dimension?[25] When Althusser, in the wake of his explicitly anti-historicist project, resorts to the spatial metaphor, 'Marx opened up the continent of History',[26] and speaks of Hegel as having understood history 'as a process without a subject',[27] exactly what sense of 'History' does Althusser intend here?

What is at stake in this section is the status of the relationship between history and time. If Althusser possesses a theory of history, he must, as a historical materialist, necessarily account for the substantial *relation* between various modes of production as he thinks that the move from essence and humanism to modes and forces of production is Marx's greatest scientific contribution. Peter Osborne describes this in the following way: as 'the impossibility of thinking [in Althusser's work] the transition from one mode of production to another – precisely that object which it is the ultimate rationale of historical materialism to think – since . . . such transitions can be thought only as breaks or ruptures between different articulated sets of times'.[28]

If, on the other hand, what Althusser actually possesses is a 'theory of the theory of history', then he is in much the same predicament as pre-Marxist thinkers such as Ludwig Feuerbach – as he reveals in his work on the post-Hegelian thinker. Althusser's incapacity to fully account for the relationship between modes of production and the 'process' of history markedly resembles Feuerbach's inability to provide a coherent account as to why alienation takes on different forms in different historical epochs. While Feuerbach's 'problematic' is undoubtedly different, retaining as it does a Hegelian emphasis on alienation, his problem in relation to history and its transition is markedly similar to Althusser's: how can Feuerbach account for the different forms of alienation he describes without being able to conceptualise transition? What is there to link the alienation of man's capacities in polytheism, for example, to the different form of alienation he sees in monotheism? The problem here is one of relationality for both Feuerbach and Althusser: namely, how the different forms of alienation or modes of production correlate to each other over time.

Badiou describes his own reading of Althusser's relation to history in the following way: 'Philosophy is guarded from the danger of confusing history and politics ... on account of itself lacking history. Philosophy authorises a non-historical perception of political events' (M 62). In other words, philosophy does not itself have a history; it can instead point out invariants or instances of a hypothesis. For Badiou, it is Althusser's work above all that provides the key to a methodology that would decouple communism from Marxism, that would return us to the question of 'political singularities' (M 58) and allow us to understand communism as such anew.

> [I]t is impossible to penetrate Althusser's work if one considers it a 'case' of Marxism, or as the (incomplete) testimony of a Marxist philosophy. In order to penetrate Althusser's work we must consider the singularity of his undertaking and his wholly particular aims. (M 59)

Althusser may well be the reason why Badiou persists in making a separation between the two terms, not least because Badiou believes that Althusser's work inaugurates a new *practice* of philosophy' (M 59), one which Badiou no doubt emulates, even as he criticises Althusser for 'suturing' politics to philosophy. But can a political practice of philosophy escape historical situatedness? Negri, for one, thinks not:

> In the French experience of 'Maoism', we witnessed the spreading of a sort of 'hatred of history', which – and this was its terrible deficiency – betrayed an extreme malaise whenever it came to defining *political objectives*.[29]

If an expressive totalising conception of history is to be abandoned, as Althusser repeatedly proposes, in favour of the 'complex whole', at what point in the present can we intervene in order to declare that history has reached a certain stage, is entertaining particular political objectives? While Feuerbach, writing in 1843, retains a concept of the philosophy to come, whose task is to 'pull [man] out of the mud in which he has been embedded',[30] Althusser posits no such task for thought or practice. Indeed, given his approving claim that Hegel ultimately posits history as 'a process without a subject', at what point can we say that this process has reached a stage in which *human* emancipation (however we determine this) will mean anything at all? If there is no subject for Althusser, neither the party nor the masses, if there are only processes without a subject, how are we to describe what politics might mean? (And I am presupposing here that politics is always constituted by the emergence of a subject – a group, a party, a class). Badiou indicates that Althusser will approach this question by trying to think of 'subjectivity without a subject', through terms such as 'partisanship', 'choice', 'decision' or 'revolutionary militant' (M 64), and in a sense, politics then can only be understood from within a process.

This leads us to a further, final, question. As Badiou puts it, how do we distinguish politics from science, another process without a subject, while preserving the specificity of politics and the political subject (M 60)? While we may appreciate the political and historical 'conjuncture' of Althusser's claims regarding the importance of anti-humanism, anti-historicism and anti-evolutionary accounts of history in the face of Stalin's 'humanist' propaganda, what is in question here is more conceptually fundamental: how can Althusser still be understood as a political thinker when politics is so undetermined as a category of action or collective practice in his work? Badiou thanks Althusser for clearing conceptual ground: 'It was . . . following his lead that we became obliged to reject the humanist vision of the bond, or the being-together, which binds an abstract and ultimately enslaved vision of politics to the theological ethics of rights' (M 66). But Badiou is perhaps too quick in dismissing the otherwise classically 'humanist' dimensions of his own notion of generic humanity by associating humanism with theology and ethics. It is evident that Badiou cannot follow Althusser in treating the subject merely as an ideological effect and not as a more substantial category. It is also clear that, despite agreeing with Althusser's criticisms of the 'humanist vision', Badiou is happy to use terms such as 'generic humanity' without thinking that these terms would also fall under the category of ideology as Althusser defines it. But what of the political subject that slips out from between the humanist–anti-humanist debate? How much existence does it have?

Which Subject?

For Althusser, according to Badiou, there is no theory of the subject; for Badiou, on the other hand, 'the declaration that there is a (formal) theory of the subject is to be taken in the strong sense: of the subject, there can only be a theory' (LW 47). In *Logics of Worlds*, Badiou explicitly dismisses experiential, moral and ideological notions of the subject, including in the last case Althusser's own, without dismissing the notion of the subject *in toto*. Subjects, Badiou declares, exist only as 'the subject of a truth', which also includes the potential denial of truth (LW 50). In this later work, Badiou attempts to fill out his formal schema of the subject with a materialist conception of 'body': 'the body is the set of everything that the trace of the event mobilises' (LW 467). This new body is, however, once again strangely purified, raising once more Negri's worry that 'the subject will remain indefinable'.

It is worth briefly juxtaposing in this final section Badiou's ongoing attempts to isolate a theory of the subject with other attempts to identify the material basis for a contemporary politics in order to position his work in relation to contemporary alternatives for any rethinking of Marx and the subject. While Badiou speaks about communism, others have returned to a discussion of 'the commons', also taking, as Badiou does, the 1840s as their point of reference. Linebaugh, for example, writes:

> In the 1840s ... communism was the new name to express the revolutionary aspirations of proletarians. It pointed to the future ... in contrast, the 'commons' belonged to the past, perhaps to the feudal era, when it was a last-ditch defence against extinction. Now in the 21st century the semantics of the two terms seems to be reversed, with communism belonging to the past of Stalinism, industrialisation of agriculture, and militarism, while the commons belongs to an international debate about the planetary future of land, water and subsistence for all.[31]

Silvia Federici similarly concentrates on the history of and ongoing struggles over the commons, summed up in part by her claim that 'What began [with enclosures in the sixteenth century] was an intense struggle, climaxing in numerous uprisings, accompanied by a long debate on the merits and demerits of land privatisation which is still continuing today, revitalised by the World Bank's

assault on the last planetary commons.'[32] Another main aspect of
the contemporary discussion of the debate regarding the commons
is, in some ways, much less historical, or at the very least, treats
history as secondary to what might be called the re-eruption of
the discovery of a human nature in the era of the commodifica-
tion and exploitation of all human materials – physical, rational,
linguistic, creative and so on. This second position may be seen
in the work of Paolo Virno, as briefly outlined in section two.
This 'return to the commons' is significant as a practical attempt
to understand the possibilities for common forms of resistance to
the ongoing process of enclosures. By taking the commons as their
starting point, Federici, Linebaugh and others point to a way in
which 'commoning' is still possible, still happening and entirely
politically necessary. Although the 'commons' approach, which
takes into consideration history, geography and grassroots political movements, seems to be operating at a quite different level
to Badiou's more theoretical take on the revival of communism,
there are parallels in the sense that both approaches depend upon
a certain notion of humanity as that which resists: capital cannot
fully 'enclose' the human, whether it be at the level of its species-
being, linguistic creativity, capacity for rational thought, practical
activity or political desire. Even if Badiou is much less interested in
the relationship of this humanity to its environs, Badiou's unwill-
ingness to give up on a term – humanity – that Althusser would
have regarded as ideological in the extreme is ultimately part and
parcel of Badiou's insistence that a theory of the subject is possible, indeed necessary:

> [A]ny political sequence that, in its principles or lack of them, stands
> in formal contradiction with the communist hypothesis in its generic
> sense, has to be judged as opposed to the emancipation of the whole of
> humanity, and thus to the properly human destiny of humanity. (MS
> 99–100)

For Badiou, the 'properly human destiny of humanity' is communism, but how do we get there? Contemporary competing theories
of the commons point to some sort of response: the material of this
communism is already there, but hidden from view because of the
way in which it is enclosed and exploited by capitalism, whether
it be labour, resources or ideas. Badiou takes communism away
from Marxism and dehistoricises it to a large degree, in part using

Althusser's attack on historical materialism to argue for a new theory of the subject that would avoid the reduction of the subject to a mere ideological effect. Yet a deeper, substantive notion of the subject re-emerges whenever Badiou talks about communism – this 'humanity', this hidden resource. But how do we get from this humanity to an active political subject? Surely the resources lie within this lump of humankind, however obscured they may be. Badiou's difficulty in naming the subject, or rather the subject's own difficulty in naming itself, is perhaps indicative of a certain political impasse – yet where else can we look but around us, to our activity and to history, for ideas? If there is a way to reconcile Badiou's communist invariants with the careful work of historical materialism in its detailed, historical mode, would that we could bring history to the subject and the subject to history: the 'invariants' we can identify can thus serve as guidelines for future successes, rather than empty echoes of failed pasts.

Notes

1. Bruno Bosteels, 'The speculative left', *South Atlantic Quarterly*, 104: 4 (2005), p. 751.
2. Antonio Negri, 'Is it possible to be a communist without Marx?', *Critical Horizons*, 12: 1 (2011), pp. 5 and 11.
3. Nick Hewlett, 'Paradoxes of Alain Badiou's theory of politics', *Contemporary Political Theory*, 5 (2006), p. 373.
4. Alain Badiou, 'The communist hypothesis', *New Left Review*, 49 (2008), p. 35.
5. Bosteels, 'The speculative left', p. 755.
6. Ibid., p. 761.
7. As Oliver Feltham states, this period comprises of three main texts, *Théorie de la contradiction*, *De l'idéologie* and *Théorie du sujet*. See the chapter 'Philosophy' in A. J. Bartlett and Justin Clemens (eds), *Alain Badiou: Key Concepts* (Durham, NC: Acumen, 2010), p. 16.
8. Bruno Bosteels, 'Post-Maoism: Badiou and politics', *positions: east asia culture critique*, 13: 3 (2005), p. 575.
9. For a serious study of Badiou's 'heterodox Maoism' in relation to other 'post-Marxist' thinkers, see Alberto Toscano's 'Marxism expatriated: Alain Badiou's turn', in Jacques Bidet and Stathis Kouvelakis (eds), *Critical Companion to Contemporary Marxism* (Leiden: Brill, 2008), pp. 529–48.
10. Chris Cutrone, 'Badiou's "communism" – a gerontic disorder'

(2011), http://chriscutrone.platypus1917.org/?p=1144. But see Bosteels' claim that 'Badiou . . . has always argued against the leftist operation that radically unties the dialectical knot between masses, classes, and state, or between communism and Marxism' ('The speculative left', p. 762).

11. A question highlighted at length by Alberto Toscano in 'From the state to the world? Badiou and anti-capitalism', *Communication & Cognition*, 37: 3–4 (2004), pp. 199–224.

12. Paolo Virno, 'Natural-historical diagrams: the "new global" movement and the biological invariant', trans. Alberto Toscano, in Lorenzo Chiesa and Alberto Toscano (eds), *The Italian Difference: Between Nihilism and Biopolitics* (Melbourne: re.press, 2009), p. 131.

13. Alain Badiou, *Peut-on penser la politique?*, trans. Bruno Bosteels (Paris: Seuil, 1985), p. 57.

14. Negri, 'Is it possible to be a communist without Marx?', p. 11.

15. Louis Althusser, *Essays in Self-Criticism*, trans. Grahame Lock (London: NLB, 1976), p. 52.

16. E. P. Thompson, *The Poverty of Theory* (London: Merlin Press, 1978), p. 206.

17. Louis Althusser, 'Marxism and humanism', in *For Marx*, trans. Ben Brewster (London: Verso, 1969), p. 222.

18. Louis Althusser, 'The humanist controversy', in *The Humanist Controversy and Other Essays*, trans. G. M. Goshgarian (London: Verso, 2003), p. 224.

19. Althusser, 'Marxism and humanism', p. 222.

20. Ibid., p. 226.

21. Ibid.

22. Ibid., p. 227.

23. Ibid., p. 229.

24. Louis Althusser, 'A complementary note on "real humanism"', in *For Marx*, trans. Ben Brewster (London: Verso, 1969), p. 246.

25. Alfred Schmidt, *History and Structure: An Essay on Hegelian-Marxist and Structuralist Theories of History*, trans. Jeffrey Herf (Cambridge, MA: MIT Press, 1983).

26. Louise Althusser, 'Marx's relation to Hegel', *Politics and History: Montesquieu, Rousseau, Marx*, trans. Ben Brewster (London: Verso, 1972), p. 166.

27. Ibid., p. 182.

28. Peter Osborne, *The Politics of Time* (London: Verso, 1996), p. 25.

29. Negri, 'Is it possible to be a communist without Marx?', p. 9.

30. Ludwig Feuerbach, *Principles of the Philosophy of the Future*, trans. Manfred Vogel (Indianapolis, IN: Hackett, 1986), p. 3.

31. Peter Linebaugh, 'Meandering: on the semantical-historical paths of communism and commons', *The Commoner*, 14 (2010), http://www.commoner.org.uk/wp-content/uploads/2010/12/meandering-linebaugh.pdf.

32. Silvia Federici, *Caliban and the Witch: Women, the Body, and Primitive Accumulation* (New York: Autonomedia, 2004).

III. Philosophical Figures

10

'The Greatest of Our Dead': Badiou and Lacan

Justin Clemens and Adam J. Bartlett

'I see that no one is putting a hand up, and thus I must go on.'[1]

In his appointment book for 11 December 1959, Louis Althusser notes: 'Introduction to Lacan'.[2] By then, Jacques Lacan's seminar had gained a reputation and Althusser, already interested in Freud, had sent one of his students to record the goings on there. On 3 December, the student reported. The student was Alain Badiou. We can't say whether this was also Badiou's first encounter with Lacan, nor whether it *alone* sowed the seed of his later break with Althusser, but we can say that Badiou has since never stopped being concerned with Lacan's 'goings on'. From his involvement with the journal *Cahiers pour l'analyse* in the mid-1960s up to his latest published works, Lacan's influence on Badiou's philosophy has been ongoing, marked and decisive.[3]

Indeed, Lacan's impact upon contemporary European philosophy more generally cannot be underestimated. From Alexandre Kojève through Jean Hyppolite to Jacques Derrida and Gilles Deleuze, reactions to Lacan's thought have integrally shaped the philosophical landscape in often unexpected and, for the most part, unexamined ways. While being no exception to what by all appearances is a rule, Badiou has gone further by explicitly nominating Lacan as 'the greatest of our dead'. Whereas many of the aforementioned luminaries have found themselves all the more Lacanian in raging against him, Badiou has dedicated an extraordinary number of essays and chapters to the work of the French psychoanalyst. If Badiou's work has been developed in explicit confrontation with a number of other contemporary thinkers, Lacan's is the most determining in this regard. From Lacan, Badiou extracts and extends doctrines regarding the status of love, science, art and even of philosophy itself; there is hardly an article or book by Badiou that does not allude to or draw upon Lacan's work. It is critical to note that for Badiou this engagement is always from the side of philosophy, from the perspective of Lacan's relation to philosophy, that is to say to the other side, and, as he notes, such an engagement is 'perilous', not least because Lacan could never finally clarify his own non-relation to Plato and thus philosophy.[4]

This perilous and essential engagement, continuous as it is, has two distinct phases divided by Badiou's 1988 magnum opus *Being and Event* and, more particularly, with his subsequent conceptualisation of 'anti-philosophy' and the ongoing development of his theory of conditions. We track this engagement with Lacan, the exemplary 'anti-philosopher' and 'educator to every philosophy to come' from the extensive use Badiou puts Lacan to in his late 1970s seminar, published in 1982 as *Theory of the Subject*, through the subsequent and consequent stages of Badiou's *oeuvre*. Even though anti-philosophy was not an operative category for Badiou prior to the early 1990s, it is helpful in understanding the character of Badiou's engagement with Lacan and this, as we will argue, holds as good for *Theory of the Subject* retrospectively as it does for *Logics of Worlds* and beyond.

Even though he doesn't use the term in *Theory of the Subject*, Lacan's 'anti-philosophical' approach to the question of the subject, to its formative and (quasi-)ontological division and its central place in the production of new knowledge, is central to Badiou's efforts to re-found the subject as a category of thought. The relation is not simply one of analogy nor, as Badiou puts it in an interview from the early 1990s, a matter of 'showing that what I was saying in philosophy was compatible with Lacanian thought'.[5] Rather, Badiou's constant references to the limits and aporias embraced by Lacan – precisely in order to keep a good analytic distance from the predations of the 'philosophical' master – become for Badiou the sites and points of a renewed philosophical encounter. This is a constant of Badiou's method: the very point at which a thought 'fails', which is to say comes to posit its own end on the supposition of that which is inaccessible to it, marks the very point at which philosophy can (re)constitute itself as the discourse capable of composing the consequences of these 'failures'. The *familiar* ethic is 'keep going' (E 52, 90–1).[6] Philosophy, in Badiou's estimation, is what takes the next step subject to this condition for, as mathematics teaches and as Lacan also teaches – 'mathematical formalisation is our goal' – the inaccessible is not a consistent concept. The paradox is that while Lacan desired mathematical formalism to render the discourse of the Other intelligible and thus integrally transmissible, he himself (knew that he had) failed to achieve it. Wedded to language, thus reducing mathematical formalism to its logicist expression, Lacan mistook the route but not the goal.[7] It's a mistake Badiou takes up and a goal he pursues. To use, somewhat enigmatically, the terms Badiou uses in *Theory of the Subject*, 'Lacan sides with Sophocles but points at Aeschylus, which is where we want to get' (TS 161).

Lacan's Philosophical *Hainamoration*

Before addressing the place of psychoanalysis in *Theory of the Subject* it is worth summarising Lacan's minimal distance from philosophy. To begin, as Lacan says, at the limit is to note that Lacan's hatred of philosophy was manifest. Aside from his long-pursued, explicit critiques of, say, G. W. F. Hegel, one could cite some of Lacan's hilarious, scabrous puns: '*faufilosophe*', '*flousophie*', etc.[8] Indeed, Lacan becomes more and more direct on the matter, to the point where he flatly states: 'I abhor philosophy, it's been a long time since it's said anything of interest.'[9]

However, it's more accurate to say, as does Jean-Claude Milner, that Lacan's engagement with philosophy took the form of *hainamoration*.[10] For references to philosophers are also endemic across the seminars and the *Ecrits* and, apart from anything else, this gives currency to Badiou's claim that anti-philosophy – of which Lacan is the exemplary contemporary figure – is a division immanent to philosophy. Further, this suggests that the method of anti-philosophy, at least in its Lacanian version, is a *subtractive* one. In other words, it builds its discourse on that which, for its rival, is *impossible to say* and *impossible to know*. Analytic *discourse* constructs itself as the truth of the other or the thought of the real.[11] When Lacan claims to situate psychoanalysis in relation to 'Science itself'[12] it is both a nod at Kant, whom he will treat at length in the essay 'Kant avec Sade' published in *Ecrits*,[13] and more potently a direct revision of the Cartesian subject.[14] That which philosophy cannot think, the unconscious, is the key to this psychoanalytic revision.[15] It is not too reductive to say that this revision even has its roots in the pre-Socratics and therefore turns on the contention whether 'being thinks', as Parmenides (Plato and Badiou) insist, or whether, as Heraclitus claims, 'it signifies', which is to put things in the dimension of the act.[16]

Summarily, then, and with regard to our contention that the key to Badiou's engagement with Lacan centres on the articulation of truth of which the subject is the effect, *hainamoration* entails analytic discourse hating, not what philosophy professed to love, truth, but rather what the love of philosophy made of truth: ostensibly an object for its contemplation alone, thus turning the animus of truth, the real as such, into something un-lovable per se. In other words, philosophy mistakes its object *for* the *object a*, that is the cause of its desire.[17] Philosophy claims not only to 'love truth', but to know the 'all' of truth as such, the whole truth. Philosophy thereby conflates truth and knowledge and, in and through this operation, truth ultimately becomes little more than a predicate of the knowledge of philosophy, i.e. 'truth' is the unjustifiable honorific philosophy gives to its own 'knowledge'.

This is the crux of philosophy's general lack of appeal, of claims to its end and of its self-serving reserve. It is philosophy's 'love' (of the One, we might say) that analysis hates, which is to say, the very form of its discourse – given that discourse is a social bond – because philosophy fails to see in truth anything other than *its* object of love, which is to say *itself*. In short, philosophy for Lacan is a sort of psychotic narcissism – to which he listens closely. For Lacan, the great exponent of this narcissism at the limit (and thus after a fashion not determined by it himself) is not Plato, with whom Lacan compares himself, but Hegel (check the index to *Ecrits*) whose concept of absolute knowledge, in this context, invokes the church ethic par excellence: 'love thy neighbour as thyself', an ethic, as has often been remarked, which requires that what is to be loved must, above all, be what is a priori lovable. Like God, then, who does not hate, philosophy, caught in its own projections, is a most ignorant being.[18] Essentially, philosophy, in love with its own knowledge, cannot think that which philosophy is not, that which is not the knowledge of philosophy (in both senses of the genitive) or that which is in excess of philosophy. This insight, first of Freud vis-à-vis the unconscious, and Lacan's vis-à-vis the sexual *non*-relation, guides Badiou's return of philosophy to itself. Badiou orients his project on the Real of this Lacanian impasse, which is for Badiou at once true *and* unknown.

Lacan was not merely intent on philosophy's destruction; indeed, he saw that, with all irony intended, as a matter for philosophy itself. Rather, he was concerned with the *subversion* of philosophy and as such with the place which philosophy, mostly by its own determination, supposed itself to occupy. That place – and the topological designation matters insofar as speaking of the *locus* of truth is, Lacan insists, anti-philosophical – is that of truth or, more accurately, of the *knowledge* of truth. Yet it is not that Lacan wanted to render that place void so much as to see it occupied by a discursive operation worthy of truth itself, one that in fact founded itself on the division of truth from knowledge and, by association, the subject from being. This meant a discourse that did not presume itself at one with that which it discoursed upon, that is to say a sovereign discourse, a discourse of mastery, of completion, retrospectively and in anticipation of all knowledge to come. Against this eternal absolutism, so to speak, and the logic upon which it was articulated, Lacan insisted on treating the structural division of knowledge as *real* – that there are fundamentally two distinct and formative sites for the production of knowledge. If there is a subject, for Lacan, the very condition of new knowledge, the goal of all analysis, then there is immediately, immanently and in-differently, that other which guarantees the very (dis)place(ment) of this subject. Philosophy, for Lacan, cannot think this subject (of love, of non-relation, thus 'hate', of the *two* 'universality/existence'), and for Lacan, that which escaped determination and was as such outside philosophy was the very point, the point at which philosophy, in thrall to the love of truth qua object (rather than process in the real), could no longer think. Thus its very presumption to mastery is a veil philosophy throws over its own lack. As he says, in this sense, 'the love of truth . . . is the love of castration', a point Badiou will take up (TW 120).[19] Mastery, in essence, is the limit of thought and not its 'completion'. One 'masters', at the limit, when one can no longer think. What Lacan shows (for Badiou, he goes astray only in not *demonstrating*) is that truth is not mastery and the absolute is not universality. Moreover, what Lacan recognised was that mastery was itself inscribed in a serial chain of positions and as such was the result of a particular turn in the becoming of truth. The problem was to force a new turn, a deposition, to aim truth at the real (the impossible) in the manner of Heraclitus *contra* Parmenides and, in a move of spectacular, speculative non-sense, Socrates *contra* Plato. Analysis, then, is anything but a 'world-view', which is a 'discourse entirely different from ours'.[20]

The Happiness of Falling Short[21]

In an interview from the late 1990s, Badiou claims that his entire philosophical effort is devoted to thinking the new, of setting out the formal procedures that trace the production of the new in situations.[22] The production of the new, which, because of its very newness, makes no sense in the established situation, requires that which affirms *both* its consistency and its 'being there'. The subject, in Badiou's conception is the name for this process or effect and is, as for Lacan, the central category of Badiou's *oeuvre*. The seminars that make up *Theory of the Subject* offer a unique perspective.[23] In this work, Badiou is most definitely engaging with Lacan in a 'conditional' sense, as we understand it from *Being and Event* onwards, and yet in *Theory of the Subject* he nowhere conceives of this engagement *as such*. Like so much else in *Theory of the Subject*, this praxical engagement with Lacan anticipates the future direction of Badiou's philosophy.

In *Theory of the Subject*, Badiou enlists Lacan to help forge a new thinking of the subject on the rubble of the old subject of revolutionary praxis, whose supposed exhaustion permeates Badiou's response to the burgeoning reactionary situation of the 1970s. The immediate identification of the subject of politics with the proletariat is now untenable. The Sartrean subject as group in fusion hit its limit in the events of 1968. Althusser's negative, nominalist and statist conception of the subject realises only the ubiquity of the state, and the classical subject of metaphysics delimited by Heidegger et al. persists as the ideological substrate of an individualism eminently manipulable by an ascendant capitalism and its attendant parliamentary administration. Basically, things are shit! What each of these efforts maintain in their various ways is the classical non-division of the subject, a formation, as we have said, that Lacan found untenable.

In *Theory of the Subject*, it is primarily the political subject that is (algebraically) in question *and* the goal (its topology).[24] Philosophy, as a discourse itself is not yet as *explicitly* at stake as it will be after *Being and Event*; however, philosophy is the site of the enquiry undertaken in *Theory of the Subject* and the requirement that philosophy be something other than a bourgeois language game or academic quibble most certainly subtends the diagnosis and prognosis of the subject. In the period of his work up until 1985's *Can Politics Be Thought*, Badiou, as Oliver Feltham argues, adopted – not without Maoist modification – Althusser's final determination of philosophy as 'class struggle in theory', and this informs the thinking of the subject in this text.[25] Yet in order to think this political subject, one tenured neither to science or knowledge nor to ideology, the text engages with an extraordinary array of subjects including contemporary poetry (Mallarmé and Hölderlin), Greek tragedy (Sophocles and Aeschylus), mathematics (algebra, set and category theory), dialectic (synthesis, division, Marx, Engels, Hegel, Lenin, Mao) and, of course, psychoanalysis.

The overriding Maoist trajectory organising *Theory of the Subject* is the prescription 'one divides into two' and indeed the entire trajectory of the work is itself immanently and minimally divided between the initial claim that philosophy is 'deserted' and the final determination that 'this is the eve'. This is opposed to the reactionary dialectic – political and amorous – wherein any 'two' is fated to become one.[26] Throughout the text, every determination is divided, and in some cases divided again, in order to formalise the 'true' instance of the subject. The exercise is devoted, on the one hand, to ensuring that deviations are analysed, delimited and pronounced upon, and, on the other, to ensuring the most rigorous and incorruptible possible conception of political and thus subjective praxis.

Ostensibly, Badiou seeks the point at which the subject is found: the point at which there is no subject of repetition. Repetition, Badiou argues, is constitutive of the subject insofar as it retains the mark of its placement within a given structure – particularly a state structure. In short, what repeats is what is recognised as rightly occupying its determined place in the structure. In turn, the latter determines the compulsion to repeat. However, this subject of repetition – and this is where psychoanalysis aids the investigation by splitting Hegel in two – is not all. That is to say, its very place(ment) can be demonstrated as lacking any ground other than the prescriptive determination of structure itself, and therefore the subject maintains as itself, so to speak, the capacity (process) to lack this very place (of subjectivisation) and, from the outplace [*horlieu*] immanent to and yet in excess of the determination of the 'splace' [*esplace*] (or state), to be that which interrupts (subjective process) the repetition supposed to condition and sustain it. In other words, the subject *is* the division of determination and lack, of subjectivisation and subjective process, put into practice. And this division is itself split into two in Lacanian fashion, that is horizontally and not vertically: on the side of subjectivisation, anxiety and superego; on the side of subjective process, courage and justice. However, it is not Badiou's position that there is a simple opposition between determination or placement and lack (or the outplace), rather that, given the immanent division which marks the subject, an entire dialectical rearticulation of its place and constitution is possible, and, under particular evental conditions, necessary. A subject is 'at once' the product of an encounter, as it takes place by force. At its most formal, then, the subject – precisely as Lacan conceives it under the condition of love – is always Two, which is to say, four.[27]

Badiou begins his analysis proper of Lacan in *Theory of the Subject* by noting Lacan's 'ambiguity', that is, his discourse on the question of the One and the Two (or of universality and the absolute). What Lacan does in Seminar XX is to interrupt Hegel's pretty little dream – *Aufhebung* – not from the side of the One, but the Two. Lacan's ambiguity is constitutive, not a folly or an inconsistency. Hegel is also a site of this ambiguity, for to be faithful to Lacan's splitting of Hegel, Badiou must himself split Lacan ('our Hegel').[28] Critically for the entire trajectory of Badiou's future (subtractive) engagement with psychoanalysis, Badiou notes that Lacan is speaking of history, Hegel's 'end of history', as the history of love. Thus Lacan goes behind Hegel's back and invokes courtly love, saying something gets split there. The implication is that what was split there, Hegel never 'sublated' and thus in the great Hegelian discourse of love there is an immanent excess, a point from which to interrupt the Hegelian 'absolute' and to begin again the analysis of the place of love. (Going *behind* philosophy is a characteristic Lacanian or 'anti-philosopher' move.) Ultimately, this displacement or splitting that Lacan originates is, for Badiou, internal to the dialectic itself. There is the structural and the historical or, psychoanalytically speaking, the symbolic ('place') and real ('force').

In contrast to Mallarmé's 'univocity', Lacan maintains the division which is not (a new) one. Badiou, in saying this, evokes the 'cunning' of Lacan as 'strategist of *lalangue*', underlining that this might mean the impossibility of the *new*, such that whatever splits is mere 'iteration' and so we have simply 'the Law of splitting' as such. Or, Badiou asks, should the emphasis fall on the *one*, such that as a consequence of splitting there is no new *one*? In this case there is something new, something beyond the law of the one, and this would entail that the one of the law is not, that 'the symbolic is ruined by the real, the one ungraspable except in the process of its destruction' (TS 114). In the rhetorical style that animates the *Theory of the Subject*, Badiou nominates Lacan as 'the theoretician of the true scission' of the 'one divides into two', against 'those repairmen of flat tyres, the revisionists, to whom is suited the syrupy conviction that Two fuse into one' (TS 113). This is the crux of things and Badiou will never waiver from this conditional axiom.

But, a propos Lacan, at crucial junctures *conditioned* by set theory *and*, contra Lacan, a *mathematised* logic, he takes it further. We should emphasise that, just as Lacan works both sides of the dialectic, Badiou works both sides of Lacan: the side of Lacan that exposes the holes in knowledge (that of lack), and the side of Lacan that distributes these expositions within a theory of the subject which is, Badiou says, 'ahead of the current' and it is up to us to 'take advantage of this advance' (TS 115).

What Badiou wants to make compatible in *Theory of the Subject* is the psychoanalytic real of two sexes and the political real of two classes, but he wants to derive a materialist articulation of the division from Lacan. This operational paradox – which will later be denoted 'fidelity' – involves following Lacan as far as Lacan can go, consistent with his own conceptions, *to the point at which it becomes impossible for Lacan himself to go on*. We are speaking here situationally, conceptually, rather than of Lacan's own 'self-image' (whatever that might have been). At this point of impossibility, Badiou seeks to divide and interrogate that point to extract the resources for its own overcoming. This means delineating the hole in this knowledge, its point of impasse, and interrupting this discourse by way of another – just as the hysteric's discourse interrupts the master without adding any elements that were not already there. Thus the philosophical freighting concerns the Real (at which truth must aim), for it is this concept whose formalisation is in question. For Lacan, what is at stake in this formalisation is the very lack of sexual relation; that is to say, *there* is, fundamentally so, such a lack and it is by this lack that all discourse is inscribed. In this case, Lacan's case, the lack is situated on the side of the subject (we will return to this, for as much as it is a problem in this text, *Theory of the Subject*, it is so differently in Badiou's texts subsequent to *Being and Event*). Further, what this lack holds together – the *non* of non-relation – for Lacan is a problem of logic or, as Badiou insists, algebraic logic. That is, he subverts Aristotle's classical logic of the four places.

Nonetheless, Lacan remains caught, due to his refusal to accord ontology any status except that of just another instance of sense. For Lacan, ontology is inevitably a matter of language in a classical algebra of places. If, as for Lacan, language is constitutive (of things, etc.), and the subject as such is reducible to a being who speaks in the place of language and, further, on the basis of its non-relation to what is other to it, then there is no *outside* place. In effect, the (algebraic) mark and the place that it inscribes as such are one and the same. Now this suturing effect, a mark of anti-philosophy, results in an idealist form of the dialectic – one advanced in terms of what passes for a thinking of the subject, but one whose materialist consequences need to be drawn. Thus we can see Badiou's conceptual movement: from Hegel's idealism to Marx's materialism, from Lacan's idealism to that which is to come: Badiou's materialist reversal of materialism. What Badiou does with Lacan's algebraic reconfiguration of the division of the sexes is topologise these placements or marks which signify as points in a differential structure.

Topology demonstrates that every point is inscribed within a set of relations or a space of placements and thus any point is 'existentially' dependent on the set of relations within which it is inscribed. A topos, falling under the rule of set theory, is an actual infinite – thus denumerable as such (there is a denumerable set of relations) – and bounded by a 'least upper bound', a limit point which marks but does not 'belong' to the determined 'world'. However, first, inscribed within this 'set' or topos (which is really just ordered relations) is that-which-is-not and, second, on the basis of this 'that-which-is-not', that which escapes its placed inscription in the order of relations, which determine the place of the elements in their place (*esplace*), these determinations are eminently subvertible, 'crossable', reversible, and so on. Badiou's 'dialectical name' for this eminence is 'torsion'.

Badiou thereby operates upon the Lacanian algebra of places – which rightly marks out the structure of the dialectic of the subject, but at the price of saving repetition – accounting for the force of this placement. That is to say that the constitutive determination of the relations hold these points of the structure in place, and do so under the veil of in-determination, which is to say, simply, ideologically. But the critique of ideology – and again, Lacan points the way for Badiou – necessarily returns to a dynamics of the structure of which ideology is mere representation. What the turn to a mathematised logic allows Badiou to show is what has been *logically* foreclosed. That is, the impossibility of the reversal of this set of determinations (thus the consistency of the 'non-repeatable') (TS 142) is already inscribed in the very abstract logic of the determination of places – a logic Badiou redescribes most abstractly in *Theory of the Subject*.

The logic itself, qua logic, excludes any other 'logic'. Now Lacan – and this will only later become a bone of contention for Badiou – opts for an intuitionist logic to break this classical bind. Badiou, as we noted, approves of Lacan's move, which insofar as it serves psychoanalysis is entirely legitimate. Formally, however, it is too limited to serve the interests of philosophy, and cannot found a formal conception of the subject, one useful for politics as for other procedures. Badiou returns to contemporary mathematics to break formally with the 'logic of the space of placement'. In effect, he goes behind the back of algebraic logic, to what it cannot think without; yet what it thinks it already determines, i.e. mathematics. The point is, for *Theory of the Subject*, that Lacan's algebraic recourse is correct insofar as it denotes the critical import of structure *and* insofar as this helps to realise the categorical import of anxiety and superego at this algebra's limit (two sites of excess as such (TS 146)), but it is delimited by the demands of structure itself, proposing as it does a structural form as the guarantee of the subject. Badiou turns to a mathematised logic to in-determine structure itself, that is to say to subject structure to force, to the effect of a torsion or subjective force, and not simply to turn structure on its head. The political point is not to put the proletariat in power, but to situate *subjective force* as that which, immanent to 'the space of placements', finally can be done with the repetitions of the latter.[29] Hence the thoroughgoing re-education enacted by the '(materialist) reversal of materialism' is the fourfold rearticulation of the subjective complex in such a way that anxiety and the superego, themselves capable of producing new knowledge of subjects under the conditions of repetition, are inscribed in a dialectic with their 'philosophical' others, courage and justice.[30] Thus the subject of analysis, resubjected to the torsion of its own division, realises itself as the subject of philosophy.

Lacan Post *Theory of the Subject*

This position soon proves inadequate for Badiou himself. There are three critical aspects to his continued engagement with Lacan and psychoanalysis beyond *Theory of the Subject*. First, there is the question of philosophy under *conditions*. The theory of conditions is fundamental to Badiou's re-formed philosophy. Lacan, the theorist of love – one of the four conditions for a philosophy – and of the *four* discourses, is naturally a central figure in this regard. Second, there is the question of anti-philosophy. This term, taken from Lacan himself (who provocatively takes it from the reactionary response to the Enlightenment encyclopaedists, those who struggle, as Colette Soler has acerbically phrased it, against the right to think), is given conceptual weight by Badiou.[31] As such, Badiou again pays philosophical homage to Master Lacan, making a concept of an operational (polemical) category. Not only does it conceptualise something essential for Badiou's renewed conception of philosophy, it allows him to designate other thinkers under the concept, thus constructing an invariance of the non-relation between anti-philosophy and philosophy. This has severe consequences for the history of philosophy itself, for it enables the rigorous drawing of new immanent lines within the philosophical heritage.

Further, denoting as it does both a distance from philosophy and a traversing of a similar territory of thought, anti-philosophy can be distinguished from sophistry, that other great 'other' of philosophy. Where the former, Badiou suggests (not unambiguously), is immanent to the philosophical project itself, the latter, sophistry, is inimical to it. Sophistry designates an outside to philosophy and is parasitical – all the more so, as he says, because 'their rhetoric is the same'. As we will see, what organises this 'triplet' (*sans plaisir*) is the relation each proposes to truth – and thus to the subject and to being. This threefold articulation also requires a reconsideration of the notion of the infinite. Here, for Badiou, Lacan is found wanting, but not irredeemably so.

The final aspect of Badiou's continued engagement with Lacan and psychoanalysis beyond *Theory of the Subject*, which will be examined below, is the role Lacan plays in Badiou's thinking of appearing in *Logics of Worlds*, specifically with regard to the '*body* of truths', the *en corps* and/or the *encore*.

Conditions

The short text, *Can Politics be Thought?*, marks the nodal point of the first of two major transitions in Badiou's work (*Being and Event*'s 'mathematics is ontology' and *Logics of Worlds*' 'topology of appearing'). The title alludes to the return of philosophy qua discourse of the other, but it also alludes to the status of those discourses that *think* politics (as well as love, science and art) and to the thinkers of these discourses at their limits. We will look at some thinkers below, but first a short exposition of the status of these discourses *for* philosophy, psychoanalysis being, for today, that discourse which thinks the truth procedure that is love.

Without conditions, there is no philosophy. For Badiou, philosophy as such does not exist. There may be some philosophy, philosophies have existed, but there is no discourse identical to itself, established for all time, that corresponds to the name. Philosophy is, properly speaking, *indiscernible*, but can come to be under the pressures and constraints of a particular epoch, an epoch wherein the discursive operations of mathematics (or science), art, politics and love are extant and are engaged in thinking and producing the truths of their time. Philosophy then appears as a discursive operation in its own right, one that is itself the formal composition of these irreducible and disparate truths. Philosophy seized, as he says in the first *Manifesto for Philosophy*, by the truths so produced, in turn seizes on the forms and structures that inhere in these productions. That is to say, the truths of love, politics, art and science will be irreducible to each other and specific to the field of their production, but the formal arrangement of their procedures vis-à-vis being, event, subject, *will have been* invariant. In thinking these discourses together, in constructing the space of the composition of these distinct generic procedures, philosophy proposes the *form* of these procedures and proposes, moreover, the eternal invariance of this form across the different procedures. Badiou, in all modesty, draws our attention to the fact that these are the discursive conditions for Plato.

While love is a condition for philosophy, the status of psychoanalysis with regard to love is not immediately straightforward. Badiou is unambiguous that psychoanalysis is the pre-eminent contemporary discourse concerning love – the science of love, even – but the status of the analytic cure is for Badiou a little more vexed. He says:

I've never resolved the issue of whether the analytic cure represents an independent, autonomous truth procedure. The difficulty is that there's something in the analytic situation that's analogous to the love situation. Transference, after all, is an encounter that is supposed to take the form of knowledge. Lacan himself was unable to clarify transference except by referring to the great philosophical works on love.[32]

In pursuing these questions, Badiou once again mercilessly re-interrogates Lacan. What is absolutely critical here is the following: (1) Lacan sustains a formal thought of the subject that is neither historicist nor philosophical, neither substantive nor active; (2) Lacan does this by means of recourse to the matheme, on the one hand, and a theory of love, on the other; (3) Lacan insists on the primacy of a practice that is extra-moral and whose maxim is 'don't give way on your desire'.

Anti-philosophy

The conceptualisation of anti-philosophy arises due to Badiou's effort to 'return philosophy to itself'. This means, as another form of the Platonic gesture, articulating the means by which to compose a philosophy on the basis of that which philosophy is not but, subsequently, cannot not be and, concomitantly, to establish the ethics of philosophy's engagement with its rival discourses. In 1989's *Manifesto for Philosophy*, the dissimulating discourse that has occupied the place of philosophy, as in ancient times, is sophistry. Badiou names as contemporary examples Nietzsche, Wittgenstein and Lyotard. It is in this text that Lacan is named 'the greatest of our dead' but, despite sharing with the named sophists an affinity for the ideal of language as constitutive (and a commitment to the deposition of being qua truth), Lacan is never labelled a sophist. In this text, Badiou notes only that Lacan nominated himself an anti-philosopher (MP 28). There is then a distinction to be made between the sophist and the anti-philosopher, one Badiou himself notes, but is not always clear in making. Wittgenstein and Nietzsche, for example, appear sometimes as sophists (great ones to be sure, 'our Gorgias and Protagoras' (C 21)), sometimes as exemplary anti-philosophers.[33] The preliminary answer to the confusion is that in 1989 Badiou had not yet properly addressed the question of the status of the anti-philosopher. Despite the fact that in *Theory of the Subject* he had put this (non-)relation into practice, he had not yet considered it categorically or conceptually, that is to say *philosophically*. The first essays in which anti-philosophy is thought as such are republished in 1992's *Conditions*.

However, the slippage between the two essential categories *for philosophy* remains, and Badiou remarks in *Logics of Worlds* that there is a mutable compact between the two positions, such that, due to the 'rhetorical forcing' inherent in the anti-philosophical act, 'every anti-philosopher is a virtual accomplice of sophistry' (LW 540–2). Despite this complicity – whose other name is 'anti-Platonism'[34] – it is possible to discern critical differences. These differences centre on the orientation each maintains in regard to the threefold schema constitutive of philosophy: being, truth and the subject. 'Modern sophistry', Badiou writes, 'seeks to replace the idea of truth with the rule' or the 'production of the true with modalities of linguistic authority'.

> The modern sophists are those that . . . maintain that thought is held to the following alternative: effects of discourse or language games, or the silent indication, the pure 'showing' of that which is subtracted from the grip of language. For sophistry, the fundamental opposition is not between truth and error or errancy but between speech and silence, between that which can be said and that which is impossible to say. Or: between statements endowed with sense and those devoid of it.[35]

Strategically, and in order to give itself historic depth, Badiou says that modern sophistry appropriates the 'Jewish epic', which is to say the 'eternal narrative of wandering, under the original authority of the law', and it combines this narrative with the method of interpretation. The combination is perilous, Badiou notes, and *not at all well founded*, not least because the 'signifier "Jew" does not lend itself to representation'. Yet it allows postmodern sophistry to support a linguistic analysis, constituted in terms of sense and meaning, and ultimately of Law, against a straw-man conception of the historical subject, in such a way that its denial of philosophy benefits from its (dubious) historicism.[36] In Badiou's eyes, philosophy must track a diagonal trajectory to the 'constructivist' determinations of its 'perverted double', sophistry, and take as its axiomatic orientation, in exception to sophistry's desire for Law or rule, that 'there are truths' and therefore also some subjects. The ethics of truths and, as such, the ethics of philosophy demand that the sophist not be done with once and for all, but that sophistry is assigned its place. Philosophy's maintenance of this sophistic place is actually crucial to the continuation of philosophy; without properly taking account of the genuinely corrosive power of the great sophists (whether by inadvertently succumbing to, or by furiously excluding them), philosophy also loses itself. Philosophy in effect displaces sophistry in and by its discursive composition of the truths of its time. These truths owe their form to what sophistry forces from philosophy: (1) that truths are local; (2) that truths are (subjectively) manifest in different and irreducible conditions and so take multiple names; (3) that being qua being is thinkable as that which thought seizes upon, and not as destiny, as the True, or as that which befalls philosophy as such. In fine, the *polemos* with sophistry must be maintained.

However, to return philosophy to itself – that is, to de-suture it and thus establish a site for its practice *without* sophistry – which is Badiou's singular goal as a philosopher, will require, Badiou comes to see, not merely keeping one's eye on what one must not be, but also on traversing the discursive subtleties and active interventions of that discourse which does not want philosophy to be at all. In other words, the fact is that it is by way of anti-philosophy that this return of philosophy to itself is established in Badiou's work. Despite the discursive slippage between the two figures, the anti-philosopher can be identified in contrast to the sophist because rather than imitate the philosopher, rhetorically and institutionally, and from the side of scepticism with regard to truth, the anti-philosopher seeks the means for a deposition of philosophy entirely, predicated in part, not on the inadmissibility of truth per se but on the 'axiomatic' contention that truth may be *experienced* (in whatever fashion current) but 'cannot be thought'.

Thus the anti-philosopher is, as the name suggests, in a dual relation to philosophy. It is 'anti' to the extent that it forges a distance between its analytic practice and philosophical enquiry, and yet the former demands that philosophy and in particular its conditions be traversed in the very constitution of itself as a formal discourse. In the case of psychoanalysis, Badiou says, and insofar as it 'touches the subject, being, truth and ethics', 'psychoanalysis is always a traverse of at least love and mathematics' (C 246).

Anti-philosophy is philosophy's rival, not its re-presentation; therefore not, in Badiou's terms, its 'state' formation (such is why anti-philosophy, like philosophy itself, runs the risk of slipping into sophistry). In fact, we can say that the effective goal of anti-philosophy is to assign philosophy, by 'punching holes in it', to the place anti-philosophy establishes as belonging to it. For Lacan, speaking from the position of the analyst, this means to designate it either 'historically' as the discourse of the master or, today, when capitalism assumes this place, as the discourse of the university and thus in the position of furnishing the 'knowledge' of the master. Nevertheless, as we have already seen, it is Lacan whose mathematical formalism comes closer than any other anti-philosopher to the 'integral transmission' of truth and thus the deposition of the threefold structure of non-philosophy: meaning, sense and experience. In Badiou's own words, psychoanalysis is not an experience so much as a thought.

We can sum up the position of anti-philosophy as follows: (1) a *subordination* of philosophical categories to language, and the concomitant destitution of philosophy's pretensions to truth and system; (2) the *diagnosis* of such pretensions as evidence of a philosophical will to power; (3) the *affirmation* of an extra-philosophical ethics that escapes such strictures.[37] What is noteworthy is that in whatever guise anti-philosophy comes – whether proselytising for Life or 'active' force, *charité*, candour, redemptive choice, etc.[38] – Badiou attends to its prescriptions philosophically, such that 'force', 'love', 'generic' and 'decision' denote, respectively, critical re-conceptualisations of these 'affects'. Badiou composes his philosophical project instructed by the anti-philosopher's discriminations, delimitations and conflations; each act of anti-philosophy, if you like, provokes the philosopher to philosophy, such that the philosopher must 'turn back frequently to what we've already said, in order to test it by looking at it backwards and forwards simultaneously'.[39] It is through anti-philosophy that philosophy can return to itself as conditional and punctual, thus being attentive to what it is not. And it is from the anti-philosopher Lacan that this term and this concept are delivered.

Lacan: The *Nec Plus Ultra* of Contemporary Anti-philosophy

In the collection *Conditions*, Badiou dedicates no less than three important essays to the study of Lacan: 'Philosophy and Psychoanalysis', 'The Subject and Infinity' and 'Anti-Philosophy:

Plato and Lacan'. The first of these delineates a key set of relationships between the two as practices of thought. The second is a detailed criticism of Lacan's use of mathematics. The third is an account of the relation between anti-philosophy and Plato in Lacan's practice. In each case, we are confronted by a rigorous statement and contextualisation of the key conceptual disagreements; next, by a thoroughgoing critique of psychoanalysis, targeting its own points of impossibility; finally, with an affirmative delimitation of psychoanalysis' importance for philosophy.

Each of these essays is of interest in its own right for what it illuminates not just about the Badiou–Lacan relation, but about the development of Badiou's thought more generally. 'Philosophy and Psychoanalysis' examines the *différend* between the two as hinging on the question: 'what is the localization of the void?' (C 201). The very posing of this question enables Badiou to enumerate what these two heterogeneous discourses in fact share: a repudiation of the doctrine of truth as adequation; that 'chance' supports what Lacan called 'the only absolute statement'; that both psychoanalysis and philosophy are praxes that aim to transform the places in which they intervene. Yet it is at the precise point regarding places that they diverge again. For Badiou, analysis locates the void in the subject – Lacanian theory notoriously figuring the subject as a void brought to becoming by a void object and supported by a void signifier – whereas philosophy locates the void as the void of Being itself. Moreover:

> According to Kant, the universality of the moral act, in the form of the void, opens onto being itself, qua being, what he called the suprasensible; whereas, according to Lacan, ethics opens, singularly, in response to the discovery of betrayal, to our being. (C 205)

Where, in this splitting, the two discourses once again coincide in a non-relation, if from entirely irregular angles, is on the problems of the matheme and on love: 'Love undergoes the void of relation, because there is no sexual relationship. Mathematics undergoes it, because it exhausts it in pure literalization' (C209). In other words, Lacan has once again pointed out for Badiou certain requisite conditions – above all, the necessity for thinking love and science together – as well as a way for a desuturing of philosophy from these conditions.

Significantly, however, the way in which Lacan organises the relation of these conditions according to the ethics of psychoanalysis is struck by a double disability. The first concerns the consistency of Lacan's deployment of mathematics; the second concerns the problem of politics, both as a practice of philosophical commentary and as a condition itself.

In 'The Subject and Infinity' Badiou intervenes primarily in Lacan's use of mathematics in supporting the latter's famous 'formulas of sexuation'. Badiou points out that, in his attempts to evade Aristotelian logic, Lacan confronted a dilemma:

> The first path consists in saying that the logic underlying the formulas of sexuation is not classical logic but a variation of intuitionist logic. The second, basing itself on Cantor's set theory, introduces, outside the field of the Φ function, the abyss of actual infinity. Now, intuitionism is defined, amongst other things, by a categorical rejection of actual infinity. We have a new and grave problem. (C 214)

Indeed. As it turns out, the situation is even worse than this. Intuitionistic logic rejects reasoning by absurdity, insofar as it rejects the law of excluded middle (often considered by intuitionists not as a 'law' at all, but merely an observed regularity in finite mathematics) and hence demands constructive, finite proofs. Yet Lacan himself constantly relies on reasoning by absurdity and the mathematical results that depend on it; to do so, he must implicitly reject intuitionist logic. If that's the case, however, and even if one overlooks his other inconsistencies, Lacan's formulas succumb to the very Aristotelian logic they were arrayed against.

Badiou's unknotting of this snarl – even more complicated than we have the space to investigate here – is decisive. He shows that Lacan merely requires the thought of an infinite point, one inaccessible to any finite creature, rather than the *actual* infinities of the Cantorian paradise. As such, for Lacan, the 'infinite is not a set, but a virtual point subtracted from the action of the finite.' Perhaps this resolution does indeed permit Lacan a certain consistent evasion of Aristotle, but it gets him into further conceptual hot water, especially regarding a blatantly sophistic 'demonstration' that 2 is already infinite qua its splitting. For Badiou, these routines underline that, despite his genuine innovations, Lacan remains pre-Cantorian. In sum, Lacan once again points the way, and it is by taking him absolutely seriously, by remorselessly tracking his thought to its symptomatic point of failure, that Badiou reveals a new impasse, and makes a decision that will take him beyond Lacan – without any simple repudiation.

This method holds too for the third and final essay to be discussed here. Badiou summarises Lacan's grievances against Plato under three headings: the gnoseological (the process of knowledge), the ethical (concerning 'well-speaking') and the ontological (the relation of truth, knowledge and being). We have elsewhere referred to Lacan's list of charges against philosophy under the headings of 'power crime', 'thought crime' and 'sex crime'.[40] Badiou shows how Lacan – in line with a rather general post-Nietzschean anti-Platonism – at once identifies Plato as the origin of philosophy, and hence the origin of all the aforementioned troubles, at the same time as he, Lacan, often essays to detach the personage of Socrates from this origin. For Lacan, Socrates sometimes looks like an exemplary hysteric, sometimes like a proto-psychoanalyst. Plato, by contrast, is pre-scientific, yet anticipates the modern episteme of science. Plato allegedly misunderstands language (the etymologies of the *Cratylus*), de facto treats reminiscence as an imaginary phenomenon and falsifies the One with his theory of participation. Finally, for Badiou, these claims rest on a symptom of Lacan's, the 'strange and restated conviction that Plato concealed his thought more than he presented it' (C 245). This, in its odd operations – 'duplicitous' will be the name Badiou gives to Lacan's procedure here – immediately puts Lacan's own very decided opinions about Plato's decided opinions into question. For Badiou, then, Lacan – like anti-philosophers more generally – finds himself contrarily split between a certain distance-taking from philosophy, and a traversal of it. In other words, even the most rigorous anti-philosophy cannot help but generate symptoms regarding philosophy, symptoms which, properly attended to, enable further steps within philosophy itself.

To give one further example: in the essay 'What is Love?' also in *Conditions*, Badiou uses Lacan to provide an orientation towards the proper matter of philosophy. Drawing from Lacan a thesis about the relation between love and being that at once assents to Lacan's proposition and takes it in a different direction, Badiou, at the moment that he affirms that the phallus may indeed function as the differentiator of the sexes from the point of analysis, splits and supplements the problem of sexuation for philosophy by way of the creation of a new function. It will no longer be the operations of the phallic function and linguistic desire that found sexuation; it is now the operations of a 'humanity function' and the procedure of love that will have founded sexuation.

Obviously, to conceive of philosophy as under conditions is already to side-step a central anti-philosophical criticism concerning philosophy's mastery or assumption of a generalised sovereignty over what is thought and what is said vis-à-vis truth. But we have to recognise, somewhat paradoxically, that this very conception of philosophy is an effect of anti-philosophy, precisely because the condition of the relation between a condition and 'philosophy' is actually their non-relation – their lack of rapport – and thus the contingent necessity of that which comes to supplement this 'lack'. Thus the *incompleteness* of this relation – to risk a logical term for rhetorical gain – has in fact an operational form. It is a condition of the continued effort to traverse the distance between the conditions and their composition, between truths and their form. Thus Badiou can say, renouncing any ambiguity: 'only those who have the courage to work through Lacan's anti-philosophy, without faltering, deserve to be called contemporary philosophers' (TW 119).

Logics of Worlds: Question of the Body

Badiou's intense, protracted encounter with Lacan continues in *Logics of Worlds*. A glance at the index would alert any reader to Lacan's importance: of the major thinkers Badiou discusses in this treatise, Deleuze receives nineteen entries, Hegel twenty, Heidegger sixteen, Kant twenty-one and Leibniz twelve. Lacan receives twenty-five, rivalled only by Plato with the same number. If it is always a little misleading to rely on quantitative analyses, this comparison is illuminating: Badiou, the self-declared Platonist, is clearly directly engaging with the ultimate contemporary anti-Platonist Lacan. Attending to the entries themselves underscores this engagement. Justifying the formalisation in his Preface, Badiou writes: 'As Lacan says, "*mathematical* par excellence", means "transmissible outside of meaning"' (LW 39). This is, as the reader should now be aware, another rephrasing of Badiou's long-held enthusiasm for this aspect of Lacan, for whom the essence of the matheme is to transmit ab-sense (note the knotting of mathematics, transmission, ab-sens) (LW 390). Moreover, as Badiou adds:

> We must recognize that we are indebted to Lacan – in the wake of Freud, but also of Descartes – for having paved the way for a formal

theory of the subject whose basis is materialist; it was indeed by opposing himself to phenomenology, to Kant and to a certain structuralism, that Lacan could stay the course. (LW 48)[41]

In this and in other remarks, Badiou is simply rephrasing positions that were already in play from *Theory of the Subject* onwards. Where Badiou does indeed seem to add something new to this reading of Lacan is regarding his own new interest in a formal theory of the body. Under Section 2 of the division 'What Is a Body?' Badiou dedicates a short chapter, titled simply 'Lacan', to precisely this question.

Here he invokes two aspects of Lacan relevant to such a question: (1) the body is of interest for Lacan insofar as it is traversed by the Other; (2) modern science for Lacan is constitutively antiperceptual, and therefore breaks the link between nature and the natural body (LW 477). As Badiou adds, 'For Lacan, affect is the body, to the extent that structure operates within it' (LW 478). He further adduces some perhaps unexpected similarities between his theories and Lacan's: (1) the extreme version is polemical against Merleau-Ponty and Sartre; (2) in Lacan, the body still thinks; (3) the split of the body in Lacan is constantly menaced by becoming reactive or occultist. As Badiou says, 'I can unhesitatingly communicate with Lacan's construction, which incorporates the natural body into the body conceived as the stigmata of the Other' (LW 480). Where Badiou parts company with Lacan on the problem of the formalisation of the body hinges, as in prior works, on the difference between process and structure. The Lacanian emphasis on the subject as a structural recurrence is integral to the subject's finitude; Badiou renders the *work* of the subject, its becoming-body, to an infinite process.

To conclude: we have demonstrated here the extraordinary priority which Badiou accords Lacan, and the utmost seriousness with which the former pursues the theses and argumentation of the latter. Without Lacan, no Badiou. On this basis, wherever Badiou goes from here, Lacanian psychoanalysis will remain of extreme importance.

Notes

1. Jacques Lacan, *On Feminine Sexuality, The Limits of Love and Knowledge, 1972–1973: Encore, The Seminar of Jacques Lacan Book XX*, trans. Bruce Fink (New York: Norton, 1999), p. 90.

2. Olivier Corpet and François Matheron, 'Introduction', in Louis Althusser, *Writings on Psychoanalysis: Freud and Lacan*, trans. Jeffrey Mehlman (New York: Columbia University Press, 1996), p. 1.

3. Links to English translations of many of the articles from *Cahiers pour l'analyse* can be found online at http://www.web.mdx.ac.uk/cahiers/.

4. See Alain Badiou, 'Lacan and the pre-Socratics', in Slavoj Žižek (ed.), *Lacan: The Silent Partners* (London: Verso, 2006), p. 7. See also Alain Badiou, 'The Formulas of *l'Étourdit*', trans. S. Saviano, *Lacan Ink*, 27 (2007), pp. 81–2.

5. Alain Badiou and Lauren Sedofsky, 'Being by Numbers', *Artforum*, 33: 2 (1994), p. 123.

6. In *Theory of the Subject* Badiou's formulation is different – 'love what you will never believe twice' (TS 324) – but the 'sentiment' is the same as in its Lacanian inspiration.

7. See 'The subject and infinity', in *Conditions* (C 211–27) and 'Formulas of *l'Étourdit*', pp. 80–95.

8. See, for example, Jacques Lacan, *Écrits* (Paris: Seuil, 1966), p. 233. One needs to hear in these puns on *philosophie* the subverted homophones: *faux* (wrong, false, fake); [il] *faut* (it is necessary); *flou* (blurry, misty, unfocused, unclear); *faufiler* (to baste, to slip through); etc.

9. See Jacques Lacan and Emilio Granzotto, 'Il ne peut pas y avoir de crise de la psychoanalyse', *Magazine Littéraire*, 428 (2004), p. 25.

10. Lacan, *Seminar XX*, pp. 90–1. 'The word [anti-philosopher] surprises. Reference to philosophers appears inseparable from Lacan's oeuvre. Where Freud remained reserved – more Austrian than German in this regard – and always more disposed to rely upon arts and letters than upon philosophy, Lacan constantly cited the *corpus philosophorum*. In speaking of antiphilosophy, had he decided to refute himself?' Jean-Claude Milner, *L'Œuvre Claire: Lacan, la science, la philosophie* (Paris: Seuil, 1995), p. 146.

11. Lacan does not equate truth and the Real. There can be a discourse of truth if the discourse aims at the Real. This is why Badiou calls psychoanalysis a thought and not a knowledge.

12. This might be most 'simply' expressed as the Real of science. He says it is the 'science in which we are caught up, which forms the context of the action of all of us in the time in which we are living . . .' Jacques Lacan, *Seminar XI: The Four Fundamental Concepts of Psychoanalysis*, trans. A. Sheridan (London: Penguin, 1994), p. 231.

13. Jacques Lacan, *Ecrits*, trans. Bruce Fink (with Héloïse Fink and Russell Grigg) (New York: W. W. Norton, 2006), pp. 645–68 (Fr. pp. 765–90).

14. See 'Descartes/Lacan' (BE 431–5).

15. Lacan, *Seminar XI*, p. 231.

16. Lacan, *Seminar XX*, p. 114. See also Badiou's comments in 'Lacan and the pre-Socratics', p. 15.

17. 'It is neither [philosophy's] virtue nor its essence to want to ground the unity of being in the One of the object' (TS 236).

18. Lacan, *Seminar XX*, pp. 14 and 91.

19. Jacques Lacan, *Seminar XVII: The Other Side of Psychoanalysis*, trans. R. Grigg (New York: Norton, 2006), p. 52.

20. Lacan, *Seminar XX*, p. 30.

21. See TS (144).

22. Alain Badiou and Bruno Bosteels, 'Can change be thought: a dialogue with Alain Badiou', in Gabriel Riera (ed.), *Alain Badiou: Philosophy and Its Conditions* (New York: SUNY Press, 2005), p. 245.

23. Badiou notes that Lacan's seminars are a 'strange appropriation of a real *Symposium*' (TW 119 and C 129). See also Bruno Bosteels' introduction to *Theory of the Subject* (TS xxvii).

24. The failure of Lacan to rigorously topologise the subject, whose algebra he had distinctly provided, is the point at which Badiou's theory of the subject is founded.

25. Oliver Feltham, 'Philosophy', in A. J. Bartlett and Justin Clemens (eds), *Badiou: Key Concepts* (Durham, NC: Acumen, 2010), pp. 16–17. Feltham goes on: 'The task of theory – "Marxist" philosophy – is then to serve the practical struggle by systematising the thinking of the masses as it emerges . . .' See also Feltham's *Alain Badiou: Live Theory* (London: Continuum, 2009), for a fuller treatment of Badiou's 'second period'.

26. This dialectical division pre-empts the division in *Logics of Worlds* between the 'materialist dialectic' and 'democratic materialism', between a body subject to truths and a 'sacred' body of opinion. In the latter, language is both constitutive and communicable while in

the former truths render communication void and language parasitical. The intelligibility of truths is integral and not representable in Badiou's formalisation, and thus in *Logics of Worlds* we see Badiou have recourse to the Idea as the instance of this transmission thus affirming a tripartite structure to the articulation of truth which invokes a fourth position – precisely that of subjectivity. This schema is commensurate with that of *Theory of the Subject* and is therefore beyond Lacan for whom mathematical intelligibility was the goal but for whom the Idea is a philosophical chimera.

27. Lacan, *Seminar XX*, p. 4.

28. Lacan: 'the one who for us French Marxists is today's Hegel' (TS 113).

29. Badiou notes the distinction between the psychoanalytic cure which seeks the 'readjustment of the subject to its own repetition', and political re-education which seeks a 'radical toppling of the subject's position, that is the interruption of repetitions' (TS 142).

30. See Jacques Lacan, *Le Séminaire: Livre I: Les écrits techniques de Freud* (Paris: Editions du Seuil, 1975), pp. 198–9 and TS (157).

31. See Colette Soler, 'Lacan en antiphilosophe', *Filozofski vestnik*, 27: 2 (2006), pp. 121–44; see also Bruno Bosteels, 'Radical antiphilosophy', *Filozofski vestnik*, 29: 2 (2008), pp. 155–87.

32. Badiou and Sedofsky, 'Being by numbers', p. 123.

33. As anti-philosophers see Alain Badiou, 'Who is Nietzsche?', trans. Alberto Toscano, *Pli*, 11 (2001), pp. 1–10; and *L'Antiphilosophie de Wittgenstein* (Paris: Nous, 2004).

34. See A. J. Bartlett, *Badiou and Plato: An Education by Truths* (Edinburgh: Edinburgh University Press, 2011), and 'Badiou and Plato', in Bartlett and Clemens (eds), *Badiou: Key Concepts*, pp. 107–17.

35. Authors' translation. See *Conditions* (Fr), p. 60. Wittgenstein is the figure here invoked. See C (6) and MP (116–17).

36. *Conditions* (Fr.), pp. 61–2; see C (7) and MP (117–18).

37. See Alain Badiou, 'Silence, solipsisme, sainteté: l'antiphilosophie de Wittgenstein', *Barca!*, 3 (1994), pp. 13–53; 'Who is Nietzsche?', *Pli*, 11 (2001), pp. 1–11; 'L'antiphilosophie: Lacan et Platon', *Conditions* (Fr.), pp. 306–26 (C 228–47).

38. Peter Hallward, *Badiou: A Subject to Truth* (Minneapolis, MN: University of Minnesota Press, 2003), pp. 20–1.

39. Plato, *Cratylus*, 428d.

40. A. J. Bartlett and Justin Clemens, 'Badiou and Lacan', in Bartlett and Clemens (eds), *Badiou: Key Concepts*, p. 158.

41. Regarding Lacan's defence of the subject, Badiou reiterates: 'That is why traversing Lacan's anti-philosophy remains an obligatory exercise today for those who wish to wrest themselves away from the reactive convergences of religion and scientism' (LW 523).

11

Badiou and Sartre: Freedom, from Imagination to Chance

Brian A. Smith

Freedom, Group and Subject: The Problem in Sartre

Sartre has a wide-ranging and continuing influence on Badiou. Initially, from his position as an important cultural figure and public intellectual, Sartre dominated Badiou's early philosophical development, also inspiring him to write novels and plays (LW 555).[1] In Badiou's mature work Sartre continues to feature as a regular interlocutor and philosophical companion, especially in relation to Badiou's development of his concepts of freedom and subjectivity from the *Theory of the Subject* to *Being and Event* (PP 35; LW 555; C 165–78).

Badiou's fidelity to Sartre is to a philosopher of decision, and of freedom as decision. Decision is key to Badiou's philosophy, and it determines his understanding of the subject as born from a moment of decision, rather than as an underlying ontological ground.[2] For this reason, the individual is not sufficient in itself to produce radical change, but requires something in excess of itself and the current situation (TS 219–20). The individual has a capacity of decision, or choice, which cannot be called freedom unless it is tested against an event, an excess that is undecidable according to any given calculable rule. I think that Badiou sees something of this philosophy of the event in all of Sartre's major works, both *Being and Nothingness* and the two volumes of the *Critique of Dialectical Reason*, but this idea is always lost or overwhelmed by Sartre's continued commitment to the phenomenological ontology of the in-itself/for-itself. There is, by Badiou's own standards, a materialist dimension to *Being and Nothingness*, which surfaces in the occasional speculative discussions of the emergence of the for-itself from the in-itself, described by Sartre as an absolute event. This theme reoccurs later, but in a different

form, in Sartre's discussion of the group and its moment of formation in the *Critique of Dialectical Reason*. Badiou's interest in and
fidelity to Sartre are specifically focused on this later development,
with its consequences for political action. But in order to develop
this positive idea of revolt and group action, in the face of an
event, Badiou must tease apart the subject from its foundational
ontological role. Central to this move is recognising the role that
chance and the event play in the *Critique of Dialectical Reason*, as
Sartre states:

> The explosion of revolt, as the liquidation of the collective, does not
> have its *direct* sources either in alienation revealed by freedom, or in
> freedom suffered as impotence; there has to be a conjunction of his-
> torical circumstances, a definite change in the situation, the danger of
> death, violence.[3]

Also, for Badiou, it is important to show how the presupposition
of the for-itself is what always leads Sartre's subject toward a pes-
simistic conclusion (PP 26–7; TS 320). Peter Hallward points out
that Badiou must remove Sartre's reliance on the for-itself's imagination as the source of change, shifting the dependence of freedom
from solely the power of the imagination to the chance, or unconditioned, nature of the event.[4] This shift in focus will allow Badiou
to mount a serious critique of Sartre's notion of the group, most
notably in Sartre's commitment to a group of subjects rather than
a group subject. This argument is crucial. Political action can only
be sustained if the group itself is the subject. If it is simply a group
of subjects it will finally fall apart back into its constituent pieces:
the inevitable decline charted in the *Critique of Dialectical Reason*,
from liberated group existence to alienated serial existence. Sartre
denies the possibility of a group subject on the basis that such a
subject would be an impossible super-organism, deriving its unity
from an unintelligible transcendent source.[5]

At the heart of Badiou's response to Sartre is an attempt to
think the philosophy of the *Critique of Dialectical Reason* without
the underlying ontology of *Being and Nothingness*. By rejecting a
phenomenological ontology that begins from the subject Badiou
can countenance the possibility that the subject only emerges as a
response to a contingent event. Badiou makes this clear in his short
essay on Sartre, where he introduces the archetypal group subject
of the political subject:

There is in the political subject . . . a principle of consistency that is neither series, nor fusion, nor pledge, nor institution. An irreducible principle, which escapes from the Sartrean totalization of practical ensembles. A principle that is no longer grounded on individual praxis. (PP 34)[6]

The main focus of this essay will be to focus on this separation of the subject from any foundational role. To that end, my analysis will be directed toward Badiou's *Theory of the Subject,* where he directly questions the value of retaining the autonomous for-itself as a simple de facto subject (TS 180). The subject is not the simple for-itself, but rather 'two processes whose combination defines that region of practical materiality that we would do better to call the "subject effect"' (TS 154, 300). This subject effect is composed of a moment of subjectification, similar to Sartre's Apocalypse and the formation of the group, and a subjective process that produces a consistent effect, again mirroring Sartre's group action (TS 155). The subject only begins with an event, a contingent set of chance circumstances. It does not pre-exist this event and, therefore, it cannot be liberated or transformed by it. Rather, it creates itself from out of this event.

This early systematic work succeeds in developing Badiou's notion of freedom as chance by retaining the idea of the Apocalypse, or event, from Sartre while removing its ontological base in the for-itself (TS 59, 260).[7] By breaking the bond between the individual and the subject Badiou is also able to assert, contra Sartre, that every subject is a group-subject (TS 20, 243, 250). But the destructive impulse in *Theory of the Subject* becomes too dominant, something Badiou later admits in *Being and Event* (BE 409). This destructive passion for the real gives rise to such a radical transformation that nothing of the old survives in the new, and it is impossible to know, or to measure, if anything has really changed at all (C 56). If everything changes, how can we really tell if anything has changed? I will address this problem toward the end of the essay, by pointing to some of the developments of *Being and Event* which recognise the limitations of *Theory of the Subject.*

To follow this development of Badiou's thought in detail, I will split this essay into two major sections, concentrating on Sartre and Badiou respectively. First, in order to appreciate Sartre's importance for Badiou it will be necessary to look at the materialist thread that runs throughout Sartre's work, something that is already present in *Being and Nothingness* before its explicit development in the *Critique of Dialectical Reason*. Despite being generally accepted as a work of phenomenological ontology, Sartre makes it clear in *Being and Nothingness* that the in-itself exists independently from the for-itself: 'the in-itself has no need of the for-itself in order to be'.[8] On Badiou's own criteria this is enough to categorise Sartre as a materialist thinker: 'Materialist is whoever recognizes the primacy of being over thinking (being does not need my thinking in order to be)' (TS 117). This materialist aspect is relegated to metaphysical speculation at the margins of *Being and Nothingness*, appearing sporadically throughout the text in Sartre's occasional discussion of the absolute event of the emergence of the for-itself from the in-itself. This has many parallels with his later discussion of the Apocalypse and the fused group in the *Critique of Dialectical Reason*, as well as forming the basis of Sartre's opposition to a group subject.

Second, in *Theory of the Subject*, Badiou introduces key ideas on subjectivity and the event for the first time. Badiou's most explicit attempt to incorporate Sartre's *Critique of Dialectical Reason* into his own work is in the *Theory of the Subject* (TS 299–300). In this section I will show how Badiou uses his reading of Lacan to incorporate Sartre's subjects, the affirmed subject of the for-itself and the denied subject of the group, into his own philosophy. By doing so Badiou is able to overcome the limitations he sees in both Sartre and Lacan. I will conclude by pointing to the weaknesses of *Theory of the Subject*, principally how it is over-reliant on a destructive phase and the difficulty it has dealing with some of Sartre's criticisms regarding the intelligibility of the change that the group creates. Only in the formal set-theoretical ontology of *Being and Event* can these problems be overcome.

The Underlying Materialism of *Being and Nothingness*

The consequence, for Sartre, of accepting that the in-itself has ontological primacy over the for-itself is that one is led to ask the question: what is the origin of the for-itself? But, as Sartre puts it: 'To this question [phenomenological] ontology can not reply, for the problem here is to explain an *event*, not to describe the structures of a being.'[9] Despite this injunction, Sartre engages with this metaphysical question on two occasions in *Being and*

Nothingness: firstly in chapter one of part two, on the 'Immediate Structures of the For-itself', and again in the final conclusion.

For anyone familiar with the structure of the for-itself, in *Being and Nothingness*, the discussion of the emergence of the for-itself from the in-itself appears strange. Sartre consistently refers to this upsurge as a project of the in-itself, as an attempt to remove contingency from its being through an attempt at self-foundation.[10] This language, which attributes an effort to the in-itself, results in the in-itself realising its singular possibility in the upsurge of the for-itself: 'Nothingness is the peculiar possibility of being and its unique possibility.'[11] What is strange is that this seems in conflict with Sartre's own discussion of possibility as belonging solely to the for-itself, in the structures of desire and lack that form the heart of the nihilating process of freedom. For Sartre, 'desire is a lack of being', and human freedom strives to satisfy this lack by seeking the fullness of being of the in-itself, that is to be what it is, to coincide with itself.[12] What is the nature of this desire at the heart of the in-itself? Sartre is forced to refer to this as an absolute event; there is no mechanism within the in-itself that can lead to this upsurge. The in-itself is pure positivity, absolutely full and without even the 'tiniest crack through which nothingness might slip in'.[13]

Sartre's suggestion is that somehow the in-itself finds its independent yet contingent being intolerable, and it seeks self-foundation in order to be a necessary being. So, being in-itself does lack something, it lacks necessity. But the necessity born of the upsurge of the for-itself is also limited. Firstly, it is no longer independent; being for-itself depends on the in-itself. Secondly, the for-itself does not ground its own being, but only its nothingness.[14] The tension at the centre of *Being and Nothingness* remains that between the in-itself as independent and contingent (absolute contingency), the for-itself as dependent and necessary (relative necessity) and the impossibility of an in-and-for-itself, or God (absolute necessary being).[15] This impossibility is Sartre's own conclusion, a reading that renders the for-itself a failed project, which only intensifies the malady already present at the heart of contingent being in-itself.[16]

At the end of *Being and Nothingness* we are left with two forms of freedom: first, the familiar freedom of the for-itself, based on lack and the negating power of the imagination, and, second, a speculative form of freedom as the interruption of the in-itself by the upsurge of the for-itself. This second form is based on

the intolerable fullness or excess of the in-itself, it lacks nothing
except nothingness, the in-itself is the lack of lack; this Lacanian
terminology will be explicitly adopted by Badiou. Sartre does not
want to recognise two radically different conceptions of freedom,
noting how if we map the freedom of the for-itself onto the in-
itself this leads to a contradiction, as it presupposes that the in-
itself is already consciousness, that is it is already a for-itself.[17] In
the end, Sartre puts a limit on our phenomenological ontological
speculation:

> Ontology will therefore limit itself to declaring that *everything takes*
> *place as if* the in-itself in a project to found itself gave itself the modi-
> fication of the for-itself. It is up to metaphysics to form the *hypotheses*
> which will allow us to conceive of this process as the absolute event
> [of the upsurge of the for-itself] which comes to crown the individual
> venture which is the existence of being.[18]

The key phrase here is 'as if', forever putting out of reach any
experience of this grounding event.

The problem with this analysis is that the metaphysical speculation is focused too intently on the big picture. Sartre's desire
to affirm our individual freedom and independence makes him
naturally opposed to any pantheistic or pan-psychic claims about
matter, or the in-itself, having an inherent unity, consciousness or
freedom. Although we might never experience the prehistoric and
primordial contingency of the in-itself, we may, nonetheless, experience situations in which my objectification and alienation lead to
an intense experience not unlike the intolerable contingency of the
original in-itself. This is precisely the move that Sartre will make
in the *Critique of Dialectical Reason*.

The *Critique of Dialectical Reason* and the Fused Group

In the *Critique of Dialectical Reason* Sartre abandons the conflict model of intersubjective experience. Instead he focuses on
reciprocity, a relation that can have both positive and negative
determinations and which lies at the heart of all human relations.[19]
Conflict is now a consequence of the contingent circumstances of
scarcity rather than a fundamental ontological relation.[20]

This new understanding of reciprocity has four aspects, all of which conform to Sartre's understanding of a for-itself working towards its own goal or project. First, the Other is a means to the extent that I am a means: the Other is their own means towards their own project, just as I am my own means towards my own project. Second, in integrating the Other as an object into my own project, I also recognise them as working toward their own project; they resist appropriation in a different way to a simple object. Third, I am aware, therefore, of the reversal of this second position, I am integrated as an object into the project of the Other. Fourth, and finally, the previous two stages are realised simultaneously as two aspects of my action, or praxis, as a whole, not as sequential moments.[21]

On this model, reciprocity spans a range of intensive degrees, from mutual antagonism, competition and conflict, through exchange and cooperation to, finally, a shared and common goal.[22] Alienation will be based on a growing asymmetry and irreversibility between the second and third aspects of reciprocity outlined above. In the liberated reciprocity of group action the other members of the group and I share the same project, there is an ideal symmetry and reversibility between appropriating the other as an object, a means to my own ends, and their appropriation of me as a means towards their ends, as these ends are the same. In the case of alienation I feel that my project is subordinated to the Other's project. This is what Sartre calls the inertia of the practico-inert situation, an alienation that increasingly makes it impossible for me to live as I choose.[23]

Although the majority of relations of reciprocity fall somewhere in the middle, between a conflict and competition for resources due to scarcity and mutual collaboration and exchange, Sartre's interest lies in the extremes. Sartre wants to understand how groups are formed, but these ideal states of reciprocity cannot be reached through the mechanisms of serial collective existence, which Sartre calls the constituent dialectic.[24] Group formation is never the result of a slow considered evolution or development; it cannot be produced through increasing levels of cooperation and integration between individuals.[25] The relation between any particular set of individuals is always objectified by an external third party, for example a pair of builders cooperatively wield a two-man saw toward a common end, but their labour and relationship is objectified by the commercial interests of the building company, present in the form of a foreman.[26] No matter how hard we work, or how well integrated our circuits of reciprocity may be, eventually these relations escape us in the objectifying gaze of an external third party.[27] The collective can only manage to internalise the third party and form a group, a perfect coordination of its members, if there is no external third party. This can only happen when the external third party changes its relation to the serial collective of individuals, when it ceases to exploit them as if they were objects and attempts to actually reduce them to objects; this is the act of violence that threatens to kill or eliminate the collective.[28] The threat of violence is only a necessary condition for group formation, not a sufficient one. The reaction of the threatened individuals is as likely to be disorganised panic as much as an organised group resistance.[29] Sartre describes this feeling of ultimate objectification, the threat of death, as the impossibility of impossibility:

> The transformation therefore occurs when impossibility itself becomes impossible, or when the synthetic event reveals that the impossibility of change is an impossibility of life. The direct result of this is to make *the impossibility of change* the very object which has to be transcended if life is to continue.[30]

The impossibility of living as I choose is the experience of serial existence, alienation and exploitation in the practico-inert; the impossibility of this impossibility is the threat of death, the threat of actually being reduced to an object. In this instant the gathering of individual for-itselfs has a window directly onto being in-itself: 'There exists *at least one case* where we experience absolute exteriority within interiority . . . violent death.'[31] But just as this threat attempts to make our humanity impossible, it also dissolves the difference between a human and non-human threat:

> Through the pitiless necessity of his death-agony, a traveller lost in the desert experiences the non-humanity of the Universe, and thereby the transcendent limit of the human adventure manifests itself to him in its full horror, as his impossibility of being a man. But an insurgent – arrested by men, sentenced and kept in custody by men, and knowing that other men will put him to death – grasps no differently . . . the impossibility, for himself and those he was seeking to deliver, of living and of being a man.[32]

In response to being targeted for elimination, actual objectification, the group responds by treating the threat as inhuman, it can no longer be an Other, an objectifying third party. The only others are now my fellow members within our gathering, each is subject to the same threat, without discrimination, and our resistance to this threat is the same, our action becomes coordinated and the group is formed.[33]

This is why group freedom cannot be a progressive achievement, it can only occur under circumstances of extreme oppression and objectification. The formation of the group in the moment of the Apocalypse is a radical reversal, from the limit of determined objectification to free subjectification. This leads Sartre to say that freedom experiences a sudden resurrection in the fused group: a sudden reversal, from its paradoxical moment of minimal intensity/inexistence to its maximal intensity in the group.[34]

Two Types of Freedom and the Super-Organism

Again, although Sartre will resist the reading, there appear to be two types of freedom, just as in *Being and Nothingness*, where there was a contrast between the freedom of the for-itself based on lack, and the speculative account of the absolute event of the upsurge of the for-itself from the in-itself, a moment of freedom based on a lack of lack. In the *Critique of Dialectical Reason* we have the constituent dialectic, the alienated freedom/existence of the individual for-itself, and the constituted dialectic of group freedom/existence, born from a moment of intolerable contingency and objectification. Just as Sartre blocks the discussion of the absolute event in *Being and Nothingness*, as metaphysical speculation, he also immediately closes down any radical discussion of group freedom even as he introduces it: 'This new dialectic, in which freedom and necessity are one, is not a new incarnation of the transcendental dialectic: it is a human construction whose sole agents are individual men as free activities.'[35]

The incarnation of the transcendental dialectic is precisely the absolute event of the upsurge of the for-itself from the in-itself, and Sartre is keen not to confer a similar stature to the event of the Apocalypse that produces the group. Sartre discusses the fused group, but spends very little time on the actual moment of Apocalypse itself, which he problematically admits is neither series nor group.[36] Sartre resists a direct comparison between group

formation and the upsurge of the for-itself because both the group
and the serial collective preceding it must be intelligible to each
other. The individual free for-itself has access to both its alienated
serial existence and its liberated group existence; it is the continuity that provides experiential access to both these situations. Sartre
maintains, in *Being and Nothingness* and now in the *Critique*,
that the radical incarnation of the for-itself from out of the in-
itself leaves no such access available. The for-itself cannot know
the intolerable contingency suffered by the in-itself, but can only
speculate, whereas the group can know their own objectification
and alienation prior to the Apocalypse. For Sartre, we as individuals would have no access to the intentions or project of such a
group subject, or super-organism. Hypothetically, Sartre asserts:

> And if it [the group] succeeded in *becoming an organism*, the organic
> unity of its action (assuming a hyper-conscious unity etc.) would
> be different in kind and would have a different intelligibility: each
> organism might have some comprehension of the hyper-organism as
> a structure connected to the *whole*, but this would be very different
> from ours.[37]

The hyper-organism haunts the group as a regulatory idea of what
its process of totalisation aims toward but can never achieve.[38]
This can be seen in the way that groups try to mimic organisms, as
a group develops it becomes organised and divided into a number
of specific roles and tasks, but this specialisation can never achieve
the natural specialisation and division of labour found within an
organism.

But this already goes too far. For Badiou, the group subject is
already there in the fused group; Sartre's problems begin when
he thinks that the fused group cannot be sustained, leading to the
pledge and the statutory group (TS 299). For Sartre, this is the
moment that the group becomes self-reflective, for the first time
it '*posits itself for itself*'.[39] This occurs when the initial threat that
provoked the Apocalypse of group fusion subsides, the group
survives the initial onslaught and repels its enemy. But the group
was nothing more than this action, a pure praxis, coordinated and
made homogenous by the threat: a pure unconditioned activity. If
the group is not to disperse and disappear, then the external threat
must be interiorised and perpetuated, most commonly by positing
the threat of the return of the enemy.[40] This is the first condition

of the group, the pledge and the beginning of fraternity terror, necessary in order to maintain integration beyond the initial intense moment of fusion.

For Sartre, this conditioning of the group always fails to capture the unconditioned unity and coordination of the fused group. The condition is taken up within each individual in the constituted unity of the group, but there is no way to know or guarantee that each individual will take it up in the same way: a possible but imperfect unity. The ideal situation is that the group forms a new constituent being, the organic unity of a hyper-organism, which need only take up the condition in one way: an impossible but perfect unity. As the group persists and develops, adding further conditions and dividing into specialised functional parts, this disconnect between the actual and ideal intensifies. Each individual's perspective on the whole becomes less likely to agree with other members of the group, or reflect any unified vision of the whole. This reaches a tipping point when the group itself becomes treated as a thing, perpetuated for its own sake, instead of existing for some shared goal or project; the institution is born and group existence lapses back into serial existence.[41] The group moves from an initial unconditioned state, where the group has no substantial reality as it is nothing more than a struggle for survival in the face of an immediate threat, through increasingly conditioned states where the substantial reality of the group grows through the multiplication of conditions and functions that the group embodies in its increasing organisation. Finally, the unifying project of the group is lost and the perpetuation of itself becomes its sole goal in the form of perpetuating its institutional organs.

Badiou will adamantly agree with Sartre that we cannot have a group subject in the sense of a hyper-organism, but he thinks that there is more to the idea of a group subject motivated by unconditioned activity than Sartre allows for in the brief existence of the Apocalypse and fused group. In fact, the theme of unconditioned activity, as the hallmark of subjective process, is central to all Badiou's later work, informally in *Theory of the Subject* and then formally in *Being and Event*, where the concept of the non-constructible is used to bring mathematical rigour to the unconditioned. This move on Badiou's part is a move to affirm the second form of freedom, which creates a subject in response to a chance event. This, for Sartre, is always hypothetical or impossible, existing only at the margins of human existence. Badiou also rejects Sartre's first form of freedom, a commitment to freedom as the negating power of the imagination. It is the recovery of this simple conscious subject, through the introduction of conditions into the fused group, which ruins group existence, limiting us to the narrow alternatives of either an imperfect group of individuals or an impossible group as hyper-organism. The existence of the fused or unconditioned group must be extended beyond the finite bounds of its appearance and first struggle.

Badiou and the Unconditioned Subject

Badiou claims that *Theory of the Subject* is an attempt to extend Lacan's theory of the subject, focusing on the underdeveloped concepts of justice and courage, to complement Lacan's developed theory based on the superego and anxiety (TS 155–6). But it is equally a development of Sartre's theory of the fused group, which gains its homogeneity through an anger and courage to fight to the end, warding off the anxiety of defeat and indecision.[42] This can be seen more clearly in Badiou's discussion of the moment of subjectification as a moment of revolt, which draws on many of the same Marxist and political themes as Sartre:

> When the popular insurrection breaks out, it is never because the calculable moment of this insurrection has arrived. It is because it is no longer worth doing anything else except to insurrect. This is what Lenin said: there is revolution when 'those from below' do not want to continue as before, and when it is everywhere imposingly evident that it is worth more to die standing than to live lying down. (TS 257)

This description echoes Sartre's Apocalypse, an incalculable and radical reversal, resulting in the upsurge of freedom in the face of intolerable oppression. The moment of decision is forced; provoked by a threat that does not allow for reflection or calculation, making haste an intrinsic part of subjectification (TS 256–8).

Theory of the Subject is not a systematic work in the way that *Being and Event* and *Logics of Worlds* are, but is a collection of seminars held between 1975 and 1979. The book unfolds a developing argument about subjectivity, with a constant mutation and creation of technical terms and ideas (TS 169). But despite this openness, a set of terms and concepts does begin to solidify: 'There are four fundamental concepts (anxiety, courage, justice, superego), two temporalities (subjectivization, subjective process), and two modalities: ψ, which links anxiety to the superego, and the mode α, which links courage to justice' (TS 258).[43]

Rather than grapple with the dynamic nature of *Theory of the Subject*, I will restrict myself to giving an account of these four terms and their relations, especially the two modalities ψ and α. These relate to the two types of freedom that I have been developing throughout this essay, and it will also shed light on Badiou's interest in, and frustration with, Sartre. Toward the end of *Theory of the Subject* Badiou explicitly tackles Sartre's *Critique of Dialectical Reason*. He states that Sartre's work is a failure as it activates the imaginary functions of dogmatism and scepticism, which trace lines from courage and justice (the fused group, or at least the moment of Apocalypse) to the superego and anxiety (the statutory group) (TS 297, 299–300). These are the diagonals of the imaginary, which transform the modality α into the modality ψ (TS 299). Ultimately, for Badiou, the true subject will be woven from both modalities, as the subject cannot be simply reduced to either one or the other; he calls this ideal process confidence (TS 330–1).

For Badiou, every situation already labours under a law of lack or, more specifically, a lack of being (TS 133). The individual that already inhabits this structured situation conforms to one of the two stages of Lacan's development of the subject, which also bears a striking similarity to Sartre's for-itself (TS 133, 138). We have already seen how the for-itself, as nothingness, clearly lacks being. From Lacan and Badiou's perspective, Sartre's being for-itself squanders the novelty of its non-coincidence by reducing it solely to the ego or consciousness (BE 3).[44] Sartre sees lack and desire in the conscious ego, or for-itself, as its fundamental structure, rather than as a completable incompleteness, leading to his constant rejection of the possibility of a being in-and-for-itself. This lack of coincidence is not something that can be overcome or fulfilled, rather the for-itself can only recognise its own projects, a succession of particular desires, a lack that once satisfied immediately gives rise to another. It can only speculate that it is itself the product of a different lack: the upsurge of the for-itself from the in-itself. Sartre excludes the foundation of the for-itself as an experience for the for-itself, and therefore the for-itself is limited to experiencing lack as possibility. This limitation is clear from Sartre's position that the in-itself only appears as phenomena to the for-itself, even while admitting that it has a pure material existence, independent from the for-itself. The full potential of the in-itself is not realised in the structured space, which recognises only the divide between the actual and the possible.

This is the difference between the lack of being and the being of lack, which represents, for Badiou, two stages in Lacan's own theory of the subject (TS 133). As such, Lacan represents a distinct step beyond Sartre in his formulation of the subject. Sartre, in positing the dialectical dualism between being and nothingness, neglects that in doing so he also splits off the full potential of the in-itself, which becomes inaccessible to the for-itself. Building on Lacan, Badiou wants to place this three-way split at the heart of the subject between the actual, the possible and the impossible (TS 135). This excluded non-being, or impossibility, is Badiou's outplace, in contrast to the structured space, or splace (TS 10–11). But this excess, though explicitly excluded from the regulated economy of the actual and the possible, is still active in a clandestine manner. It bubbles beneath the surface and is capable of rupturing and destroying the current status quo:

> To define the subject as 'the metonymy of the lack of being' only identifies half of its essence, the other half being *that which gives being to the lack*, that is, destruction, which is irreducible to the act of pure substitution. Thus the subject, as the placed product of the law of lack, brings out a 'more-than-real' in its domain through which lack itself, in the tracks of destruction, comes to lack. (TS 141)

The excess as excluded and absent from the structured space is that which makes that regulated space possible. When it interrupts this structure, through its sudden upsurge, it destroys the law that is currently in place. Every subject, for Lacan and Badiou, encompasses these two sides: it is founded in a destructive moment, an event in which the old subject and order are destroyed, leading to a new split between a structured situation and an excluded excess. Every subject has two effects or processes: subjectification, which is initially the destruction of a previous formation, which then becomes the excluded excess that makes the regulated functioning of a new subject possible (this is its unconscious aspect); and the subjective process, which is the regulated functioning of the subject in a structured situation (this is its conscious aspect). Sartre's subject is, according to this model, one-sided, being totally committed to only a conscious subject. The subject is born from the decision that something happened in the moment of subjectification, and the nature of its reaction to this event is its subjective process.

Badiou's Break with Lacan: ψ and α

Having given a basic account of Badiou's two subjective effects, it is time to focus on his critique of Lacan's subject and his own alternative. This is grounded in the difference between the two modalities of ψ and α, and their different treatment of the destructive upsurge of the excess.

Taken separately, each modality can be viewed as a form of subjectivity, comprising a moment of radical punctuation and interruption of the status quo, the subjectification of decision that introduces a destructive excess and a means of accommodating that excess through a new subjective process. The difference between the two arises from how they treat this excess, and the nature of the change that this produces. The modality ψ corresponds to a transgression that sees the current law destroyed, but the idea of law in general is only suspended, since anxiety and the superego will eventually replace the old law with a new law: law as non-law (TS 145, 175). The recomposition that ψ enacts will, eventually, be a conditioned recomposition: a new law succeeds the old law. The modality α also enacts a destruction of the current law, but it permanently suspends the idea of law in favour of a free expression of force as an unconditioned recomposition: non-law as law (TS 175). This modality expresses courage and justice.

Badiou names these two modalities in terms of an algebraic and topological response for the modalities ψ and α respectively. For Badiou, the algebraic focuses on elements of a set, while the topological focuses on the subsets of a set (TS 211). Badiou can then play on the difference between a set's elements and its subsets, a concept central to *Being and Event*. The set of all subsets (the power set) of a set always has more elements than the initial set; this, for Badiou, is the source of an inexhaustible excess (TS 217). If the initial set has n elements then its power set has 2^n elements, and if n is finite then the excess is calculable within the given framework, but if n is infinite, such as ω, the set of all natural numbers, then the excess is no longer calculable within the given framework and a decision is necessary regarding the magnitude of this excess. To avoid getting bogged down in a technical discussion, I will relate these ideas to the concepts that I have been developing throughout this essay.

The first response is to deny that this excess introduces anything new, to try and accommodate it within the given framework: this is to limit the subsets to constructible subsets only. Here, only subsets that satisfy a finite set of conditions are allowed. The excess is managed under the old law.

The second response is to acknowledge that the excess is in excess of the current situation and law: there are some subsets that are non-constructible within the given situation. These subsets do not satisfy any set of conditions of the given situation, but a new law can be established that will accommodate this excess. This is the modality ψ, or, in set theory, the introduction of new higher cardinal axioms that can be used to construct and control the excess.[45] The non-constructible is made constructible and the unconditioned becomes conditioned. This is a repetition of a law-governed situation, a repetition that can be repeated, as there is no consistent totality of all sets, so a consistent extension of a given situation can always be made (TS 263–4).

The third response maintains the unconditioned excess, in the form of non-constructible sets, without giving in to the desire for a new transcendent law that would condition and eliminate this excess. This is the modality α, and Badiou finds his prime example in the technique of forcing introduced by Paul Cohen to prove the independence of the continuum hypothesis (TS 271–4). The unconditioned is no longer just a temporary feature of a situation, rupturing and interrupting a process, only to disappear in a recomposition that either regulates or expels the unconditioned. It remains operative in the recomposition precisely as unconditioned.

Although this is not the more considered use of set theory used in *Being and Event*, it is already supplying Badiou with the formal rigour to be able to point to the actual and continuing role of the unconditioned, or non-constructible, within a situation. This is important for working out how freedom appears within these situations, either as a self-sufficient power embodied within a subject, or as a decision in the face of an incalculable chance event that something happened: does the free subject give in and become subjected to a new law or does it respect the unconditioned nature of the event?

Badiou thinks that Lacan favours the algebraic over the topological, and that his subject is either explicitly operating in the mode ψ or, if it is operating in the mode α, then this is only temporary and it will necessarily lapse back into the mode ψ (TS 239–44). Courage and justice will always collapse into anxiety and the superego: Badiou calls this model the saturation of the subject by the imaginary functions of dogmatism and scepticism (TS 297–9). The ultimate return of the algebraic repetition of the structured space is inevitable, the topological interruption is only temporary: α gives way to ψ which finally establishes a new situation, or splace, under a new law. Badiou wants to resist this particular braiding of the two modalities for the same reason that Sartre would: the dominance of the mode ψ, in the group political context to which Badiou elevates it, is tantamount to positing the group as a transcendent hyper-organism. The disruption experienced through the upsurge of the excess is deferred to some transcendent unifying power outside of the current situation. That which appears as unintelligible within the current situation is intelligible to something outside of this situation; the immediate subject is dissolved as it submits and is incorporated into a new subject. Badiou, echoing Sartre, will want to affirm that whatever happens as the result of an event is accessible and intelligible within the immanent resources of the current situation. Where he differs will be in his affirmation of this intelligibility as unknowable, that is, as not conforming to any condition. The imaginary, through its exclusion of the full power of the real, seeks to understand the freedom experienced in the event as a conscious phenomenon, this reduces freedom from chance to the illusion of conscious activity in the ego.[46]

Sartre also does not escape from the reductive power of the imaginary or the imagination. From the analysis in the first part of this essay we can see how his persistence to hold onto the for-itself ruins the moment of the Apocalypse, such that even the group in fusion is already tainted by a reduction of the freedom experienced in this moment of pure chance, or contingency, to being dominated by consciousness, and never having been anything but a conscious action. This is Badiou's own criticism of Sartre: even if we are generous enough to grant that the fused group operates in the modality α, the for-itself soon returns and reasserts itself, saturating the process with its imaginary function, the illusion of consciousness as the free power of the negating imagination, and pulling the group back towards the modality ψ through organisation and institutionalisation (TS 299–300).

We can no more understand the fragile nature of the subject by refusing to shift from its current configuration (Sartre) as we can if we simply posit the subject as prey to a succession of egoic conscious forms (Lacan). For Badiou, the most powerful form of the subject resides between these two positions. Sartre and Lacan are beholden to the power of the imaginary. In Sartre it is locked within the for-itself as, literally, the imagination, which is the negating power of nothingness: freedom is not chance, it is the power/activity of consciousness. For Lacan, the imaginary reduces the unconditioned to the conditioned within the illusion of consciousness: freedom is a response to a chance event, but this element of chance, the unconditioned, is retroactively made to give way in a new consciousness. Freedom can never maintain the element of chance in the event, in the form of a continuing explicit functioning of the unconditioned.

Even Badiou, in *Theory of the Subject*, has trouble realising this goal. The subject cannot simply affirm the modality α and ignore ψ – this would simply reverse Sartre's position. The destruction of the law in the modality α is too extreme. If left unchecked it would simply reduce everything to an unconditioned chaos; it would have no context in which to stand, no conditioned framework against which to affect its novelty as unconditioned. We have seen how this context, or continuity, against which change can be measured and made intelligible is for Sartre the for-itself, and for Lacan it is the repetition of the same structure, the excluded real and the economy of the symbolic and imaginary. What provides this continuity for Badiou? In *Theory of the Subject* Badiou calls this subjective confidence the interlacing of α and ψ in such a way that ψ constantly intervenes in the process α to regulate it and guarantee that its change is real change (TS 311, 316).

Courage and justice are not without anxiety and the superego: the two strands are related. Justice invokes anxiety, but it must resist it: 'Justice is escorted by a vacillation of certainties . . . "There has never been any rule": such is the antagonizing diagonal fiction by which justice wards off the restorationist drives that are polarized by anxiety' (TS 300). Courage, like anxiety, is a break with the status quo, it is a liquidation of the current law, but anxiety leads to the superego, which destroys this destruction in the name of a new law, while courage entails justice which preserves the destruction (TS 300). At every moment the subjective process of justice must ward off anxiety as the desire for certainty and the fear of following justice wherever it may lead. Justice must continue to proceed in a lawless and unconditioned recomposition; it destroys not only the initial law governing the situation but also every law that anxiety presents. This structure allows Badiou to counter Sartre's criticism of group subjectivity: the group of individuals who compose the subject of courage and justice are a group subject but it is not a hyper-organism. There is no appeal to an external unity – the constant process of warding off the effects of anxiety and the superego provide this unity. Also, this process is potentially ongoing. There is no final goal for the subject of courage and justice, no finitude to its project, and it can therefore avoid the pessimism attributed to the finitude of unified group action in Sartre's fused group (TS 330).

What is missing from Badiou's model of subjective confidence is still any continuity or background against which the novelty of the subject can be measured. His focus at this stage is fixed too firmly on the destructive nature of the subject of α, preserving a constant destruction and warding off any stability or establishing any future law. The constant invocation and resistance to ψ cannot provide the background continuity, because here ψ is providing a succession of possible recompositions, which α constantly negates, rather than a single continuous threat. We can only see how Badiou overcomes this by briefly looking towards *Being and Event* and the adoption of set theory as ontology rather than just as an illustrative example. There are two key points that I want to conclude with. First, Badiou gives a formal account of the subject of courage and justice by returning to Cohen's theory of forcing. This theory incorporates non-constructible, or unconditioned, sets into a situation in what is called a generic extension of the situation. These sets remain unconditioned and have their specific generic quality by partially satisfying, but ultimately negating, every given condition of a situation; there is no substantial quality in itself to being unconditioned aside from not satisfying any of the possible conditions of the situation (BE 371).[47] This is the fully-fledged subject of *Being and Event*, which codifies this ability to take up the unconditioned trace of the event and preserve its unconditioned nature through the Axiom of Choice.[48] This axiom finally gives us a formal definition of what we mean by freedom as chance or, more precisely, the ability to affirm and remain faithful to a chance event.

Second, by fully taking on set theory as his ontology Badiou is able to gain the necessary background stability and continuity necessary in order to demonstrate that the event, and subject, introduces real measurable change into a situation. This absolute background is grounded in Badiou's definition of natural multiples and situations, as opposed to historical multiples and situations. Badiou notes that natural multiples have an absolute structure that is 'indifferent to the situation in which the multiple is presented' (BE 133). Badiou contrasts this to an evental site, the point of uptake necessary for a subject to transform a historical situation:

> One should note that the concept of an evental site, unlike that of a natural multiplicity, is neither intrinsic nor absolute. A multiple could quite easily be singular [a site] in one situation . . . yet normal in another situation. In contrast, a natural multiple, which is normal . . . conserves these qualities wherever it appears. Nature is absolute, historicity relative. (BE 176)

Badiou is now able to use these natural multiples as a stable framework which cannot be destroyed or altered through the activity of the subject against which the change that the subject does introduce can be contrasted as real change and novelty. This ontology is the final step, allowing Badiou to reject the subject, especially the Sartrean subject, as a starting point, or as a point of experiential continuity necessary for confirming the difference between the liberated group and their prior alienation.

Badiou is keen to affirm his fidelity to Sartre, but this is a fidelity to Sartre's political works and his philosophy of decision rather than the autonomous existential phenomenology of *Being and Nothingness*. This can be seen especially in Badiou's somewhat narrow characterisation of Sartre in *Logics of Worlds*, where he is reduced simply to being a philosopher of the decision, of the yes or no (LW 404–5). In this essay I have traced how Badiou takes the inspiration he finds in Sartre, in the form of the fused group and the moment of decision, and separates it off from Sartre's underlying ontology. This fidelity to an idea in Sartre's work allows Badiou to develop an optimistic theory of the subject and group action, something that would have been impossible for Sartre himself.

Notes

1. At the conference *Paul, Political Fidelity and the Philosophy of Alain Badiou: A Discussion of the Incident at Antioch*, held at the University of Glasgow on 13–14 February 2009, Badiou commented, during an interview, that he had been inspired to write both novels and plays in emulation of Sartre.

2. Peter Hallward, *Badiou: A Subject to Truth* (Minneaolis, MN: Minnesota University Press, 2003), p. 43.

3. Jean-Paul Sartre, *Critique of Dialectical Reason: Volume 1*, trans. Alan Sheridan-Smith, ed. Jonathan Rée (London: Verso, 1991), p. 401.

4. Hallward, *Badiou*, p. xxxii.

5. Sartre, *Critique of Dialectical Reason 1*, pp. 342, 345, 348, 516, 537–8. Jean-Paul Sartre, *Critique of Dialectical Reason: Volume 2*, trans. Quintin Hoare (London: Verso, 2006), pp. 305, 330.

6. My translation.

7. Hallward, *Badiou*, p. xxxii. Peter Hallward is the first person to note this as a key aspect that Badiou takes and modifies from Sartre.

8. Jean-Paul Sartre, *Being and Nothingness: An Essay on Phenomenological Ontology*, trans. Hazel E. Barnes (London: Routledge, 1969), p. 622.

9. Ibid., p. 620, my emphasis.

10. Ibid., pp. 79, 84, 621.

11. Ibid., p. 79.

12. Ibid., p. 89.

13. Ibid., p. 74.

14. Ibid., p. 94.

15. Ibid., p. 623.

16. Ibid., p. 621.

17. Ibid.

18. Ibid.

19. Sartre, *Critique of Dialectical Reason 1*, pp. 111, 113.

20. Ibid., p. 13.

21. Ibid., pp. 112–13.

22. Ibid., p. 113.

23. Ibid., p. 349.

24. Ibid., pp. 342, 349.

25. Ibid., p. 395.

26. Ibid., p. 114.

27. Ibid., p. 115.

28. Ibid., p. 401.
29. Ibid., p. 404, n. 16.
30. Ibid., p. 350.
31. Sartre, *Critique of Dialectical Reason* 2, p. 310.
32. Ibid., pp. 313–14.
33. *Critique of Dialectical Reason* 1, pp. 402–3.
34. Ibid., p. 401.
35. Ibid., p. 342.
36. Ibid., p. 357.
37. Ibid., p. 538.
38. Ibid., pp. 538–9.
39. Ibid., p. 414.
40. Ibid., p. 413.
41. Ibid., pp. 603, 606.
42. Ibid., p. 404.
43. A detailed table of these concepts can also be found earlier at TS (175).
44. Jacques Lacan, *The Seminars of Jacques Lacan: Book II: The Ego in Freud's Theory and in the Technique of Psychoanalysis*, trans. Sylvana Tomaselli, ed. Jacques-Alain Miller (New York: W. W. Norton, 1991), p. 44.
45. Michael Potter, *Set Theory and Its Philosophy* (Oxford: Oxford University Press, 2004), pp. 209–10.
46. Lacan, *The Seminars of Jacques Lacan: Book II*, pp. 52–3.
47. Alain Badiou, 'Gilles Deleuze, *The Fold: Leibniz and the Baroque*', trans. T. Sowley, in Constantin V. Boundas and Dorothea Olkowski (eds), *Gilles Deleuze and the Theatre of Philosophy* (New York and London: Routledge, 1994), p. 66.
48. I discuss the importance of the Axiom of Choice for Badiou in detail in my essay 'The limits of the subject in Badiou's *Being and Event*', in Paul Ashton, A. J. Bartlett and Justin Clemens (eds), *The Praxis of Alain Badiou* (Melbourne: re.press, 2006), pp. 71–101.

12

Badiou's Relation to Heidegger in *Theory of the Subject*

Graham Harman

Badiou's references to Heidegger are surprisingly infrequent, given his obvious admiration for the great German thinker: 'Our epoch can be said to have been stamped and signed by the return of the question of Being. This is why it is dominated by Heidegger' (D 18). He does not build his philosophy atop Heidegger's own, as might fairly be said of other recent French thinkers such as Derrida, Levinas, Merleau-Ponty or Sartre. While Badiou's references to Heidegger are often tantalising, they are never quite central to his own ambitions, which emerge more explicitly in dialogue with Hegel and Lacan. At times his admiration for Heidegger resembles that of a jazz saxophonist for a jazz drummer: two performers working in the same idiom and sometimes able to collaborate, but generally incapable of direct technical influence.

It is interesting that this attitude is shared by Badiou's kindred spirit Slavoj Žižek, who also speaks admiringly of Heidegger without doing so frequently or centrally. We need only look at Žižek's jacket endorsement of Badiou's *Theory of the Subject*, which concludes enthusiastically as follows: '. . . you hold in your hands proof that philosophers of the status of Plato, Hegel, and Heidegger are still walking around today!' (TS dust jacket). Whether or not one agrees that Badiou belongs in such illustrious company, the point here is that Žižek takes it for granted that Heidegger does. In short, Badiou and Žižek (surely the world's most prominent living continental philosophers as of 2011) both salute Heidegger as the dominant thinker of the past century, while also showing little aspiration to follow in his lineage. This fact is so striking that it might even serve to guide all interpretations of Badiou and Žižek. Given that the major thinker of the twentieth century so clearly fascinates them, why does he matter so little for their own declared philosophical paths? Or is it really the case that he does matter so little to them?

The present article will consider this question only with respect to Badiou, and only in connection with his 1982 *Theory of the Subject*, the first of his three major systematic books so far (the others, of course, are *Being and Event* and *Logics of Worlds*). As with most thinkers of consequence, this first systematic effort already contains the major themes of Badiou's later and more emblematic works, and articulates them with an energetic youthful candour. Here as usual we find Badiou spending much more time on Hegel than Heidegger. In fact, Hegel is listed among those names so ubiquitous in *Theory of the Subject* that Badiou does not even bother listing them in the index (TS xl). By contrast, Heidegger is mentioned only three times, one of them a passing reference of little importance (TS 69). But the other two citations are of great interest. In the first, Badiou situates Heidegger's pivotal concept of the ontological difference amid the key ideas of *Theory of the Subject* (TS 7). In the second, Badiou claims that Heidegger wishes to put an end to 'the guarantee of consistency by the cause' (TS 234–5), a project endorsed by Badiou as well. At this point some interesting questions can be raised in connection with these passages: Is Badiou's interpretation of the ontological difference in Heidegger correct? What does it mean that Heidegger wishes to end 'the guarantee of consistency by the cause'? And more generally, what are the true points of congruence and tension between Heidegger and the Badiou of *Theory of the Subject*?

Hegel and the Ontological Difference

For Badiou (as for Žižek), the major partners for philosophical dialogue are Hegel and Lacan rather than Heidegger. In *Theory of the Subject* Badiou's attitude towards these partners is ambivalent, despite his admiration for both. At times he treats them as masters who saw everything essential in advance, while at other times he openly announces his deviation from them. The question for us is what role in such deviation can be ascribed to the silent background influence of Heidegger. In the present section I will consider this topic in connection with Hegel, and in the next section with Lacan.

In the opening pages of *Theory of the Subject*, Badiou claims that Hegel's dialectic is subtler than usually believed. 'There are two dialectical matrices in Hegel' (TS 3). We must take Lenin's hint, he says, and read Hegel as a good materialist. But Hegel is not just a materialist who happened to have a lamentable idealist side into which he accidentally stumbled. Instead, both the materialist and idealist sides belong to the dialectic itself: 'At the heart of the Hegelian dialectic we must disentangle two processes, two concepts of movement, and not just one proper system of becoming that would have been corrupted by a subjective system of knowing' (TS 3). The idealist dialectic gives us the Hegel of the textbooks; by means of alienation, an initially immediate term gives way to a movement of negativity before returning in higher, sublated form. But Badiou asserts that there is also a 'materialist' side of Hegel that operates according to 'a dialectical matrix whose operator is scission, and whose theme is that there is no unity that is not split. [Here] there is not the least bit of return into itself, nor any connection between the final and the inaugural' (TS 4). On the one hand, Badiou refers to the 'idealist propensity' of Hegel and describes his philosophy with mild sarcasm as a 'journey through the galleries of the One' (TS 4–5). On the other, Badiou asserts nonetheless that with the dialectic between something and something other,[1] Hegel is already aware of the never healed 'scission' in being that is the hallmark of Badiou's own position (TS 5). But if Hegel 'is right, as always', there are still 'all sorts of contortions on [his] part that serve to mask [his] recognition' of the fact that the dialectic must be based on the incurable Two rather than the unified One, and that scission rather than completion should be viewed as the true pillar of Hegelian philosophy (TS 4–5). If Hegel is always right, he never fully realises why.

In the famous beginning of Hegel's *Science of Logic*, being and nothing turn out to be mutually indistinguishable.[2] In their sameness they vanish into one another in the movement of becoming, though not because they are in any way different: 'Alterity has here no qualitative support' (TS 6). This 'indexical stasis' of contradiction gives us the same term twice: 'It is the same A twice named, twice placed. This will more than suffice for them to corrupt one another' (TS 6). But there is some ambiguity in Badiou's presentation of this point. The observation that there is no qualitative difference between being and nothing in Hegel would indeed yield the claim that we have A and then A once again, the same name twice. But although Badiou does put it this way more than once, his true interest lies not in such contradiction between A and another A, but rather in the 'constitutive scission' between any term A in its specific place and A 'in its pure, closed identity' (TS 6). Stated differently, what really fascinates Badiou is not the repetition of two indistinguishable As, but rather A considered in relation with the world and in independence of any such relation. In other words: 'the givenness of A as being-itself [splits] into: its pure being, A [and] its being-placed, A_p' (TS 7, punctuation modified). It is not a matter of two indistinguishable As, but of A in its own right and A for another.

Having told us that A splits into A and A_p, Badiou immediately adds a surprising parenthesis: 'Heidegger would say [that A splits] into its ontological being and its ontic being . . .' (TS 7). The reason for surprise is that Heidegger never sees himself as a Hegelian. Instead Hegel is treated, for all his greatness, as one of the most desolate thinkers of the forgetting of being, which for Heidegger means the reduction of being to presence. None of Heidegger's key terms for what being does – concealing, withdrawing, veiling, sheltering, preserving – could possibly be of interest to Hegel, for whom any supposed reality-in-itself is no better than an abstract exteriority produced in the heart of an internal movement. For Heidegger, Hegel's description of being as 'the indeterminate immediate' is not just a provisionally deficient opening move that is later redeemed in the subtly enfolded draperies of the *Logic*. Instead, it is a doomed approach from the start, since it reduces being to its series of manifestations for the logician who describes them. Stated in terms of the Badiouian scission between A and A_p, Heidegger would describe the Hegelian dialectic as unfolding entirely within the realm of A_p: being as placed or present with respect to something else, not being in its own right.

What then are we to make of Badiou's unlikely bundling of Hegel and Heidegger? One possibility is that Badiou is simply another Hegelian, blinded by the forgetting of being. Another is that Heidegger has merely reinvented the wheel, failing to understand that Hegel's dialectic has already done a sufficient job of undercutting presence. A third possibility is that Badiou mimics Heidegger without realising or admitting it. A fourth is that Badiou subtly draws on Heideggerian resources to escape Hegel's shadow, establishing a new philosophy somewhere between these two great predecessors. This question can be left to the end of the article; for now we will simply follow Badiou's model of scission and see where it leads.

For Hegel, 'something' always splits into 'something-for-itself' and 'something-for-other'. Badiou takes this for 'proof that in order to think anything at all, something no matter what, it must be split in two' (TS 6). Every thing is necessarily both A and A_p. Nonetheless, 'what Hegel does not state clearly' (TS 7) is that the contrary of A is not A_p, but P itself. The thing is not contradicted by another thing, but by the fact that it is placed anywhere at all. To give one of Badiou's own political examples, the contrary of the proletariat is not the bourgeoisie but rather the bourgeois *world*. Here Badiou coins the portmanteau word 'splace' [*esplace*, or space/place] to designate any thing's structural-relational place in a situation, and 'outplace' [*horlieu*] for its non-placed reality outside the situation. These poles are not to be treated in isolation. If we attempt to assert the 'lost purity' of an outplace outside all places, this is just as bad as the opposite tactic of asserting that everything is thoroughly determined by its current situation (TS 11). Badiou calls the former the 'Leftist deviation' (Deleuze in philosophy, China's Lin Biao in politics) and the latter the 'Rightist deviation' (Lévi-Strauss in philosophy, the revisionist French Communist Party in politics). Thinkers of flux and desire can no more assert the purity of A than structuralists can insist on the dominance of A_p. Things are neither entirely inscribed in a given place nor liberated into a placeless nowhere. Instead, in overtly Hegelian fashion, Badiou proclaims that the thing is *determined* by the indexical effect that place has upon it, while the resulting determinate thing is *limited* by an indeterminate excess capable of subverting it. This two-faced reality of each thing is nicely expressed in 1982 by a pair of terms familiar to readers of Badiou's 1988 classic *Being and Event*: namely, 'belonging' and 'inclusion'. Belonging refers to elements explicitly contained in the structure of a situation, while inclusion is a matter of parts exceeding the literal terms of that situation even while pertaining to it in some way. As Badiou puts it: 'Everything that belongs to a whole is an obstacle to this whole insofar as it is included in it' (TS 12, emphasis removed).

The contradiction between A and P is never symmetrical, since 'one of the terms sustains a relation of inclusion to the other' (TS 13). Stated differently: 'It is A that is indexed in A_p according to P. The inverse makes no sense' (TS 13). Badiou claims that Hegel misses this asymmetry and always returns to the idea of a whole that includes both terms. Hegelian circularity needs to be reworked as a periodicity or spiralling movement in which nothing ever returns to the same place without a difference. We find an example of Hegel's circularity in his treatment of Christian doctrine, a treatment that Badiou otherwise deeply admires. If God is A or the outplace, and the world is P or the splace, God is indexed in the incarnation as A_p, or father-placed-in-the-finite (the Son). As we know, this principle was established as orthodoxy in the Nicene Creed. It is flouted by the Arian heresy in which Christ has no divine transcendence but is purely immanent in the world ('Right deviation'), and Docetism in which the worldly suffering of Christ is treated as illusory ('Left deviation'). Badiou favours the orthodoxy over the deviations, but laments nonetheless that the passion of Christ followed by the resurrection merely leads us to a heaven with 'a God who reconciles in himself . . . the finite and the infinite' (TS 16). Here Badiou proposes dividing Hegel yet again, offering a materialist periodisation in place of idealist circularity (TS 18). In circularity 'the outplace finds a space in the place' (TS 20), without excess or remainder. What is called for instead is a principle of 'the irreducibility of action' (TS 19), and of 'discontinuity, even [of] failure' (TS 20). The Bolshevik revolution of 1917 is not a mere come-full-circle return of the Paris Commune, but a periodisation of it, which 'Lenin seals by dancing in the snow when power is held in Moscow for one day longer than had been the case in Paris in 1871' (TS 20). To escape the circularity, one of the terms of the new contradiction needs 'to become the bearer of the intelligibility of the preceding sequence' (TS 20), and this is how 'it comes about as subject' (TS 20). Here the decisive break with Hegel is announced: 'Now that Hegel has been given the proper salute . . . we must think periodization through to the end' (TS 21).

The key to periodicity lies in distinguishing between the One and the Whole: 'in this gap lies the whole question of the Subject' (TS 30). This occurs by breaking free from structure towards something outside the splace that is admittedly difficult to express, given that 'every discourse fixes the splace of the very thing that it passes over in silence' (TS 31). Consider the supposed case of the duality between active and passive, which Badiou views as mistaken. The idea of an actively malevolent government abusing a passively innocent populace is said to be the root of an 'anti-repressive' humanitarian politics that Badiou associates with the 'indignant petit bourgeois' (TS 31). For Badiou this sells short the genuine outplace represented by the masses. Insofar as this anti-repressive vision interprets the masses as docile clay in the cruel hands of the state, 'the splace . . . [still] fixes the place of the outplace' (TS 31). Nonetheless, this correlation between the active and passive terms not only marks an imprisonment in the structural conditions of the splace; for Badiou, it is also the gateway to a deeper speculative profundity. For even though the structural dialectic tolerates nothing but 'vacillation' (TS 34) or correlation between two terms, 'correlation is force against force. It is the *relation of forces*' (TS 31). Whereas Hegel claims to derive force from the very oscillation between the terms, for Badiou 'force is only the [oscillation's] essential, originary, and undeducible overdetermination' (TS 34), with 'overdetermination' meaning something like 'surplus' rather than what it usually means. Force is what escapes the correlate, remaining irreducible to it. In short, force belongs to what Badiou calls the historical rather than the structural side of the dialectic. It 'keeps in movement the parts of the whole' (TS 34), by remaining outside the terms of the current structure. The singular force of anything, even of an individual person (TS 35), requires a 'radical anteriority of practical existence' (TS 34).

Force comes from the outplace, but is not identical with it: 'force is impure because it is always placed' (TS 38). This contrasts with the Left deviation of the pure outplace, which Badiou describes in barbed terms aimed obviously at Deleuze: 'the metaphysics of desire, that is, the substantial and nomadic assumption of the outplace from which place itself comes to be inferred . . . Nothing new on this end ever since Spinoza' (TS 37). In Badiou's eyes the impurity of force even explains the need for Stalinist purges: to say that the Party is strengthened by purges is 'an understatement', even if 'on this bloody path Stalin arrived at nothing but disaster' (TS 38). An image even more to Badiou's liking is Mao's 'struggle of old and new', since 'every rightness and every justice are, in principle, novelties' (TS 39). What is always needed between thinkers in quest of truth is not a tepid harmony, but 'an essential nonlove'. If you want to be a subject you must resist the dead splace of pedagogy (TS 39) and form a Party of your own (TS 41). This also leads Badiou to a new definition of subjective and objective: 'Inasmuch as it concentrates and purifies itself *qua* affirmative scission, every force is therefore a subjective force, and inasmuch as it is assigned to its place, structured, splaced, it is an objective force' (TS 41). And inevitably, 'the being of force is to divide itself according to the objective and the subjective' (TS 41). We can neither deduce nor predict the emergence of force but must wait for it. By contrast, Hegel '[takes] up his position at the end of time, whereby the circle is traced, in order to know who is who in the unity of the progressive and the retroactive. One remains dismayed by the fine arrogance to which Hegel thenceforth bears witness' (TS 49).

There is a logic of places and a logic of forces (TS 53), or a structural dialectic and a historical one. Despite the generally dismal role ascribed to structure in his book, Badiou praises the dialectical correlation between two terms within structure for upholding 'the primacy of process over equilibrium, of the movement of transformation over the movement of identity' and for its 'primacy of the Two over the One' (TS 54). There is the structural/horizontal dialectic between two correlated terms, but also the deeper historical/vertical dialectic between force and place in which the outplace wreaks havoc on the structured world. For Badiou, 'everything that exists in thought is the result of weak differences' (TS 60, emphasis removed), but only because of the 'retroactive effacement of the cause' (TS 63), in which the outplace vanishes in favour of its surface legibility within a given structure. As Badiou puts it: 'In the structural dialectic, any term is split into its place, on the one hand, and its vanishing capacity for linkage, on the other.' He continues: 'For us, this is as good as place and force. But, as I said before, the structural dialectic is reluctant to *name* the force, and breaks its back trying to keep it in place' (TS 71). All terms are split between old and new. And we now come to an unusually intriguing part of Badiou's model, one already prefigured in the treatment of correlations as composed of forces surging up from the outplace. Despite the vanishing of forces as they are filtered into the world of structure, the outplace is not completely erased from the visible figures we encounter: 'A term is that which presents the vanishing term to another term, in order together to form a chain' (TS 72). One split term has the remarkable ability to signal depths to another, rather than meeting it in a purely structural embrace in which nothing lies beneath the surface of their relation. Or stated differently, 'to function as a combinable element amounts to presenting the absent cause to another element' (TS 72). But this obviously cannot be done in a direct manner, since that would entail a reduction of each term to mere structure in the eyes of the other. And thus, according to

Badiou, we must learn from the poetry of Mallarmé that if we are always dealing with an absent cause, 'the effect of its lack lies in affecting each written term, forced to be "allusive", "never direct" . . . The allusive is the vanishing border of the written term' (TS 72). Force is force and not just a placed force, precisely because force is allusion.

Badiou's approach to the ontological difference can now be summarised. There is a tension between any term A and A_p as placed in the world, or between the outplace of non-relation and the splace of relation. The former affects the latter by means of force, which never occurs in pure form but is always placed, though thanks to the ineffaceable depth of this force any term can be present to another term through indirect allusion. Circularity is abandoned in favour of a spiral or periodic movement, in which one of the terms of the new contradiction bears witness to the previous one. There is a structural/horizontal dialectic between two correlated forces that gives way to a historical/vertical one in which the outplace affects the splace via force. Badiou has already told us how he thinks this model differs from Hegel's. We can leave until later our reflections on how it resembles or differs from Heidegger's ontological difference.

Lacan and Topology

We have seen that Badiou claims a similarity between Heidegger's ontological difference and Hegel's dialectic, though in doing so he partly concedes that his interpretation of the dialectic is unorthodox. Badiou's major objection to the Hegelian version of the dialectic is that it falls into circularity, rather than accomplishing a spiralling movement or periodicity in which something unpredictable is held in reserve behind the visible figures correlated in any structure. We have briefly followed Badiou's exposition of what he thinks the dialectic ought to entail.

The present section turns to a related Heideggerian theme: the critique of ontotheology. It is well known that for Heidegger, being itself is not a being. No privileged entity can be taken as the explanation for being as such. Badiou glosses this principle as follows:

Heidegger intends to deconstruct metaphysics, previously defined as the concealment of the [ontological] question by the [theological

question]. I say that he seeks to dissipate the algebraic precision
of God, localization of simple belonging, placed being from which
all beings take their place. It is a question of opening up onto the
topological unlimitation of being, for which it is not for nothing that
Heidegger evokes ad nauseam the dialectic of the near and the far.
Heidegger would like to put an end to the philosophical idea of a *guarantee of consistency by the cause.* (TS 235)

Here we encounter a number of new terms: algebra, topology,
consistency and cause. In order to explain what Badiou means by
these, we need to consider the remarks in *Theory of the Subject*
concerning Lacan, which show the same mixture of praise and
deviation as Badiou's statements about Hegel.

For Badiou, Lacan 'for us French Marxists is today's Hegel – the
only one whom it is our task to divide' (TS 113). In fact Badiou
is even closer to Lacan, whose challenge to Hegel's key term
Aufhebung he cites rather approvingly. Badiou also maps his own
interpretation of the dialectic directly onto Lacanian terminology:
the structural dialectic is the Lacanian 'symbolic', and the historical dialectic is the Lacanian 'real' (TS 114). He adds another pair
of new terms, telling us that the symbolic is 'algebra' and the real is
'topology' (TS 133). By working out the relations between algebra
and topology, Badiou aims to push philosophy a bit further than
Lacan, another hero who falls somewhat short of bona fide materialism: 'Lacan . . . is our Hegel, that is, he presents the (idealist)
dialectic of our time' (TS 132).

Badiou also begins to clarify what 'subject' means in the title
Theory of the Subject: 'We must reserve the name *subject* for that
which cannot be inscribed on the splaced ground of repetition
except destructively as the excess over that which keeps it in place'
(TS 141). As that which tears free from the current configuration
of beings, 'subject' plays a role for Badiou not unlike 'being' for
Heidegger. For Badiou there are not two opposing subjects locked
in a duel, since this would lead only to a correlation and thus to a
mere structural dialectic. In any given predicament there is at most
one subject. And here we note the first appearance in the book of
a key Badiouian term: 'Just as there is only one subject, there is
also only one force, whose existence always surfaces as an *event*.
This *event*, trace of the subject, crosses the lack with the destruction' (TS 142, emphasis added). Or as he puts it later, 'the subject
placed as force can force the excess over the place' (TS 157). We

see this happen, for instance, in both justice and courage: 'Justice names the possibility that what is nonlaw may function as law' (TS 159), while 'courage is insubordination to symbolic order at the urging of the dissolutive injunction of the real' (TS 160). Justice and courage are not equally distributed, but emerge along with a specific political class: while 'the dominant class derives its position from keeping the splace as is', the proletariat 'is the political name of the truth that is not-all' (TS 173). And this is where Badiou thinks that Lacan falls short: 'Regarding the double division which determines the subject effect, it would be fair to say that Lacan has exhaustively named only one half' (TS 174). We will soon see why.

Unlike typical idealist philosophies of the subject, Badiou's theory of the subject is diametrically opposed to any model of the subject that would treat it as the site of an elucidating transparency. 'Immediacy and self-transparency are idealist attributes . . .' (TS 180). For Badiou the subject is a scission without reconciliation. He claims to offer a 'conceptual black sheep – a materialism centred upon a theory of the subject . . .' (TS 189). This materialism entails a much stronger sense of the real than the 'idealinguistery' of figures such as Foucault (TS 187–8), in which 'discourse' or 'language' function as non-idealist alibis for what is in fact an idealist position. In response to those who accuse Badiou of mimicking Kant in his focus on the borderlands between representation and that which exceeds it, he counters that at least he does not make *one* of the two terms of the correlate into the subject (TS 191): the subject is not one region of being among others. For 'we are materialists' (TS 192), and thus we follow 'the axiom of the crossing' (TS 200) in which knowledge is not merely the cause of the subject but is rather a knot tying thought to the real.

In what is surely his least Heideggerian moment, Badiou declares that 'there exists no intrinsic unknowable' (TS 201). He describes a tension between the accessible space of 'reflection' and the elusive zone of the 'asymptote' of knowledge (TS 201), but insists that this is different from Kant's noumenal vs. phenomenal pair. While Kant sets a mournful limit to human knowledge, Badiou holds by contrast 'that the sphinx is nameable, once the questioning limit from where Oedipus's answer provisorily appeared to be well adapted, through a forced event, comes to the light of history' (TS 202). While the real of knowledge is impossible to know at any given moment, it 'asymptotically fixes the future of the reflection.

This impossible, therefore, *will be known* . . .' (TS 202, emphasis added). In fact, the whole point of what Badiou calls justice is that 'forms of knowledge previously considered as absurd can now function as reflections' (TS 204). Any time we untie the knot of knowledge, this 'makes for a revolution, by positing a name for the impossible of the subject' (TS 204). What currently has no name will someday find one.

We now return to the theme of algebra vs. topology, already familiar to us as the difference between the structural dialectic of splace and the historical dialectic in which the outplace exerts destruction on the splace. Algebra deals with the explicit elements belonging to a set, and is thus the domain of structure without remainder: 'It excludes all thought of tendencies and asymptotes. Homogeneous identity of belonging, elementary structuring, species distinguished in terms of types of legal constraint: the algebraic universe is limited to combinatory materialism' (TS 210). Algebra deals with both individuals and relations, which Badiou takes to be partners: 'Algebra explores [the Whole] under the aegis of the individuals that belong to it and the rules according to which they relate to one another' (TS 215). By contrast, 'topology [explores the Whole] under the aegis of the varied subsets of which each individual makes its site within the Whole' (TS 215). If algebra deals with belonging, topology is a matter of 'adherence'. But once again we are told that *individual* things belong entirely on the algebraic side of the fence: 'The "micro-revolutions" of the desiring individual . . . stay in their place. No individual has the power to exceed the era and its constraints, except by the mediation of the parts . . .' (TS 219–20).

And here we begin to approach the heart of Badiou's position, which works simultaneously in two paradoxical directions. The paradox of the algebraic or structural realm is that while it is supposedly the zone of discrete individuals, these individuals are initially defined without remainder by their place in the structure, thereby depriving them of individuality. Conversely, the paradox of topology is that it supposedly points to that which exceeds all relational structure. And while this ought to be autonomous and individual, it turns out that we cannot really speak of topological individuals at all: 'One sees how topology is *disidentifying* in nature' (TS 223). Everything is connected more or less closely with everything else, linked through a series of neighbourhoods and sub-neighbourhoods: 'In topological thinking there exists no neighbourhood in exteriority' (TS 221). This is what 'establishes a link between the elements of a set, which is the basis of belonging for algebraic materialism, and the surrounding adherence by which the elements are locatable, [the] basis for topological materialism' (TS 221). In this way the elements in a set are not just hopeless structural encrustations without a future, but '[points] of flight for a set of collectives' (TS 221). This is Badiou's attempt, following Lacan, to solve 'the supreme problem of materialism, which is correctly to tie together its own division according to algebra and according to topology' (TS 228). The set that is close to you includes you as well. 'If you are part of two processes, you are part of their crossing . . .' (TS 222). A factory revolt may begin with the working class but then spread to some nearby collectives and not others. History is never universal; the contagion is never limitless. These processes of topological expansion, intersection and constriction show how topological neighbourhoods can do the work of the traditional concepts of universal and particular (TS 221). Lacan already has two concepts of the real: the vanishing cause (algebra) and the knot (topology) (TS 228). And this properly double sense of reality on Lacan's part 'shows the extent to which the real is the unity of the algebraic and the topological, unity of the cause and the consistency. It is object, but *not only*' (TS 230).

With this move towards the model of neighbourhoods, Badiou also tries to account for the periodisation that he deployed against Hegel's circularity. As Badiou puts it, 'we thus pass from the algebraic punctuality, by which a materialist domain opens itself up to knowledge, to the topological adherence, which saturates the recurrence of conflict with memory and neighbourhoods' (TS 231). And this is where Badiou tries to settle his accounts with Lacan for not having a sufficiently vigorous sense of the real: 'because the Lacanian concept of consistency is too restrictive. By failing to oppose and conjoin explicitly the algebra and the topology, he exposes himself to the risk of thinking of consistency only as an attribute of algebra' (TS 231). This can be seen not only in the early Lacan's view that the subject has access only to a certain structural syntax rather than the real itself, but even in the later Lacan's fascination with the 'Borromean knot' linking symbolic, real and imaginary, in which cutting any one link makes the whole knot come undone. In Badiou's eyes this comes 'dangerously close to being a simple principle of existential interdependence'

(TS 232), turning everything back into correlates within a structure rather than leaving room for the excessively real. Badiou on the other hand insists on a distinction between 'weak' consistency which 'is resolved in structural cohesion' and 'makes a knot of what is only a chain' (TS 232, emphasis removed), and 'strong' consistency which rightly 'overdetermines the algebra, as consistency of neighbourhoods' (TS 232). In other words, Lacan does not have a sufficiently powerful sense of 'destruction', and thus he becomes 'the norn of his own errancy' (TS 234). Badiou follows with an expression of 'disdain' for 'Lacan's sectarians' who 'boast about being daring antiphilosophers . . . [but rather] protect the algebraic indivisibility of the object' (TS 234). What is needed instead is a strict division between what Heidegger calls the 'ontological' and 'theological' questions. It is interesting that at the precise moment when Lacan supposedly entangles himself in the weave of his own algebraic fate, and hence in ontotheology, Badiou turns with admiration to Heidegger.

The Proximity of Heidegger

It is often the case that important philosophy begins as a deviation from one or more selected ancestral heroes. We see this happen between Aristotle and Plato, Heidegger and Husserl, and many other pairs. In *Theory of the Subject* Badiou sketches his relation to his own philosophical models: Hegel and Lacan, whom he both endorses and subverts. It is remarkable that in both cases Heidegger can be found in the vicinity, despite just three occurrences of his name in the book.

Let's begin with Hegel. By interpreting the dialectic as a tension between any term A and its relational placement A_p, and by associating both Hegel and Heidegger with this idea, Badiou ventures to interpret both philosophers as anti-relationists. But this is far from the standard reading of either. Hegel is generally credited with taking Kant's world of fixed determinations of the understanding and setting it into motion by showing the internal relations that every determination has to every other. As for Heidegger, his critique of presence-at-hand often takes the form of equating presence with non-relationality. For this very reason, it is said, his first step in *Being and Time* is to dissolve the world's apparently autonomous chunks of presence into a global, relational system of tools in which everything has its being in relation to human Dasein.

Although it seems dubious to me that Badiou uses the term 'materialist' to describe his position (I have similar misgivings in the cases of Žižek and Meillassoux), his purpose in doing so is clear. Every thing marks a twofold scission; every thing is out of place. There is never one world as the set of all sets, but always an excess or remainder over what explicitly belongs to any apparent whole. Now, in Badiou's eyes Hegel is a materialist no less than an idealist. There is not just the dialectic between correlated terms in a structure, but also a 'historical' tension between the terms in a situation and something that is always held in reserve but never fully thematised. While Badiou celebrates this 'materialist' side of Hegel, he charges him with emphasising circularity over periodicity or theory over praxis. Here again, non-relationality is the standard to which Badiou holds himself and others, with Hegel apparently not going quite far enough in this respect. Hegel now stands accused of a robotic dialectic in which each moment passes without remainder into its successor. He does not appreciate the obscure kernel of praxis that no theory can fully master, and which entails that history at any moment might go in one of several possible directions rather than automatically leading in just one.

In some respects Heidegger is an even more unlikely candidate than Hegel to be read as a non-relational thinker who distinguishes profoundly between A and A_p. After all, Heidegger is the great critic of presence in philosophy, and as already mentioned he often seems to equate presence with self-subsistent reality apart from all relation. In these moments relationality is treated as the great hero that frees us from metaphysics in the bad sense. Indeed, Heidegger might seem to abolish autonomous individual entities altogether and dissolve them into a holistic network of equipment in which each thing gains reality only from a total system of meaning. But despite the unorthodox flavour of Badiou's brief remarks on Heidegger's ontological difference, his instincts are basically correct. In fact, Badiou and I are practically alone among readers of Heidegger in viewing him as a champion of non-relational being.[3] What Heidegger shows is not that non-relational presence is grounded in the relational usefulness of tools, but that the presence of entities to humans *and* the presence of tools to other tools are both forms of relation, and are equally deficient for this very reason. Both theory and praxis are able to be subverted by surprises, because both are relations undergirded by an obscure surplus or reservoir: the being that is not itself a being.

But regardless of how he interprets Hegel and Heidegger, the real question is whether Badiou remains true to his program of a non-relational outplace that is irreducible to splace even while exerting forces of destruction upon it. In one sense he remains entirely faithful to the cause, given the lesson he draws from Mallarmé: that forces signal their depths to each other through an indirect or allusive form of contact. Yet this insistence on indirect contact creates tension with the other Badiou, the one who holds that nothing is intrinsically unknowable. Though in *Theory of the Subject* he claims to insist on a difference between thought and being, it is not clear that he does so in sufficiently vigorous fashion. All that Badiou really means when he insists on a gap between thought and being is that the subject is a special rip or tear in the cosmos rather than just one entity among others. Continuing the Cartesian tradition with its two distinct substances, Badiou holds that being has sufficient independence from thought as long as it continues to exist in the absence of that thought. Yet when he says that nothing is inherently unknowable, he risks the same idealist backslide of which he accuses both Hegel and Lacan. For if the outplace is supposedly treated by Badiou as an asymptote to be approached but never reached, the claim that nothing is unknowable clearly means that whatever is now asymptote will eventually be reflection, with a new asymptote simply replacing the old one. For Badiou there is an unknown at any given moment, but nothing remains unknown forever. And here we must question whether Badiou breaks free from splace and structure as much as Heidegger himself does: for if Badiou thinks *nothing* is inherently unknowable, Heidegger holds that *everything* is, given the permanent rift between being and any form of presence. And this seems even more true to Badiou's stated principles than Badiou's own conclusions are. If A is not inherently unknowable and comes to be known, then precisely by being known it is converted from A into A_p, since by being known it is now in relation to us. Here Badiou loses his Mallarméan commitment to indirect allusion.

It is similar with Lacan, the man Badiou describes as 'today's Hegel' (TS 113) who 'presents the (idealist) dialectic of our time' (TS 132). Since 'idealism' is never used by Badiou as a complimentary term, we can take this to be a moment of critical distancing from his admired psychoanalyst forerunner. Recall that Badiou identifies the Lacanian symbolic with 'algebra' and the Lacanian real with 'topology'. Recall further that Badiou criticises not only the early Lacan for claiming that the subject has access merely to a syntax rather than to the real, but also the later Lacan for treating the imaginary-real-symbolic as an intertwined Borromean knot that verges dangerously close to an existential interdependence of three terms, and thus to a relationally determined structure of the sort that Badiou is so keen to avoid. The figure of the knot is viewed positively by Badiou, but only if the knot ties together two terms (thought and the real) that are genuinely *distinct* even as they frequently interact.

And here once more, Heidegger emerges as a key ally in Badiou's deviation from an admired hero. While Badiou laments that algebra 'excludes all thought of tendencies and asymptotes' (TS 210), and that it thereby remains tied to the relational world of individuals correlated as elements within a structure, he also credits Heidegger with wanting 'to dissipate the algebraic precision of God [and the] localization of simple belonging, placed being from which all beings take their place' (TS 235). The word 'God' is metaphorical here, referring to any privileged being of the ontotheological tradition in which philosophy forever attempts to replace being itself with one specific kind of being. In this sense Badiou endorses Heidegger's aim of trying to make room for a being different from all beings (the ontological difference), which Heidegger employs with the critical aim of a destruction of the history of metaphysics. Lacan apparently does not succeed in this, since as concerns 'the subject effect, it would be fair to say that Lacan has exhaustively named only one half' (TS 174).

On a related note, we have also seen Badiou distance himself from the usage of Kant and most other philosophers in which 'subject' refers specifically to the thinking human. Badiou's 'subject' is rather depersonalised, in much the same manner as Heidegger's *Sein*. Although Badiou does speak of individual humans freeing themselves from algebraic networks in order to attain their own proper force, for the most part 'subject' is mentioned only in connection with the proletariat (even though each proletariat is historical and local), and in *Theory of the Subject* 'proletariat' often verges on functioning as a name for being as such, not for a particular assembly of downtrodden humans.

Now, for Badiou, when algebra is treated as a free-standing realm in which vanishing terms have been entirely used up by structure, it becomes an ontotheological kingdom of the sort that he like Heidegger aspires to avoid. For Heidegger the non-algebraic term is 'being', and with his ontological difference he tends to conflate two points that are in fact quite distinct. In one sense being is treated as that which resists presence, which Badiou reads (correctly, though unusually) as meaning: 'resists any sort of relationality at all'. Being is that which simply is what it is, rather than in its placement for something else: *Sein* is A rather than A$_\text{p}$. But in another sense, Heidegger also tends to interpret the ontological difference as a difference between one and many. Here, being is that which is not carved up into multiple individuals which are found only within the 'ontic' realm. In this way, individuality and relationality are treated as basically the same problem. This remains the case even in Heidegger's later period, when he moves towards a reflection on 'the thing' in which individual entities such as jugs and bridges are granted a foothold in a sort of subrelational autonomy. For even here, this autonomy is treated in terms of 'earth', and earth is always treated by Heidegger as a one.

Despite his rejection of the 'one' in philosophy, Badiou shares Heidegger's basic assumption that individuality and relationality always come as a pair. We have already heard him say that algebra is concerned both with 'individuals' *and* with 'the rules according to which they relate to one another' (TS 215). He criticises the notion that individuals are capable of 'micro-revolutions' (TS 219–20) and tells us that topology, always his counterweight to algebra, is 'disidentifying' (TS 223). Yet this is where Badiou adds another possible solution that we never find in Heidegger. For Heidegger, the escape from identifiable and relational individuals occurs only by appeal to an ominous being that rumbles like a quasi-articulate lump, forever withdrawn from all access. There are times when Badiou seems to suggest the same thing. But what his theory of topology really says is that individuals belong to 'varied subsets' (TS 215); they are '[points] of flight for a set of collectives' (TS 221) and belong to multiple neighbourhoods and subneighbourhoods, none of which is entirely distant from the others. A subject becomes more universal by expanding outward from an initially constricted location, as when a factory revolt catches fire among ever wider collectives. Individuals are always specific and local, but by communicating through closer neighbourhoods towards more distant ones, they exert indirect force on an ever-widening circle of neighbours.

Badiou initially sides with Heidegger in countering encrusted relational individuals with a rather shapeless outplace, thereby pointing outside structure altogether towards something that escapes it. But when it comes to the theme of topology he does not actually repeat this gesture. Instead, he enacts the rather non-Heideggerian programme of partially entangled horizontal collectives, for which change comes not by drawing on a vast indeterminate surplus, but by triggering chain reactions from one local neighbourhood to another. Instead of being undermined by an indeterminate mass of multiplicity, they are shaken up by lateral glidings between the current neighbourhood and others, which are partly but not entirely distant from one another. If there is a point where Badiou veers sharply away from Heidegger no less than from Hegel and Lacan, it is here. And if there is a point where Badiou most resembles Heidegger, it is with the rather different notion of an unformatted excess that undercuts all individual beings. It would be interesting to examine the future development of this tension, whose two sides both unfold in the vicinity of Heidegger. For the difference between eruptions from an unformatted outplace and lateral overlappings of various situations seems strikingly similar to the different emphases of *Being and Event* and *Logics of Worlds*.

Notes

1. G. W. F. Hegel, *Science of Logic*, trans. A. V. Miller (Amherst, NY: Humanity Books, 1969), pp. 114–22.
2. Ibid., p. 82.
3. See Graham Harman, *Tool-Being: Heidegger and the Metaphysics of Objects* (Chicago: Open Court, 2002).

13

One Divides into Two: Badiou's Critique of Deleuze

Jon Roffe

What human language can adequately portray that astonishment, that horror which possessed me at the spectacle then presented to view? The brief moment in which I averted my eyes had been sufficient to produce, apparently, a material change in the arrangements at the upper or farther end of the room. A large mirror – so at first it seemed to me in my confusion – now stood where none had been perceptible before; and, as I stepped up to it in extremity of terror, mine own image, but with features all pale and dabbled in blood, advanced to meet me with a feeble and tottering gait. (Edgar Allen Poe, 'William Wilson')

In his review of two translations of Badiou's work, *Manifesto for Philosophy* and *Deleuze: The Clamor of Being*, Alberto Toscano registers a puzzling feature of Badiou's account of Deleuze:

> What is particularly confusing is that were we to concur with Badiou on the aims of Deleuze's work, i.e., the formulation of a metaphysics of the One, we would most probably be unable to notice its alleged failures. After all, if the essential in Deleuze's philosophy is the approximation towards an 'immutable One (immutable qua perpetual mutation)', towards the truth of Being over against the fictive character of beings, the Deleuze which emerges at the end of Badiou's book, an ascetic apologist for One-Being, would be an eminently successful philosopher.[1]

Insofar as Badiou's reading is construed as a *critique* of Deleuze, it takes on a peculiar chimerical character: a fierce multilateral assault on an impregnable target. What seems to have been overlooked for the most part is that Badiou's reading of Deleuze, above all in *The Clamor of Being*, is not in fact a critique at all. Its general goal is different: to present a revealing *contrast* between

Deleuze's philosophy and Badiou's own. Badiou himself presents his methodology in the following way, claiming that his goal was to '[revive] the great classical controversies, that were neither closed, self-engrossed altercations nor petty "debates", but rather, forceful oppositions seeking to cut straight to the *sensitive point* at which different conceptual creations separate' (D 5). That this is Badiou's goal is borne out at every turn in *The Clamor of Being*, while also marking his general approach to Deleuze from his early polemical and occasionally pseudonymous texts, to his more recent sober denunciations.

Nonetheless, Badiou does in fact pursue a single substantial critical point in *The Clamor of Being*, one which, ironically enough, has been all but overlooked in the fairly polarised responses that have arisen in the nearly twenty years since the book first appeared. It is found in his account of the relationship between the virtual and the actual, which he takes to be the pair of concepts which 'exhaust the deployment of univocal Being' (D 43) in Deleuze's metaphysics, marking the pinnacle of not just the latter but also *The Clamor of Being* itself. There Badiou argues not just that Deleuze's philosophy departs from his own in ways that he 'cannot bring himself' (D 91) to agree with, but that Deleuze's own philosophy is internally flawed. The flaw lies in the way in which the thematic of the *image* is brought into play in order to bind together the virtual/actual pair. The failure of this move dashes any hope that Deleuze, on Badiou's account, could present a coherent ontology:

> The more Deleuze attempts to wrest the virtual from irreality, indetermination, and nonobjectivity, the more irreal, indetermined and finally non-objective the actual (or beings) becomes, because it phantasmatically splits in two. (D 53)

These points taken into account, we are presented with a peculiar state of affairs: the point at which Deleuze's philosophy *fails* – becomes fatally exposed to critical attention – for Badiou is found not in the seminal works of sober philosophy from the late 1960s, but in his philosophy of cinema, where the notion of the virtual image is elaborated. In turn, the measure of the strength of the critique Badiou presents of the formulation of the virtual/actual pair in *The Time Image* is also the measure of the specifically *critical* value of Badiou's reading of Deleuze.

Now, the goal of this chapter is not to investigate the complex network of questions that underpin Badiou's approach to Deleuze as a whole such that it gives rise to this peculiar situation; it is simply to examine the cogency of this single (and singular) critique of Deleuze's account of the virtual and the actual. I would like to demonstrate that the accounts of the virtual that appear in *Difference and Repetition* and *The Time Image*, and which form the two loci around which Badiou's argument turns, are not homologous, and thus the critique fails.

Before turning to this examination, we ought to register a second irony: the only substantial critique of Deleuze presented by Badiou concludes that he is in the final analysis an ontological *dualist* and not a philosopher of the One at all. If this criticism is well-founded and taken seriously, the figure of the One would thus shift position in Deleuze on Badiou's account, adopting the role of a *rhetorical* rather than *metaphysical* investment. Thus the chimera appears even stranger again: a critique that is in fact in substance an encomium, a writ of praise for a philosophy that radically fails at its most significant junction.

'The Virtual Is *Ignorantiae Asylum*'

The general framework of Badiou's reading of Deleuze is well-known. He claims that, contrary to a certain widespread second-order doxography, not to mention certain explicit assertions made by Deleuze himself, the theme of difference and multiplicity is of ancillary interest in Deleuze's metaphysics. In perhaps the most well-known formulation, Badiou's claim is as follows: 'Deleuze's fundamental problem is most certainly not to liberate the multiple but to submit thinking to a renewed concept of the One' (D 11). Badiou claims that this commitment to an ontological figure of the One organises both Deleuze's method and all of the theoretical commitments that are found throughout his work, specifically his account of the event and of subjectivity, his account of the relationship between truth and time, and above all the structure of the virtual–actual pair.

In this pair, Badiou asserts, the virtual is synonymous with Being as such and functions as the ontological ground of the secondary regime of simulacra that manifest Being's productive effervescence, what is named by the term 'actual'. Badiou's critique of Deleuze arises in this context. Given that '"Virtual" is without any doubt the principal name of Being in Deleuze's work' (D 43), it stands to reason that the relationship between the One and its multiple products will be most clearly and decisively elaborated in relation to this concept. Badiou's essential references here are two in number: the fourth chapter of *Difference and Repetition*, specifically those passages that address the virtual/possible distinction and the invocation of mathematics, and the two *Cinema* books, above all the second section of the chapter devoted to 'The Crystals of Time' in *The Time Image*.[2] In fact, in elaborating his outline and critique of the virtual, Badiou only makes explicit reference to three successive pages in the former case, and two pages in the latter. This paucity of textual evidence will, as we will see, prove to be problematic.

Badiou begins by asserting that the virtual, qua name of the One, is ground to the actual, 'the real basis of singular beings' (D 45). Consequently, in every existing singular thing, we must be able to think its relationship to the virtual that grounds it. However, given Deleuze's commitment to the notion of univocity, Badiou argues, what is essential is that actual entities not be split from their virtual ground, since this would give rise to a dualism, ruining the fundamental unicity of being.

Here, the key touchstone is what Deleuze writes in *Difference and Repetition* concerning the two sides of the object: 'The virtual must be defined as strictly a part of the real object – as though the object had one part of itself in the virtual into which it plunged as though into an objective dimension.'[3] In other words, the entire relationship between the One and the multiple, considered on the basis of the nominations virtual and actual, is present *in nuce* at the level of the object itself. Just as, on Badiou's account, Deleuze's philosophy is devoted to the infinite dynamism of the simulacra that play across the surface of the One, the simplest of objects must also disclose the same ontological relationship.

The issue, however, is what is to be made of the notion that the object has two sides without being two objects engaged in an external relationship (or, writ large, how the virtual can be supereminent with respect to the simulacra it produces without being thought as transcendent to those simulacra). According to Badiou, Deleuze addresses this concern by recasting the double-sided nature of the object in terms of a thematic of the image:

Deleuze himself poses the question: 'How . . . can we speak simultaneously of both complete determination and only a part of the object?' In my opinion, the answer he gives is far from satisfactory and it is here that I see the stumbling block for the theory of the virtual. This answer stipulates that 'Every object is double without it being the case that the two halves resemble one another, one being a virtual image and the other an actual image. They are unequal odd halves.' . . . [Thus] Deleuze exemplarily demonstrates that the most magnificent contemporary attempt to restore the power of the One is at the price – as regards the thought of the actual object, inevitably determined as an image – of a very precarious theory of the Double. (D 51–2)

The problem, as Badiou sees it, is threefold. In the first instance, the resolution of the virtual-actual relationship on the basis of the notion of the doubled image does little to temper concerns about the notion that the object has two unequal but intrinsic halves, since it remains on the same terrain, however convincing the newly introduced framework of 'an optical metaphor' (D 52) may seem.

Badiou also wishes to insist that there does not seem to be any convincing way to conceive of the virtual as an image that does not also mean no longer thinking of the virtual as the name for the One-Being – since the notion of the image is always, it would seem, an image *of* something (hence he notes that 'it would be more fitting to say that an actual being is a "virtual image"' (D 52)).

Finally, he feels that Deleuze does not and indeed cannot provide an account of the distinction between the virtual and actual images that constitute the object. Turning now to *The Time Image*, Badiou notes that Deleuze himself insists that the pair virtual image/actual image is engaged in a form of relationship that renders the two halves radically indistinguishable. Quoting from this later work, Badiou asserts the following:

> Deleuze ends up positing that . . . the virtual and the actual cannot in fact be thought of as separate. No mark or criterion exists by which to distinguish them. They are 'distinct and yet indiscernible, and all the more indiscernible because indistinct, because we do not know which is one and which is the other.' (D 53, translation modified)

At the end of this set of concepts, it thus seems to Badiou that the house of cards collapses. If the virtual and the actual are indiscernible in the metaphorical register of the double image, then this is also true of the two sides of every object, and in turn of the pair virtual-actual as such, which is to say, as it accounts for the relationship between the One and its multiple simulacra: 'This heroic effort therefore seems to me incapable of succeeding' (D 53).

Thus the argumentative chain or order of reasons that Badiou's critique unfolds is as follows: the virtual grounds the actual; the double-sided nature of the object manifests the virtual/actual relation; the two faces of the object correspond to the two faces of the image; the two faces of the image cannot be thought as both unified and different on Deleuze's own criteria, and consequently, the Deleuzean thought of the virtual is incompatible with a genuine thought of univocal being.

Given this, we can see that the force of Badiou's argument rests upon the assumption that the accounts of the virtual presented in *Difference and Repetition* and *The Time Image* respectively are homologous. This is because the theme of the indiscernibility of the virtual and the actual appears only in *The Time Image*. As we will see, though, this is far from the case. Moreover, this assumption is not an insignificant one. Near the beginning of *The Clamor of Being*, Badiou asserts that Deleuze's corpus constitutes a series of 'monotonous productions' (D 14). Thus, just as the strength of Badiou's explicit critical case rests on the metonymy that holds between the case of the virtual/actual pair and the pair constituted by the One and the multiple, the strength of his exposition more generally relies upon the underlying homogeneity of Deleuze's work.

To demonstrate the weakness of Badiou's critique, we must begin by considering, however briefly, the two accounts of the virtual in question.

The Virtual in *Difference and Repetition*

The fourth chapter of *Difference and Repetition*, determined by a set of theoretical investments that in many respects remain to be fully unearthed, is the most thoroughly elaborated presentation of the concept of the virtual in Deleuze's work, and as such Badiou is right to draw on it, however fleetingly, in *The Clamor of Being*. This text presents three broad claims about the nature of the virtual.

The first of these is that the virtual must be conceived of as *transcendental*. The two philosophical figures who dominate Deleuze's presentation are Immanuel Kant and his contemporary, critic and

fellow transcendental philosopher, Solomon Maimon. From Kant
he takes three central ideas. The first is the significance of Kant's
conception of the Ideas of reason as objective problematic structures in the constitution of experience. The second is the formulation Kant uses to explain the determination of these objectively
indeterminate Ideas. They are in themselves indeterminate (this is
their problematic character), but are able to be determined in relation to the conceptualised manifold of experience, and are completely determined in principle in relation to the operation of the
faculty of the understanding, which provides – at least with respect
to cognitive judgements – the faculty of reason with its legitimate
ambit. The third is the very notion of the transcendental itself, as
a formal structure necessary for the constitution of experience.
Neither material nor simply customary (as the empirical conditions of experience are in Hume), the transcendental occupies a
level in the confection of experience never examined or explored
before Kant.

This triple heritage is filtered in *Difference and Repetition*
through the Maimonian critique of Kant's metaphysics.[4] For
Deleuze, Maimon is able to advance transcendental philosophy
by liberating it from certain of the flaws that bedevil the Kantian
edifice. He maintains that the Ideas are indeed the central problematic structures in the constitution of experience, but that these
Ideas have an objective reality that exceeds any formal logic of
experience – in other words, Maimon's philosophy frees the transcendental from the human subject. Moreover – on the basis of
crippling flaws in Kant's doctrine of the faculties – Maimon comes
to insist that the Ideas must be constitutive and not simply regulative as Kant thought.

Given Maimon's transgression of the subjective basis of Kantian
metaphysics, it is easy to see – and this is the second key claim
made of the virtual in the fourth chapter of *Difference and
Repetition* – why Deleuze might want to say that the virtual is
above all to be considered a *structural* notion: 'The reality of the
virtual is structure.'[5] By treating the Ideas as at once ontologically
real, relational and extra-subjective, they take on the characteris-
tics of a set of structural determinants that contribute their part to
the constitution of actual reality for Deleuze.

However, there is, at least in this context, a more important
reason why the virtual should be considered as structural for
Deleuze, and this – the third characteristic – is that its presentation

is above all undertaken in the vocabulary and on the basis of the conceptual apparatus of the differential calculus. For Deleuze, as Daniel W. Smith asserts, differential calculus provides 'the primary mathematical tool we have at our disposal to explain the nature of reality, the nature of the real – the *conditions of the real*',[6] that is to say, the virtual. The role of the calculus in Deleuze's discussion is thus to provide the most rigorous scaffold for his account of the transcendental structure that plays a central role in the constitution of reality.[7] Essentially, Deleuze argues that the virtual–actual relationship can be conceived in terms of the relationship between a given function (the actual part) and the differential relations that attend it. More precisely, following Weierstrass, Deleuze conceives of the differential relation as the logically prior genetic instance rather than a derived product, which is to say that the virtual is not derived from the regime of the actual – a point that Badiou heavily emphasises throughout *The Clamor of Being*. Instead, Deleuze conceives of this relation as formally but not ontologically distinct from the actual without being explained on the basis of the actual. Deleuze will write that 'the reality of the virtual consists of the differential elements and relations along with the singular points which correspond to them.'[8] Or, to recapitulate the triple-faceted Kantian account of determination in the terms of the calculus: dx is, in relation to x, 'completely undetermined',[9] as is dy in relation to y; both dx and dy are reciprocally determined in relation to one another (dy/dx); and finally, there are the singularities or distinctive points of the differentiated equation according to which it is the object of a complete determination. Thus, to connect back to the Kantian provenance of the virtual – which, given that Maimon himself makes heavy use of the Leibnizian framework of the calculus, is more than just an extrinsic association of concepts – that Deleuze elaborates from Kant to the calculus: 'dx is the Idea . . . the "problem" and its being.'[10]

With these points in mind, we can now turn to the invocation of the double image that forms a crucial moment in Badiou's argument. The first thing to note is that the figure of the image itself only arises once and in passing in *Difference and Repetition*, in contrast to the preponderance of other more elaborate and thoroughly worked out moments in the argument, whose characteristic claims we have just briefly seen. While Deleuze does indeed write that 'Every object is double without it being the case that the two halves resemble one another, one being a virtual image and

the other an actual image',[11] this image of the image is of little use
in grasping Deleuze's argument in this work. What is of use are the
structural (indeed, structuralist), transcendental and mathematical
resources that are deployed. Indeed, against this backdrop, it is as
though Badiou's use of these claims has been carefully extracted
from the passages in which they appear, as if directly avoiding the
bulk of Deleuze's argument. The passages in question are fundamentally couched not in terms of the theme of the virtual image,
but in terms of the mathematical account of the virtual part – qua
differential – that we have just touched on. Given Badiou's own
fundamental commitment to mathematics qua ontology, it is more
than a little surprising that he goes out of his way to avoid including Deleuze's first answer to the question of the virtual and actual
parts that, on Badiou's account, leads to the problematic assertion
of the virtual image. Immediately after the sentence that opens
Badiou's critical attention ('the virtual must be defined as strictly a
part of the real object – as though the object had one part of itself
in the virtual into which it plunged as though into an objective
dimension'[12]) Deleuze writes:

> Accounts of the differential calculus often liken the differential to
> a 'portion of the difference'. Or, following Lagrange's method, the
> question is asked which part of the mathematical object presents the
> relations in question and must be considered derived. The reality of
> the virtual consists of the differential elements and relations along with
> the singular points which correspond to them.[13]

In other words, the complete determination proper to the virtual
is primarily thought by Deleuze in terms of the internal structure
of the differential relations and their attendant singularities. There
is no need for any intervention from the side of the actual, or
any basis to think that – within the framework of *Difference and
Repetition* – the virtual and the actual exist in some form of indeterminate reciprocal relationship, since the virtual is, in itself, fully
determined.

Later on the same page, Deleuze turns to the second, actual, half
of the object in the same terms:

> There is thus another part of the object which is determined by actuali-
> sation. Mathematicians ask: What is this other part represented by the
> so-called primitive function? In this sense, integration is by no means

the inverse of differen*t*iation but, rather, forms an original process of differen*c*iation. Whereas differentiation determines the virtual content of the Idea as problem, differenciation expresses the actualisation of this virtual and the constitution of solutions (by local integrations). Differenciation is like the second part of difference, and in order to designate the integrity or integrality of the object we require the complex notion of different/ciation. The *t* and the *c* here are the distinctive feature or phonological relation of difference in person.[14]

If I cite at length, it is to show the extent to which Deleuze's discussion of the relationship between the virtual and the actual, precisely in the only passage Badiou explicitly attends to, is couched in terms of mathematics. In making sense of the invocation – admittedly peculiar – of the virtual image here, we must take into account this context: it is immediately after the passage cited above that we read that 'Every object is double without it being the case that the two halves resemble one another, one being a virtual image and the other an actual image.'[15] Moreover, when presented with this passage as a discussion of the relationship between the virtual and the actual, the essential claim that Deleuze seems to make is that, 'In order to designate the integrity or integrality of the object we require the complex notion of different/ciation.'[16] How are the virtual and actual halves of the object to be thought together? Through the concept of different/ciation, Deleuze argues. But rather than pursuing this explicit indication, one which both concerns the very point at which he finds the internal structure of Deleuze's argument lacking and takes place on a theoretical terrain (mathematics) with which he is intimately familiar, Badiou's attention is taken by the figure of the virtual image – which may facilitate a rather unjustified leap to the much later *Time Image*, but which also ignores a manifest response to the question at hand. *The Clamor of Being* never mentions the notion of different/citation – a strange feature, given the excessive attention it gives to a passing use of the word 'image' that is deemed to be simply metaphorical – but nonetheless Badiou does recognise, without, it would seem, understanding what he has seen, that there is an obvious sense in which the virtual when thought in terms of the mathematical framework is perfectly well-determined, even if it is not independent of the actual: 'Deleuze's favourite comparison, to make us understand that the virtual is just as determined as the actual, is with mathematics. A mathematical problem is perfectly determined, just as is its solution' (D 50).

In sum, the critical assertion that summarises these texts in Badiou's study appears at least prima facie incorrect: it does not seem that:

> We can ... state that the complete determination of the ground as virtual implies *an essential indetermination of that for which it serves as a ground*. For any intuitive determination is necessarily disoriented when, regarding the two parts of the object, 'we do not know which is one and which is the other' (D 53)

precisely because Deleuze's means of accounting for the complete determination of the virtual does not rest, at least in *Difference and Repetition*, on any 'analytic of the indiscernible' (D 52) with respect to images, but to the relationship between the differential and the function in the calculus. And there is one more peculiarity here: when Deleuze comes to situate the value of this mathematical account with respect to the virtual in the passage in question, it is on the basis of 'suggestions made by Descartes'[17] – that philosopher who, according to Badiou, 'Deleuze is unable to love' (LW 527).

The Virtual in *The Time Image*

However problematic Badiou's reading of the virtual in *Difference and Repetition* may be, my contention is that the more suspect move in his critique of Deleuze lies in the assumption of an homology between this text and the *Time Image*, a work published seventeen years later. The passing reference to the image in the former provides Badiou with (extremely minimal) textual means by which to transition between the two books, which is to say that his account of the idea of the virtual image in Deleuze is a confected entity that is extracted from two disparate sources. Here is Badiou's argument for the inadequacy of the virtual image:

> We can see clearly how Deleuze takes advantage here [in the sentence from *Difference and Repetition* in which the virtual image is invoked] of the fact that every object, or every being, is a mere simulacrum; for this allows the timely injection of an immanent theory of the double, backed up by an optical metaphor (the possible double status of

images). But it is extremely difficult to understand how the virtual can be ranked as an image, for this would seem to be the status proper to the actual, whereas it is impossible for the virtual, as the power proper to the One, to be a simulacrum. Doubtlessly, the virtual can give rise to images, but in no way can an image be given of it, nor can it itself be an image. The optical metaphor does not hold up. (D 51–2)

This passage is not only a *non sequitur*, it clearly displays the distracted, question-begging character that can be registered throughout Badiou's reading of Deleuze: we pass from 'it is extremely difficult to understand how the virtual can be ranked as an image' to 'the virtual cannot be an image' in the space of a few lines without any real justification. Underlying this swift passage is Badiou's conviction – which, let's recall, is the conclusion that the *Clamor of Being* aims to demonstrate – that the One, of which the virtual is the principal name, is super-eminent with respect to its products.

More significant though is what we find when we turn directly to the claims made of the virtual in *The Time Image*. Despite the well-known ubiquity of reference to Bergson throughout both of his books on cinema, the category of the virtual only appears there somewhat diffidently, in passing and subordinate to other concerns, with the exception of the key chapter devoted to 'The Crystals of Time'.[18] Deleuze's primary concern in this chapter is to account for the possibility of the independence of a first genre of direct time-image – opsigns and sonsigns, which he locates first in Ozu and then in Italian neo-realism,[19] along with mnemosigns and onirosigns – from a recuperation by the pact that governs the classic cinema, the pact between the sensori-motor schema, the action-image and the secondary structural manifestation of narrative.

Deleuze argues that the emergence of the direct time-image only becomes possible when no organising principles beyond those provided by the structure of time itself are put into play in the ensemble of images that constitute the film in question. There are, broadly, two varieties of modern cinema that manage this. The first deploys chronosigns, those time-images that manifest either the order of time (the integral relations of the past and the present in particular) or time as an irruptive and ungoverned creative series or surging-forth. The second deploys hyalosigns or crystal-images. Unlike chronosigns, hyalosigns are located by Deleuze not at the level of particular sequences in a film but with respect to whole films (his analyses of the various crystalline states is broader again, encompassing the entire bodies of work of Fellini, Ophuls, Renoir and Visconti).[20]

Simply put, a crystal-image or hyalosign is a film constituted by a self-enclosed set of images, organised in such a way that the distinction between what is real and what is imaginary is rendered terminally undecidable (in contrast to the dream images or flashbacks which, however destabilising, can always be recouped back into the narrative structure of the film, as in the famous flashback at the start of Hitchcock's *Stage Fright*).[21] Thus, in Fellini's *And the Ship Sailed On*,[22] the viewer is unable to find any set of images that form the real sequence of events which does not later appear as potentially unreal. Thus 'the crystal reveals a direct time-image, and no longer an indirect image of time deriving from movement.'[23]

The philosophical underpinning of this indiscernibility between the real and the imaginary in the hyalosign is derived from a key feature of Bergson's conception of time. For Bergson, we must conceive of time as necessarily splitting into two jets or streams, one constituting the passing time of the present and the other time that constitutes the past, in order to properly account for memory.[24] This is what leads to the important conclusion for Deleuze that there must be a memory of the present (arising at the point at which time splits into the two streams in Bergson's liquid metaphor) that coexists with the perception of the present itself. It is this doubling of a perception – which also accounts, in Bergson, for the phenomenon of déjà vu – that gives rise to an irrecuperable indiscernibility at the level of images themselves. Because the present perception and the memory of the present coexist, they cannot be rigorously held apart, even though they belong to two formally distinct ontological regimes: this is the indiscernibility proper to the actual image (perception) and its virtual counterpart (memory of the present).

Accordingly, crystal-images in the cinema constitute 'the smallest internal circuit',[25] or the point at which an image reveals its own proper grounding in an obscure local background from which it cannot be separated; this is the point at which the image (which is actual) and its virtual double 'coalesce'.[26] The crystal is thus the smallest figure of the relation between the virtual and the actual as it is presented in *The Time Image*. According to Deleuze, these two halves of the crystal – the two images-in-tandem – are equally irreducible, figuring in a relationship described as 'reciprocal presupposition'.[27] But they are also for the same reason essentially *indistinguishable*. It is important to be clear on this point. Deleuze's account turns around the reciprocal relationship between the two instances *which form the crystal image*. It is not a claim about the virtual and the actual as such. The crystal therefore forms not only the smallest circuit, but also a horizon where earth and sky finally become unable to be disentangled – or, a set of images in a film that are related to another set of images in such a way that they reciprocally challenge the reality of one another, their status with respect to the truth of the situation that they evoke in the viewer.

Finally, the two halves of the crystal image are entirely *reversible*: 'There is no virtual which does not become actual in relation to the actual, the latter becoming virtual through the same relation.'[28] This is what explains the basic structure that Deleuze is concerned with in this context. He begins with the claim that 'The cinema does not just present images, it surrounds them with a world',[29] which is nothing other than an alternative presentation of the relation between an actual image and its virtual context or, taken together, the large circuit. If the actual and virtual are reversible at the level of the crystal or the small circuit, it is because any image can become a part of the context for any other: the reflection, having taken on a life of its own, now finds itself among a world of its own, including that which it also reflects. If the actual can itself become virtual, it is not so *en masse* but in the case of particular images. The 'world' which surrounds every image, that obscure underbelly of each distinct image which the image 'frays' into and fulgurates from, is the virtual – but what constitutes this world is perpetually shifting, relating to new determinations which are not at present themselves actual.

Note that, for Deleuze, the small circuit is not, contrary to Badiou's occasional assertions, another name for the actual.[30] Rather, the small circuit and the large circuit both include the virtual and the actual. The difference is one of specificity or generality. Each actual image is in relation to the virtual Whole, the world or the cosmos (this is the large circuit), but is locally intertwined with its own enigmatic double (the small circuit). In place of the structural account of the virtual in *Difference and Repetition*, we find in *The Time Image* that the difference between virtual and actual is itself a matter of a location or specificity *within a broader structure* constituted by the ensemble of images.

What is perhaps most significant about this thesis in the current context is that the Whole is not the source or origin of the actual, but rather the *de jure* projection of the expanse of the virtual (reminiscent of the refrain of the cosmos celebrated in *A Thousand Plateaus*) which is never presented or presentable in total. In *The Time Image*, Deleuze is clear: we need not go as far as the posited Whole (which is, to repeat, not crystallised but only ever locally *crystallisable*) in order to encounter the virtual, since this latter doubles the present and permeates every image with its capacity to emerge anew in the world. Omnipresent in the smallest of details, the virtual resonates with its actual double. It is this capacity for novelty that is out of *this* world, indeed – but not *beyond* it – and to which cinema provides us access.

To summarise then, we can see, first, that Deleuze certainly does account for the virtual as image, in accordance with the Bergsonian framework of the *Cinema* books, contrary to Badiou's almost brute force rejection of such a possibility. However, this elaboration is only found in *The Time Image* and, given its structure and role, seems impossible to extract and to generalise. While *The Time Image* presents us with a concept of the virtual image which has a clear theoretical provenance, which is in turn the object of a thorough explication (only touched upon here), and is of a piece with the general framework of the *Cinema* books (if not any other of Deleuze's work), none of this is true for the single, passing reference to the image in *Difference and Repetition*.

In other words, Badiou makes three interpretive errors here with respect to the thematics of the image. The first is to assert that, within the framework of Deleuze's metaphysics, the virtual cannot be image. The second, correlative, error is to conceive, no doubt because for Badiou the notion of a virtual image is incomprehensible, that the use of the term image can only have a metaphorical status, and that it is as a metaphor that the figure of the image is used by Deleuze to cover over the logical flaw in his argument. Finally, Badiou assumes that the use of the phrase 'virtual image' in both *Difference and Repetition* and *The Time Image* provides enough reason to consider that the same concept is at work in them both. Even the thumbnail sketches presented here are enough to indicate that this cannot be the case.

Hagiography and Heresy

Consequently, the single direct critique levelled by Badiou at Deleuze's project does not seem to me able to succeed. Indeed, he seems to operate on the basis of the same defective mode that he accuses Deleuze of perpetrating with respect to Plato: a fictional Deleuzean philosophy is confected for the purposes of illicitly establishing his own position.

I do not think, however, that Badiou's error-prone reading of Deleuze is the product of any kind of malice or wilful cruelty, as some have claimed.[31] It is the product of a thought whose compass is skewed by, peculiarly enough, something like his uncanny double, a thinker who is too close to properly see. What is more, great errors, which is to say – to use Deleuze's criteria – interesting, provocative errors, are worth more in their own way than any solid exposition, because they do damage to the narcissistic progeny of scholarship. Hagiography may be inevitable, and the history of thought may be nothing but the condescending parade of the saints of old, our mighty dead. The greater our hagiographic respect, though, the more the might of our progenitors is made weak, precisely insofar as they become more and more – and in the end only – *our* saints.

We dream sometimes of a history of philosophy that would be nothing but the portraits of those thinkers whom we can no longer understand, whose strangeness is foregrounded as much as those parts of their thought worn smooth by their deployment. If, after all these years, Badiou's critique of Deleuze is the only one that still really matters, it is because he has shown a Deleuze that we do not recognise – a feat, all in all, worthy of a philosopher.

Notes

1. Alberto Toscano, 'To have done with the end of philosophy', *Pli*, 9 (2000), p. 235.
2. Gilles Deleuze, *Difference and Repetition*, trans. Paul Patton (New York: Columbia University Press, 1994); *Cinema 2: The Time Image*, trans. Hugh Tomlinson and Robert Galeta (Minneapolis, MN: University of Minnesota Press, 1989).
3. Deleuze, *Difference and Repetition*, p. 209.
4. Most helpful on the Maimonian reception of Kantian metaphysics in Deleuze is the text by Graham Jones on Maimon published in

Graham Jones and Jon Roffe (eds), *Deleuze's Philosophical Lineage* (Edinburgh: Edinburgh University Press, 2009), pp. 104–29.

5. Deleuze, *Difference and Repetition*, p. 209.

6. Daniel W. Smith, 'The conditions of the new', *Deleuze Studies*, 1: 1 (2007), p. 14.

7. Simon Duffy's 'Schizo-Math: The logic of different/ciation and the philosophy of difference', *Angelaki*, 9: 3 (2004), pp. 199–215, remains the best summary treatment of Deleuze's use of the calculus in *Difference and Repetition*.

8. Deleuze, *Difference and Repetition*, p. 209.

9. Ibid., p. 172.

10. Ibid., p. 171.

11. Ibid., p. 209.

12. Ibid.

13. Ibid.

14. Ibid.

15. Ibid.

16. Ibid.

17. Ibid.

18. Deleuze, *The Time Image*, pp. 68–97.

19. Though, it should be noted, the *de jure* form or genetic sign of the affection-mage, the *un-espace-quelconque*, opens onto the regime of the opsign too, insofar as its dissolution of metric spatial context renders it 'indigestible' by the form of the action-image that otherwise governs the deployment of qualisigns and potisigns. See Gilles Deleuze, *Cinema 1: The Movement Image*, trans. Hugh Tomlinson and Barbara Habberjam (Minneapolis, MN: University of Minnesota Press, 1986), pp. 123–4; and Deleuze, *The Time Image*, pp. 82–3. Deleuze also conceives of the skeleton-spaces of Mann and Mizoguchi as bearing in this direction. See Deleuze, *The Movement Image*, pp. 168 and 193.

20. On the broad compass of the concept of the hyalosign, see Ronald Bogue, *Deleuze on Cinema* (New York: Routledge, 2003), pp. 124–6.

21. I thank Mairéad Phillips for calling my attention to this example.

22. See Deleuze, *The Time Image*, p. 73; this example is superbly analysed by Bogue in *Deleuze on Cinema*, pp. 124–5.

23. Deleuze, *The Time Image*, p. 95.

24. On all of these points, see once again Bogue, *Deleuze on Cinema*, pp. 111–15 and in particular pp. 117–24.

25. Deleuze, *The Time Image*, p. 68.

26. Ibid., p. 66.
27. Ibid., p. 67.
28. Ibid.
29. Ibid., p. 66.
30. For example: 'The stakes of philosophy consist in adequately thinking the greatest possible number of particular things (this is the "empiricist" aspect in Deleuze – the disjunctive synthesis or the "small circuit"), in order to adequately think Substance, or the One (which is the "transcendental" aspect, Relation or the "great circuit")' (TW 69).
31. Emblematic in this respect is the ironically counter-Deleuzean assault by José Gil, 'Quatre méchantes notes sur un livre méchant', *Futur Antérieur*, 43 (1998), http://multitudes.samizdat.net/article.php3?id_article=411.

Bibliography

Works by Alain Badiou

Peut-on penser la politique? (Paris: Seuil, 1985).

Conditions (Fr.) (Paris: Seuil, 1992).

'Gilles Deleuze, *The Fold: Leibniz and the Baroque*', trans. T. Sowley, in Constantin V. Boundas and Dorothea Olkowski (eds), *Gilles Deleuze and the Theatre of Philosophy* (New York and London: Routledge, 1994), pp. 51–69.

'Silence, solipsisme, sainteté: L'Antiphilosophie de Wittgenstein', *Barca!*, 3 (1994), pp. 13–53.

Manifesto for Philosophy, trans. Norman Madarasz (Albany, NY: SUNY Press, 1999).

Deleuze: The Clamour of Being, trans. Louise Burchill (Minneapolis, MN: University of Minnesota Press, 2000).

Ethics: An Essay on the Understanding of Evil, trans. Peter Hallward (London: Continuum, 2001).

'Who is Nietzsche?', trans. Alberto Toscano, *Pli*, 11 (2001), pp. 1–10.

L'Antiphilosophie de Wittgenstein (Paris: Nous, 2004).

Theoretical Writings, trans. Alberto Toscano and Ray Brassier (London: Continuum, 2004).

Being and Event, trans. Oliver Feltham (London: Continuum, 2005).

Metapolitics, trans. Jason Barker (London: Verso, 2005).

Briefings on Existence: A Short Treatise on Transitory Ontology, trans. Norman Madarasz (New York: SUNY Press, 2006).

'Lacan and the pre-Socratics', in Slavoj Žižek (ed.), *Lacan: The Silent Partners* (London: Verso, 2006), pp. 7–16.

'Mathematics and philosophy', trans. Simon Duffy, in Simon Duffy (ed.), *Virtual Mathematics: The Logic of Difference* (Manchester: Clinamen, 2006), pp. 15–38.

The Century, trans. Alberto Toscano (Cambridge: Polity, 2007).

The Concept of Model: An Introduction to the Materialist Epistemology of Mathematics, trans. Zachary Luke Fraser and Tzuchien Tho (Melbourne: re.press: 2007).

'The Formulas of *l'Étourdit*', trans. S. Saviano, *Lacan Ink*, 27 (2007), pp. 80–95.

Meaning of Sarkozy, trans. David Fernback (London: Verso, 2008).

Number and Numbers, trans. Robin Mackay (Cambridge: Polity, 2008).

'The communist hypothesis', *New Left Review*, 49 (2008), pp. 29–42.

Conditions, trans. Steven Corcoran (London: Continuum, 2009).

Logics of Worlds, trans. Alberto Toscano (London: Continuum, 2009).

Pocket Pantheon, trans. David Macey (London: Verso, 2009).

Theory of the Subject, trans. Bruno Bosteels (London: Continuum, 2009).

The Communist Hypothesis, trans. David Macey and Steven Corcoran (London: Verso, 2010).

Second Manifesto for Philosophy, trans. Louise Burchill (Cambridge: Polity, 2011).

with Bruno Bosteels, 'Can change be thought: a dialogue with Alain Badiou', in Gabriel Riera (ed.), *Alain Badiou: Philosophy and Its Conditions* (New York: SUNY Press, 2005), pp. 237–62.

with Lauren Sedofsky, 'Being by numbers', *Artforum*, 33: 2 (1994), pp. 84–7, 118, 123–4.

Other Works Cited

Althusser, Louis, 'A complementary note on "real humanism"', in *For Marx*, trans. Ben Brewster (London: Verso, 1969), pp. 242–7.

Althusser, Louis, 'Marxism and humanism', in *For Marx*, trans. Ben Brewster (London: Verso, 1969), pp. 219–41.

Althusser, Louis, 'Marx's Relation to Hegel', in *Politics and History: Montesquieu, Rousseau, Marx*, trans. Ben Brewster (London: Verso, 1972), pp. 161–86.

Althusser, Louis, *Essays in Self-Criticism*, trans. Grahame Lock (London: NLB, 1976).

Althusser, Louis, 'The humanist controversy', trans. G. M. Goshgarian, in *The Humanist Controversy and Other Essays* (London: Verso, 2003), pp. 221–306.

Alunni, Charles, 'Continental genealogies. mathematical confrontations in Albert Lautman and Gaston Bachelard', in Simon Duffy (ed.), *Virtual Mathematics – The Logic of Difference* (Manchester: Clinamen Press, 2006), pp. 65–80.

Balibar, Étienne, 'Gewalt', in Wolfgang Fritz Haug (ed.), *Historisch-Kritisches Wörterbuch des Marxismus*, Vol. 5 (Hamburg: Argument Verlag, 2001).

Bartlett, A. J., *Badiou and Plato: An Education by Truths* (Edinburgh: Edinburgh University Press, 2011).

Bartlett, A. J. and Clemens, Justin (eds), *Alain Badiou: Key Concepts* (Durham, NC: Acumen, 2010).

Benacerraf, Paul, 'Mathematical truth', *Journal of Philosophy*, 70: 19 (1973), pp. 661–79.

Blackburn, Simon, 'Hume's diffuse effects cannot be reduced to Hefce narrow vision', *Times Higher Education Supplement*, 21 April 2011, http://www.timeshighereducation.co.uk/story.asp?storyCode=415873&sectioncode=26.

Bogue, Ronald, *Deleuze on Cinema* (New York: Routledge, 2003).

Bosteels, Bruno, 'Post-Maoism: Badiou and politics', *positions: east asia culture critique*, 13: 3 (2005), pp. 576–634.

Bosteels, Bruno, 'The speculative left', *South Atlantic Quarterly*, 104: 4 (2005), pp. 751–67.

Bosteels, Bruno, 'Radical antiphilosophy', *Filozofski vestnik*, 29: 2 (2008), pp. 155–87.

Bowden, Sean, *The Priority of Events: Deleuze's* Logic of Sense (Edinburgh: Edinburgh University Press, 2011).

Brassier, Ray, 'Badiou's materialist epistemology of mathematics', *Angelaki Journal of the Theoretical Humanities*, 10: 2 (2005), pp. 135–50.

Calcagnio, Antonio, *Badiou and Derrida: Politics, Events and Their Time* (New York: Continuum, 2007).

Cantor, Georg, *Contributions to the Founding of the Theory of Transfinite Numbers* (New York: Dover, 1915).

Cantor, Georg, 'Letter to Dedekind', in Jean Van Heijenoort (ed.), *From Frege to Gödel* (Cambridge, MA: Harvard University Press, 1967), pp. 113–17.

Cassou-Noguès, Pierre, 'L'excès de l'état par rapport à la situation dans *L'Être et l'événement* de A. Badiou', *Methodos*, 6 (2006), http://methodos.revues.org/471

Chevalley, Catherine, 'Albert Lautman et le souci logique', *Revue d'histoire des sciences*, 40: 1 (1987), pp. 49–77.

Cohen, Paul J., *Set Theory and the Continuum Hypothesis* (New York: W. A. Benjamin, 1966).

Corpet, Olivier and Matheron, François, 'Introduction', in Louis Althusser, *Writings on Psychoanalysis: Freud and Lacan*, trans.

Jeffrey Mehlman (New York: Columbia University Press, 1996), pp. 1–6.

Cutrone, Chris, 'Badiou's "communism" – a gerontic disorder' (2011), http://chriscutrone.platypus1917.org/?p=1144.

Dauben, Joseph W., *Georg Cantor: His Mathematics and Philosophy of the Infinite* (Princeton, NJ: Princeton University Press, 1990).

Dedekind, Richard, *Essays on the Theory of Numbers* (New York: Dover, 1963).

Deleuze, Gilles, *Cinema 1: The Movement-Image*, trans. Hugh Tomlinson and Barbara Habberjam (Minneapolis, MN: University of Minnesota Press, 1986).

Deleuze, Gilles, *Cinema 2: The Time-Image*, trans. Hugh Tomlinson and Robert Galeta (Minneapolis, MN: University of Minnesota Press, 1989).

Deleuze, Gilles, *Difference and Repetition*, trans. Paul Patton (New York: Columbia University Press, 1994).

Duffy, Simon, 'Schizo-math: the logic of different/ciation and the philosophy of difference', *Angelaki*, 9: 3 (2004), pp. 199–215.

Duffy, Simon, 'Deleuze and Lautman', in Graham Jones and Jon Roffe (eds), *Deleuze's Philosophical Lineage* (Edinburgh: Edinburgh University Press, 2009), pp. 356–79.

Düttmann, Alex García, 'What remains of fidelity after serious thought?', in Peter Hallward (ed.), *Think Again: Alain Badiou and the Future of Philosophy* (London: Continuum, 2004), pp. 202–7.

Easton, William B., 'Powers of regular cardinals', *Annals of Mathematical Logic*, 1 (1970), pp. 139–78.

Federici, Silvia, *Caliban and the Witch: Women, the Body, and Primitive Accumulation* (New York: Autonomedia, 2004).

Feferman, Solomon, *In the Light of Logic* (Oxford: Oxford University Press, 1989).

Feltham, Oliver, *Alain Badiou: Live Theory* (London: Continuum, 2009).

Feuerbach, Ludwig, *Principles of the Philosophy of the Future*, trans. Manfred Vogel (Indianapolis, IN: Hackett, 1986).

Freud, Sigmund, 'From the history of an infantile neurosis', in *The Standard Edition of the Complete Psychological Work of Sigmund Freud, Volume XVII*, trans. James Strachey (London: Hogarth Press, 1955).

Freud, Sigmund, 'Negation', in *The Standard Edition of the Complete Psychological Work of Sigmund Freud, Volume XIX*, trans. James Strachey (London: Hogarth Press, 1961).

Giere, Ronald N., *Science without Laws* (Chicago: University of Chicago Press, 1999).

Gil, José, 'Quatre méchantes notes sur un livre méchant', *Futur Antérieur*, 43 (1998), http://multitudes.samizdat.net/article.php3?id_article=411.

Gödel, Kurt, 'On formally undecidable propositions of *Principia Mathematica* and related systems I' [1931], in Martin Davis (ed.), *The Undecidable* (Mineola, NY: Dover, 1965).

Gödel, Kurt, 'What is Cantor's continuum problem?' [1947, revised and expanded 1964], in Paul Benacerraf and Hilary Putnam (eds), *Philosophy of Mathematics: Selected Readings*, 2nd edn (Cambridge: Cambridge University Press, 1983).

Green, André, *The Work of Negative*, trans. Andrew Weller (London: Free Association Books, 1999).

Hacking, Ian, *Rewriting the Soul: Multiple Personality and the Sciences of Memory* (Princeton, NJ: Princeton University Press, 1995).

Hallward, Peter, *Badiou: A Subject to Truth* (Minneapolis, MN: University of Minnesota Press, 2003).

Harman, Graham, *Tool-Being: Heidegger and the Metaphysics of Objects* (Chicago: Open Court, 2002).

Hegel, G. W. F., *Science of Logic*, trans. A. V. Miller (Amherst, NY: Humanity Books, 1969).

Heidegger, Martin, *The Metaphysical Foundations of Logic*, trans. M. Heim (Bloomington, IN: Indiana University Press, 1984).

Hewlett, Nick, 'Paradoxes of Alain Badiou's theory of politics', *Contemporary Political Theory*, 5 (2006), pp. 371–404.

Hilbert, David, 'On the infinite', in Jean Van Heijenoort (ed.), *From Frege to Gödel* (Cambridge, MA: Harvard University Press, 1967), pp. 367–92.

James, William, 'The one and the many', in *Pragmatism (A New Name for Some Old Ways of Thinking): A Series of Lectures* [1906–7] (Rockville, MD: Arc Manor, 2008), pp. 58–72.

James, William, 'What pragmatism means', in *Pragmatism (A New Name for Some Old Ways of Thinking): A Series of Lectures* [1906–7] (Rockville, MD: Arc Manor, 2008), pp. 26–41.

Johnston, Adrian, 'What matter(s) in ontology: Alain Badiou, the Hebb-event, and materialism split from within', *Angelaki*, 13: 1 (2008), pp. 27–49.

Jones, Graham, 'Solomon Maimon', in Graham Jones and Jon Roffe (eds), *Deleuze's Philosophical Lineage* (Edinburgh: Edinburgh University Press, 2009), pp. 104–29.

Kanamori, Akihiro, *The Higher Infinite. Large Cardinals in Set Theory from Their Beginnings*, Perspectives in Mathematical Logic (New York: Springer, 1994).

Kanamori, Akihiro, 'Cohen and set theory', *Bulletin of Symbolic Logic*, 14: 3 (2008), pp. 351–78.

Kanamori, Akihiro and Menachem Magidor, 'The evolution of large cardinal axioms in set theory', *Higher Set Theory: Lecture Notes in Mathematics*, 669 (New York: Springer-Verlag, 1978), pp. 99–275.

Klein, Jacob, *Greek Mathematical Thought and the Origin of Algebra*, trans. Eva Brann (Cambridge, MA: MIT Press, 1968).

Kunen, Kenneth, *Set Theory: An Introduction to Independence Proofs* (Amsterdam: North Holland, 1983).

Lacan, Jacques, *Ecrits* (Paris: Seuil, 1966).

Lacan, Jacques, *Le Séminaire: Livre I: Les Écrits techniques de Freud* (Paris: Editions du Seuil, 1975).

Lacan, Jacques, *The Seminars of Jacques Lacan: Book II: The Ego in Freud's Theory and in the Technique of Psychoanalysis*, trans. Sylvana Tomaselli, ed. Jacques-Alain Miller (New York: W. W. Norton, 1991).

Lacan, Jacques, *Seminar XI: The Four Fundamental Concepts of Psychoanalysis*, trans. A. Sheridan (London: Penguin, 1994).

Lacan, Jacques, *On Feminine Sexuality, The Limits of Love and Knowledge, 1972–1973: Encore, The Seminar of Jacques Lacan Book XX*, trans. Bruce Fink (New York: Norton, 1999).

Lacan, Jacques and Granzotto, Emilio, 'Il ne peut pas y avoir de crise de la psychoanalyse', *Magazine Littéraire*, 428 (2004), pp. 24–9.

Lacan, Jacques, *Ecrits*, trans. Bruce Fink (with Héloïse Fink and Russell Grigg) (New York: W. W. Norton, 2006).

Lacan, Jacques, *Seminar XVII: The Other Side of Psychoanalysis*, trans. Russell Grigg (New York: Norton, 2006).

Lautman, Albert, *Essai sur les notions de structure et d'existence en mathématiques. I. Les Schémas de structure. II. Les Schémas de genèse* (Paris: Hermann, 1938).

Lautman, Albert, *Essai sur l'unité des sciences mathématiques dans leur développement actuel* (Paris: Herman, 1938).

Lautman, Albert, *Essai sur l'unité des mathématiques et divers écrits* (Paris: Union générale d'éditions, 1977).

Lautman, Albert, *Les mathématiques, les idées et le réel physique* (Paris: Vrin, 2006).

Lautman, Albert, *Mathematics, Ideas and the Physical Real*, trans. Simon Duffy (London: Continuum, 2011).

Lewis, David, 'New work for a theory of universals', *Australasian Journal of Philosophy*, 61: 4 (1983), pp. 343–77.

Linebaugh, Peter, 'Meandering: on the semantical-historical paths of communism and commons', *The Commoner*, 14 (2010), http://www.commoner.org.uk/wp-content/uploads/2010/12/meandering-linebaugh.pdf.

Livingston, Paul, 'Review of *Being and Event*', *Inquiry*, 51: 2 (2008), pp. 217–38.

Mac Lane, Saunders and Eilenberg, Samuel, *Eilenberg-Mac Lane, Collected Works* (New York: Academic Press, 1986).

Macarthur, David, 'Pragmatism, metaphysical quietism and the problem of normativity', *Philosophical Topics*, 36: 1 (2009).

Marker, David, 'Model theory and exponentiation', *Notices of the American Mathematical Society*, 43 (1996), pp. 753–9.

Milner, Jean-Claude, *L'Œuvre Claire: Lacan, la science, la philosophie* (Paris: Seuil, 1995).

Morag, Talia 'Alain Badiou within neo-pragmatism: objectivity and change', *Cardozo Law Review*, 29: 5 (2008), pp. 2239–67.

Negri, Antonio, 'Is it possible to be a communist without Marx?', *Critical Horizons*, 12: 1 (2011), pp. 5–14.

Osborne, Peter, *The Politics of Time* (London: Verso, 1996).

Peirce, Charles, 'Some consequences of four incapacities', *Journal of Speculative Philosophy*, 2 (1868), pp. 140–57.

Peirce, Charles, 'What pragmatism is', *The Monist* (1905), pp. 161–81.

Petitot, Jean, 'Refaire le "Timée" – Introduction à la philosophie mathématique d'Albert Lautman', *Revue d'histoire des sciences*, 40: 1 (1987), pp. 79–115.

Plato, *Plato: Complete Works*, ed. John M. Cooper (Indianapolis, IN and Cambridge: Hackett, 1997).

Pluth, Ed and Hoens, Dominiek, 'What if the Other is stupid? Badiou and Lacan on "logical time"', in Peter Hallward (ed.), *Think Again: Alain Badiou and the Future of Philosophy* (London: Continuum, 2004), pp. 182–90.

Potter, Michael, *Set Theory and Its Philosophy* (Oxford: Oxford University Press, 2004).

Putnam, Hilary, 'What is mathematical truth', in *Mathematics Matter and Method: Philosophical Papers, Volume 1*, 2nd edn (Cambridge: Cambridge University Press, 1979), pp. 60–78.

Putnam, Hilary, *Reason, Truth and History* (Cambridge: Cambridge University Press, 1981).

Putnam, Hilary, *Ethics Without Ontology* (Cambridge, MA: Harvard University Press, 2004).

Quine, W. V., *Word and Object* (Cambridge, MA: MIT, 1960).

Quine, W. V., *From a Logical Point of View* (Cambridge, MA: Harvard University Press, 1964).

Quine, W. V., *Ontological Relativity and Other Essays* (New York: Columbia University Press, 1969).

Quine, W. V., *Theories and Things* (Cambridge, MA: Harvard University Press, 1981).

Quine, W. V., *From Stimulus to Science* (Cambridge, MA: Harvard University Press, [1995] reprint 1998).

Roffe, Jon, *Badiou's Deleuze* (Durham, NC: Acumen, 2011).

Roitman, Judith, *Introduction to Modern Set Theory* (New York: John Wiley & Sons, 1990).

Rosch, Eleanor, 'Natural categories', *Cognitive Psychology* (1973), pp. 328–50.

Rosch, Eleanor, 'On the internal structure of perceptual and semantic categories', in Timothy E. Moore (ed.), *Cognitive Development and the Acquisition of Language* (New York, San Francisco and London: Academic Press, 1973).

Rosch, Eleanor, 'Principles of categorization', in Eleanor Rosch and Barbara B. Lloyd (eds), *Cognition and Categorization* (Hillsdale, NJ: Lawrence Erlbaum Associates, 1978).

Rosch, Eleanor and Mervis, Carolyn B., 'Family resemblances: studies in the internal structure of categories', *Cognitive Psychology*, 7 (1975), pp. 573–605.

Rosch, Eleanor, Mervis, Carolyn B., Gray, Wayne D., Johnson, David M. and Boyes-Bream, Penny, 'Basic object in natural categories', *Cognitive Psychology*, 8 (1976), pp. 382–439.

Sartre, Jean-Paul, *Being and Nothingness: An Essay on Phenomenological Ontology*, trans. Hazel E. Barnes (London: Routledge, 1969).

Sartre, Jean-Paul, *Critique of Dialectical Reason: Volume 1*, trans. Alan Sheridan-Smith, ed. Jonathan Rée (London: Verso, 1991).

Sartre, Jean-Paul, *Critique of Dialectical Reason: Volume 2*, trans. Quintin Hoare (London: Verso, 2006).

Schmidt, Alfred, *History and Structure: An Essay on Hegelian-Marxist and Structuralist Theories of History*, trans. Jeffrey Herf (Cambridge, MA: MIT Press, 1983).

Shapiro, Stewart, *Philosophy of Mathematics, Structure and Ontology* (Oxford: Oxford University Press, 2000).

Smith, Brian Anthony, 'The limits of the subject in Badiou's *Being and Event*', in Paul Ashton, A. J. Bartlett and Justin Clemens (eds), *The Praxis of Alain Badiou* (Melbourne: re.press, 2006), pp. 71–101.

Smith, Daniel W., 'The Conditions of the New', *Deleuze Studies*, 1: 1 (2007), pp. 1–21.

Soler, Colette, 'Lacan en antiphilosophe', *Filozofski vestnik*, 27: 2 (2006), pp. 121–44.

Thompson, E. P., *The Poverty of Theory* (London: Merlin Press, 1978).

Toscano, Alberto, 'To have done with the end of philosophy', *Pli: The Warwick Journal of Philosophy*, 9 (2000), pp. 220–38.

Toscano, Alberto, 'From the state to the world? Badiou and anti-capitalism', *Communication and Cognition*, 37: 3–4 (2004), pp. 199–224.

Toscano, Alberto, 'Can violence be thought? Notes on Badiou and on the possibility of (Marxist) politics', *Identities: Journal for Politics, Gender and Culture*, 5: 1 (2006), pp. 9–38.

Toscano, Alberto, 'Marxism expatriated: Alain Badiou's turn', in Jacques Bidet and Stathis Kouvelakis (eds), *Critical Companion to Contemporary Marxism* (Leiden: Brill, 2008), pp. 529–48.

Virno, Paolo, 'Natural-historical diagrams: the 'new global' movement and the biological invariant', trans. Alberto Toscano, in Lorenzo Chiesa and Alberto Toscano (eds), *The Italian Difference: Between Nihilism and Biopolitics* (Melbourne: re.press, 2009), pp. 131–47.

Winn, Phillip (ed.), *Dictionary of Biological Psychology* (London: Routledge, 2001).

Index